programming concepts

concepts
a second course

Prentice-Hall Software Series

Brian W. Kernighan, advisor

programming

concepts

a second course

(with examples in Pascal)

WILLIAM B. JONES
California State University
Dominguez Hills

PRENTICE-HALL, INC.
Englewood Cliffs, N.J. 07632

Library of Congress Cataloging in Publication Data

Jones, William B. 1939–
    Programming concepts, a second course (with examples in PASCAL)

    (Prentice-Hall software series)
    Bibliography: p.
    Includes index.
    1. PASCAL (Computer program language) 2. Elec-
tronic digital computers—Programming. I. Title.
II. Series.
QA76.73.P2J66   001.64′24   81–12081
ISBN 0–13–729970–2   AACR2

Editorial/production supervision and interior design
    by Kathryn Gollin Marshak
Cover Design by Edsal Enterprises
Manufacturing Buyer: Gordon Osbourne

Printed in the United States of America

10 9 8 7 6 5 4

ISBN 0-13-729970-2

Prentice-Hall International, Inc., *London*
Prentice-Hall of Australia Pty. Limited, *Sydney*
Prentice-Hall of Canada, Ltd., *Toronto*
Prentice-Hall of India Private Limited, *New Delhi*
Prentice-Hall of Japan, Inc., *Tokyo*
Prentice-Hall of Southeast Asia Pte. Ltd., *Singapore*
Whitehall Books Limited, *Wellington, New Zealand*

contents

preface   ix

note to the reader   xiii

chapter **1**   introduction to Pascal   1

    1.1   NUMERIC DATA   *2*

    1.2   OPERATIONS ON NUMBERS   *3*

    1.3   THE ASSIGNMENT STATEMENT   *5*

    1.4   THE WRITE AND WRITELN
STATEMENTS   *6*

    1.5   THE PASCAL PROGRAM   *8*

    1.6   THE READ STATEMENT   *10*

    1.7   THE IF STATEMENT AND SEMICOLONS   *11*

    1.8   LOOPS   *17*

    1.9   ARRAYS   *22*

1.10   BOOLEAN AND CHAR DATA TYPES   26
1.11   MORE ON DATA TYPES   29
1.12   THE CASE STATEMENT   36
1.13   READ AND READLN   38
1.14   ERROR EXITS AND THE GOTO
       STATEMENT   46
1.15   FORMATING PASCAL PROGRAMS   47
1.16   SUMMARY   49

chapter **2**   structured programming and all that   51

2.1   AN EXAMPLE: LINEAR SEARCHING   52
2.2   TOP-DOWN DESIGN   55
2.3   PROCEDURES AND FUNCTIONS   67

chapter **3**   files: searching and sorting   77

3.1   FILES AND FILE TERMINOLOGY   77
3.2   THE LINEAR SEARCH   79
3.3   THE BINARY SEARCH   81
3.4   RELATIVE EFFICIENCY
       OF ALGORITHMS   87
3.5   SORTING   89
3.6   PASCAL TEXT FILES   94

chapter **4**   dynamic data structures: linear representation   101

4.1   LISTS   101
4.2   LINEAR REPRESENTATION
       OF STACKS   103
4.3   POLISH NOTATION   113
4.4   LINEAR REPRESENTATION OF QUEUES
       AND DEQUES   120

chapter **5**   dynamic data structures: linked
                representations   128

5.1   LINKED LISTS   128
5.2   POINTERS IN PASCAL   132
5.3   BASIC OPERATIONS WITH LINKED
       LISTS   135
5.4   POINTERS AND SORTING   147
5.5   STACKS AND QUEUES   151

chapter **6**   recursion   **155**

        6.1   TREES   *156*
        6.2   TREES AND RECURSION   *163*
        6.3   TRACING RECURSIVE PROGRAMS   *171*
        6.4   QUICKSORT: A RECURSIVE SORTING
              PROCEDURE   *181*
        6.5   INFIX TO RPN REVISITED   *188*
        6.6   POSTSCRIPT: WHEN NOT TO USE
              RECURSION   *191*

chapter **7**   random numbers   **195**

        7.1   INTRODUCTION   *195*
        7.2   APPLICATION TO SORTING   *197*
        7.3   PROPERTIES OF PSEUDO-RANDOM
              NUMBER GENERATORS   *201*
        7.4   GAMES   *205*
        7.5   PROBABILITY AND THE EXPONENTIAL
              DISTRIBUTION   *209*
        7.6   SIMULATION   *216*

chapter **8**   hash-table searching   **220**

        8.1   HASH TABLES   *220*
        8.2   AN APPLICATION: FINITE-STATE
              MACHINES   *232*
        8.3   SUMMARY OF SEARCHING METHODS   *241*

chapter **9**   sequential file processing   **244**

        9.1   NON-TEXT FILES IN PASCAL   *244*
        9.2   GROUP TOTALS   *249*
        9.3   MERGING   *253*
        9.4   MERGE SORTING EXTERNAL FILES   *259*
        9.5   SEQUENTIAL FILE UPDATE   *266*

chapter **10**   real numbers   **273**

        10.1 FLOATING-POINT NUMBERS   *274*
        10.2 RULES OF REALS   *278*

appendix **A**   the STATES file   288

appendix **B**   selected nonstandard Pascal features   290

        B.1 CDC 6000 AND CYBER 70 AND 170
             COMPUTERS   *291*
        B.2 DEC PDP-11 COMPUTERS   *292*
        B.3 MOST MICROCOMPUTERS   *292*
        B.4 DEC VAX-11   *293*
        B.5 SPERRY UNIVAC 1100 COMPUTERS   *293*
        B.6 IBM STANDARD 360/370
             COMPUTERS   *294*
        B.7 PROPOSED ISO PASCAL STANDARD   *294*

appendix **C**   a pseudo-random number generator   295

appendix **D**   the WITH statement   297

appendix **E**   Pascal pointers, principles, and model
        programs   303

        E.1 PASCAL POINTERS   *303*
        E.2 PRINCIPLES   *304*
        E.3 MODEL PROGRAMS   *305*

        bibliography   308

        program index   311

        general index   315

preface

This book is intended for those who have had an introduction to programming but don't know much of anything to do with that knowledge. It attempts to cover the basic methods (mostly non-numeric) and skills needed by *all* programmers and serves as a transition to more advanced computer science courses, chiefly data structures. The book includes (and goes beyond) the material of course CS-2 of the ACM's Curriculum '78 (*Communications of the ACM*, March 1979). The Pascal language and a structured approach are used in all programs. There are more than forty complete example programs, all of which have been tested on a CDC Cyber 174 or a DEC PDP-11 or both, as well as numerous program segments.

In more detail, the book's goals are threefold:

1. Introduction to the fundamental algorithms all programmers should know, such as searching and sorting, stacks and allied structures, linked lists, trees, recursion, random numbers, and

file processing — much of the simpler material traditionally found in courses on data structures as well as material which seems to have no convenient place in the usual undergraduate courses.

2. Standard techniques of program construction and analysis, e.g., top-down design, simple run time estimations, loop invariants, and contour diagrams.

3. The necessary features of a particular programming language, Pascal, to express these ideas.

As far as possible the algorithms themselves are used to organize and motivate the material, with items in (2) and (3) introduced as needed. Programming principles of various kinds are emphasized typographically (see the note following this preface); extensive use is made of examples and diagrams in explaining important concepts; there are numerous exercises; and there are over twenty-five complete, meaningful programming assignments distributed at the ends of the chapters.

The Pascal language was chosen for several reasons, despite reservations which will appear from time to time. I consider it important to use a "real" language instead of a made-up one, as the latter choice requires the student to learn *two* languages. I feel that there are only two "real" languages (FORTRAN '77 included) which are generally available and which are suitable for structured programming: PL/I and Pascal. PL/I is a very large cumbersome language which doesn't handle data structures, particularly pointers, as well as Pascal. I also have a certain awe for a language (Pascal) which could survive the extra end-of-line blank this long.

Having chosen Pascal, there is then the question of which version. Pascal, like BASIC, is really a toy language in its standard form and in my opinion is not suitable for general purpose programming. This has led in BASIC to numerous uncontrolled extensions giving mutually unintelligible dialects, and Pascal seems headed in that direction to a lesser extent. As a compromise, I have limited myself here to a few commonly available extensions to the language which greatly improve the readability of programs without, I feel, doing violence to the spirit of the language. I will assume

1. Interactive I/O with "lazy" input (see section 1.13).

2. A character array READ facility: for X a PACKED ARRAY OF CHAR, READ(X) reads to end-of-line or end of X and blank fills X if necessary (see section 1.13 and Appendix B for other ways of doing this).

3. Dynamic association of external files with file variables via RESET and REWRITE statements (see section 3.6). Many use-

ful programs are impossible without such a facility. These include the Pascal compiler itself, if it includes the $I text
inclusion pseudo-comment.

4. A HALT built-in procedure (see section 1.14), without which
   it is very awkward to avoid using GOTO.

5. EXTERNally compiled procedures (see section 7.1).

Appendix B discusses availability of (1) through (4) in selected
Pascals. Unfortunately, none is specified in the proposed Pascal standard.
I feel that the standardizers have abdicated their responsibility in not at
least specifying standard forms for common extensions (thus leaving us
with problems like EXTERN in some versions, EXTERNAL in others).

This book is designed to be usable by students who already know
how to program but have not yet seen Pascal. Chapters 1 and 2 contain
a brief resume of what I would consider a good first course in Pascal. I
have found this satisfactory for the better students, but the weaker
students without background in Pascal tend to find the course heavy
going. Features of the language which are covered, and their locations
are

Chapter 1: LABEL, CONST, VAR, TYPE (real, integer, char,
Boolean, enumerated, subrange, array), READ and WRITE,
BEGIN-END, IF, WHILE, REPEAT, FOR, CASE, GOTO, HALT,
assignment, and type conversion.

Chapter 2: PROCEDURE and FUNCTION; value and VAR parameters.

Chapter 3: RECORDs without variants, TEXT files, RESET, RE-
WRITE.

Chapter 5: pointers, NEW.

Chapter 6: recursion, FORWARD.

Chapter 7: EXTERN.

Chapter 8: FILE OF, GET, PUT, RECORD variants.

Appendix D: WITH.

LABEL and GOTO are covered early on to give an alternative for
Pascals without HALT. They are never used in the book. SETs are not
covered at all. At this level I find them a positive hindrance to the
student, and essentially worthless since SET OF CHAR usually isn't
supported.

The book has too much material to be covered in a quarter, probably even in a semester unless extensive background in Pascal is assumed.
In a one quarter course I generally cover

Chapters 1 and 2 (about 2 weeks, very hurriedly).

Chapter 3, Sorting and searching (all).

Chapter 4, Stacks, queues, etc., array representation (all but example 4.2.3). Particular emphasis on RPN and infix to Polish translation.

Chapter 5, Linked representations (in great detail).

Chapter 6, Trees, recursion, and Quicksort (some; I'm often pressed for time here).

Chapter 7, Random numbers and applications (briefly).

Chapter 10, Real numbers (very briefly).

I have on occasion also been able to cover some of Chapter 8 (hashing). I generally assign five or six of the Programming Problems and give four or so others as extra credit.

ACKNOWLEDGEMENTS

I would like to thank eight years of students who suffered through the development of the course which ultimately gave birth to this book. Special thanks are due to Frank Miles who also taught from various versions and suggested many useful corrections, and to the staff of Computer Services at California State University, Dominguez Hills, particularly Marvin Malasky and Sophie Chow, for their help with the many computer generated versions of the text.

  CDC and CYBER are trademarks of Control Data Corporation.

  DEC, LSI-11, PDP-11, RSTS, VAX, and VMS are trademarks of Digital Equipment Corporation.

  Sperry Univac is a trademark of the Sperry Corporation.

William B. Jones
Hermosa Beach, California

note to the reader

At various times in this book special typography will be used for emphasis. Three cases will be distinguished: General programming *principles*, applicable to most languages, *Pascal Pointers*, particularly sticky features specific to the Pascal language, and *Model Programs*, which provide standard ways of doing standard things in Pascal. The typography used is as follows:

principles:

> **The XXX Principle:**
>
> Whatever it is

pointers:

```
┌─────────────────────┐
│  Pascal Pointer n   ╲
└─────────────────────╱     Whatever it is
```

models:

```
┌────────────────────────────────────────────────────────┐
│  Model Program to do . . .                              │
│                                                         │
│      The Program                                        │
└────────────────────────────────────────────────────────┘
```

For your convenience, lists of each of these are collected in Appendix E.

programming
concepts
a second course

chapter 1

introduction to Pascal

In this chapter we will describe the central features of the Pascal language. This and Chapter 2 cover the material of what I would consider to be a good first course in Pascal (very rapidly, of course). I am assuming that you are already familiar with some programming language, and if that language is not Pascal, would recommend that you also consult one of the elementary texts listed in the Bibliography at the end of the book. A summary of the topics covered in this chapter is found at the end in Section 1.16. Even if you have seen Pascal before, it would be a good idea to at least skim this chapter to get an idea of my approach.

It is difficult to give an account which covers the compilers offered by all manufacturers, as there are small but maddening variations between implementations. We will generally follow the "standard" implementation on large CDC computers. This is substantially the version described in Jensen and Wirth (see Bibliography). The deviations I assume are described as encountered and are summarized in the preface.

1.1 NUMERIC DATA

Numeric data items come in two varieties, *real* and *integer*. Real numbers are used to approximate any decimal number; integers are exact representations of whole numbers in a limited range.

A numeric *literal* is a string of digits, possibly with decimal point and/or an E-part. (A literal might also be called a constant except that the term "constant" has another meaning in Pascal. A literal is something whose value is literally given.) The E-part, if present, positions the decimal point as in the usual scientific notation, where E can be read as "times 10 to the." For example,

20   -3.645   0.032E5 (representing 3200)
        -32E+2 (representing -3200)   2.3E-5 (representing 0.000023)

are valid numeric literals. Numbers must not contain commas or blanks. Thus 22,345 and 2 E3 are invalid. Numeric literals without decimal point or E-part represent integers; all others represent reals.

Pascal Pointer 1

Literals with decimal point must have digits both before and after the decimal point.

Thus .52 and 3. are not legal literals in Pascal, but may be written legally as 0.52 and 3.0, respectively.

Most computers will represent at least the first six significant digits of a number and an E-part up to plus or minus 35 or so. 1.2345678E20 would be a valid literal, but in many computers it would be represented internally as 1.23457E20. 2.0E400 would probably be invalid on any computer, and its use would result in an error message to the user. For further information, see Chapter 10.

Integers to at least plus or minus 32767 are representable. The exact largest integer is given by MAXINT, a quantity built into all Pascals, which varies from computer to computer.

Variables, as well as programs, data types, files, and so on, are named by Pascal words called *identifiers*. An identifier consists of a letter optionally followed by several more letters and digits. Some legal identifiers are

A   SUM   SQUAREROOT   K374Q3

while

3X   CO-OP   R34.2   SQUARE ROOT

are all illegal. The only upper limit to the length of identifiers is how much can be gotten on one line, but in many Pascals all characters after the first eight are ignored. Thus SQUAREROOT and SQUAREROUTE would be considered to be the same identifier.

All variables must be declared as to type of value they contain in the heading of the program (see Section 1.5). In particular, numeric variables must be declared to be either real or integer. There is no implicit declaration or typing as in FORTRAN, PL/I, or BASIC.

1.2 OPERATIONS ON NUMBERS

Real Operations

$$+, \quad -, \quad * \quad \text{(times)}, \quad /$$

Integer Operations

$$+, \quad -, \quad * \quad \text{(times)}, \quad / \quad \text{(division, real result)}$$

DIV (division, integer result), MOD (remainder from integer division)

DIV and MOD apply only to integers and satisfy

$$A = (A \text{ DIV } B) * B + A \text{ MOD } B$$

For example,

$$8 \text{ DIV } 5 = 1 \quad \text{and} \quad 8 \text{ MOD } 5 = 3$$

| Pascal Pointer 2 ⟩ | $8/5 = 1.6$, not 1. |

Order of Operations

When more than one operation is present in an expression, the following rules are used to order the operations:

1. Evaluate expressions inside parentheses completely before applying any outside operations.
2. Evaluate operations *, /, DIV, and MOD first.
3. Then evaluate + and –.
4. If there is more than one operation in the same category, proceed left to right.

Thus

$$2 + 3 * 4 = 14, \quad 8 - 5 - 2 = 1, \quad \text{and} \quad 10 / 5 * 2 = 4.0$$

You may have noticed that Pascal does not have a "to the power" operation. This is probably because exponentiation is not a simple operation on a computer, as are +, –, and others, and the language designer did not wish to hide that fact. For typographical convenience, we will often use ** to mean the "to the power" operator in the text, but methods must be found to compute powers in Pascal. Two such are as follows:

1. The built-in functions SQR (square) and SQRT (square root). Thus

$$SQR(X + Y) = (X + Y)**2$$

and

$$SQRT(X + Y) \text{ is the square root of } X + Y$$

The well-known formula for one root of a quadratic equation could thus be written

$$(-B + SQRT(SQR(B) - 4*A*C))/(2 * A)$$

(Note that all parentheses are necessary!)

2. Use the built-in functions LN (natural logarithm, log to the base *e*, where *e* = 2.71828 . . .) and EXP (*e* to the power). Then

$$X ** Y = EXP(Y * LN(X))$$

This is in fact how X ** Y is usually computed even in languages with a "to the power" operation. *N*th roots are obtained by taking *X* to the 1/*N*th power. Thus the cube root of X is EXP(LN(X)/3).

Real and integer numbers may be freely intermixed in expressions, with integers being converted to reals automatically when combined with reals.

> Pascal Pointer 3 ⟩   *Pascal* never *converts reals to integers automatically.*

This is presumably because there is more than one way to do so. Pascal provides two built-in functions for converting real to integer:

1. ROUND, which rounds to the nearest integer.
2. TRUNC, which truncates, that is in effect removes the decimal point and following digits.

Thus

ROUND(3.4) = 3   ROUND(-3.7) = -4   ROUND(3.8) = 4
TRUNC(3.4) = 3   TRUNC(-3.7) = -3   TRUNC(3.8) = 3

Exercises 1.2

1. Evaluate each of the following expressions:

    $2 + 3 * 4 + 5$ $(2 + 3) * 4 + 5$
    $2 + 3 * (4 + 5)$ $(2 + 3) * (4 + 5)$
    $15 / 4$ 15 DIV 4   15 MOD 4
    TRUNC(5 / 3)   ROUND(5 / 3)   ROUND(SQRT(15))

2. Write Pascal expressions for

    $$\frac{a + b}{2 + c/d} \qquad (1 + x)^4 \qquad a^{2.2/x}$$

3. What is wrong with the expression

    $$375 / 4 \text{ MOD } 7$$

(*Hint:* see Pointer 3.)

1.3 THE ASSIGNMENT STATEMENT

To assign a value to a variable, a statement of the form

    variable := expression

must be executed. For example, we could write

```
      A := 5
    X2 := (B – 3.2)/(2 –A)
```

and so on. When an assignment statement is executed, the expression to the right of the := is evaluated using the current values of the variables involved. The resulting number then becomes the new value of the variable to the left of the :=. Note that the statement A := B is not the same as the statement B := A; the := does not have the same meaning as the intuitive meaning of =, and the : should help remind you of that fact. Statements like

```
    X := X + 1
```

are perfectly valid; if for instance X had the value 15 before execution of X := X + 1, the expression X+1 would be evaluated (to 16) and X given that value. It can be seen that the statement X := X + 1 has the effect of adding 1 to the variable X, whatever its previous value.

The variable and the expression must be of the same type. The one exception is that we can set

    real variable := integer expression

An important special case of Pointer 3 is

Pascal Pointer 4

"integer variable := real expression"
is not allowed.

Note that even a statement like A := 3.0∗5.0 is not allowed if A is an integer variable.

Exercises 1.3

1. Suppose R is a real variable equal to 3.6 and I an integer variable equal to 24. Which of the following assignment statements are legal, and for each legal assignment, what are the values of R and I after it is executed (assuming the same initial values for each)?

$$R := I + 1 \quad I := R + 1 \quad R := R + 1$$
$$I := I + 1 \quad I := I + 1.0 \quad I := I / 2$$

2. Write assignment statements which (a) replace X by twice its original value, and (b) replace SUM by its original value less DIF.

3. Write a Pascal statement which sets DOLS to AMT, rounded to the nearest hundredth.

1.4 THE WRITE AND WRITELN STATEMENTS

The value of an expression or a sequence of expressions may be printed at the terminal or standard output device by executing the statement

WRITELN(expression1, expression2, . . .)

For example, the statement WRITELN(A + B, 3 ∗ Q34C5) prints two quantities.

Output may be labeled using a character string literal of the form

'any string of characters'

Blanks are significant characters in such a string. For example, the statement

WRITELN('SUM =', A)

would produce the line of output

SUM =   5

assuming that A is the integer 5. Note that the quotes are not printed.

To represent a quote (') in a string, two consecutive quotes are used. For example, CAN'T is represented as 'CAN''T' and a string consisting of a single quote is represented by `''''`. Be sure to use two single quotes, not one double quote.

Integer and real numbers are printed in a fixed standard form. In CDC implementations, for instance, integers are printed right-justified in a field 10 characters long and reals are printed right-justified in a field 22 characters long and in the form $\pm X.XXXXXXXXXXXXXE\pm XXX$. To change these formats, follow the variable or expression to be printed with a colon (:) and an integer expression giving the number of columns to be printed. Thus, if A is the integer 5 and X the real 273.53, the statement WRITELN('A=',A, X, A:3, X:12) will produce

```
A=        5  2.7353000000000E+002   5 2.735E+002
```

In addition, reals can be printed in nonscientific form by following them by :n:d, where n is the total number of columns to be printed in and d is the number of digits to the right of the decimal point. (For those familiar with FORTRAN, this is more or less the Fn.d format.) Thus with X as before,

```
WRITELN('X=',X:7:1, X:10:5)
```

gives the output

```
X=    273.5  273.53000
```

Note that the decimal point counts as a column position. If the number of columns is too small to hold the number to be printed, the field is expanded to be as large as necessary. This is a useful feature allowing *left* justification of numbers. For example,

```
WRITELN('A  =  ',A:1,'  X  =  ', X:1:5)
```

gives

```
A  =  5  X  =  273.53000
```

For real numbers, the sign field is always printed in some implementations, even if blank for +. Some care is required to avoid running fields together. For instance,

```
WRITELN(X:1:5, A:1)
```

produces

```
273.530005
```

In situations where a line printer is being used, the first character of every line is a nonprinting character called the *carriage control* character. In Pascal, this can be specified by making the first item written on each line a single character string containing the character required.

The most commonly used are '1' for "new page" and ' ' for single spacing. As we are assuming an interactive situation, the examples here will not use carriage control.

Note the difference between the statements WRITELN(A) and WRITELN('A'). If A = 5, the former causes 5 to be printed while the latter causes the letter A to be printed.

In addition to the WRITELN statement, there is also a WRITE statement which is the same as WRITELN except that, following a WRITELN, subsequent output appears at the beginning of the next line, and after a WRITE, output continues on the same line. Thus the statements

```
WRITELN('A'); WRITELN('B')
```

produce the output

```
A
B
```

while the statements

```
WRITE('A'); WRITELN('B')
```

produce the output

```
AB
```

The statement

```
WRITELN(A, B, C)
```

is equivalent to

```
WRITE(A); WRITE(B); WRITELN(C)
```

and

```
WRITE(A, B, C); WRITELN
```

among others.

1.5   THE PASCAL PROGRAM

The simplest form of a Pascal program is

```
PROGRAM Name(INPUT, OUTPUT);
VAR variable declarations
BEGIN
     program statements, separated by semicolons(;)
END. (note the ".")
```

"Name" is an identifier naming the program. Lines are free form; extra blanks can and should be added so as to make the program more readable. An end of line is interpreted as a blank, so statements can be freely continued over several lines. At least one blank must occur between consecutive "words"; that is, BEGINX := 14 is incorrect if BEGIN X := 14 is intended. Blanks may not occur within words and numbers (and, since the end of a line is interpreted as a blank, words and numbers cannot be split between lines). The words PROGRAM, VAR, BEGIN, END, and others to be introduced later are called *keywords*. They must be spelled and used exactly as we have them here. In Pascal, keywords are *reserved words;* that is, they may not also be used for identifiers.

As previously mentioned, all variables used in Pascal programs must be declared in the VAR statement. Declaration of all variables helps the programmer in that Pascal can catch many spelling errors. Variable declarations are of the form

variable-name1, variable-name2, . . . : type;

This may be repeated as many times as necessary. However, the word VAR occurs only once.

It is always wise to include sufficient comments to explain a program to a reader. In Pascal, a comment may appear anywhere a blank can. Comments are strings of characters surrounded by braces:

{this is a comment}

or pairs (* and *):

(* and this is too *)

We prefer the latter as it is more attention-grabbing, and many systems do not have the { and } characters.

For all our programs we will start with a standard heading comment, describe the use of each variable in comments, and give the program's name in comments in the matching BEGIN and END.

EXAMPLE 1.5.1   The complete program

```
(* EXAMPLE 1.5.1:    SIMPLE        *)
(* COMPLETE PROGRAM DEMON-  *)
(* STRATING ROUND AND TRUNC *)

PROGRAM SIMPLE (INPUT, OUTPUT);

VAR    X: REAL;        (* THE REAL VERSION          *)
       A, B: INTEGER; (* INTEGER VERSIONS OF X  *)
```

```
BEGIN (* SIMPLE *)
  X := 14.7;
  A := ROUND(X);
  B := TRUNC(X);
  WRITELN(A, B)
END.   (* SIMPLE *)
```

will produce the output

      15   14

Note that there is no semicolon after BEGIN or after the WRITELN statement. That is because semicolons are required only *between* statements, and BEGIN and END do not constitute statements. They are interpreted as punctuation, a sort of left and right parentheses. In the preceding example, semicolons could be used in those places but only because Pascal has an *empty statement* as a matter of convenience. Thus

```
BEGIN;
  X := 14.7; . . .
```

is interpreted internally as

```
BEGIN empty statement;
  X := 14.7; . . .
```

We will discuss the semicolon problem further in Section 1.7.

1.6 THE READ STATEMENT

A Pascal program uses the READ statement to obtain input from the standard input file: the card reader in batch systems or the terminal in time-sharing systems. It is of the form

```
READ(variable1, variable2, . . .)
```

For example, the following program segment READs values of A, B, and C, and solves the equation $A*X + B = C$ for X:

```
READ(A, B, C);
WRITELN('X =', (C–B)/A:1:5)
```

If we now execute this program segment in a time-shared environment, we assume the computer prompts us with

    ?

and waits for us to type in the three values, *separated by blanks:*

    8   2   5

The computer then responds

    X = 0.37500

If fewer than three numbers had been typed, the program would come back with another "?" asking for further data. If more than three numbers were entered, the remainder would be available to further READ statements.

If your Pascal does not have an automatic prompt, it may appear to be in an infinite loop when in fact it is waiting for input.

It is always advisable to prompt the program's user as to what data are required. For instance, consider the following program piece, which computes the area of a circle:

```
WRITELN('RADIUS');
READ(R);
WRITELN('AREA =', 3.1415926535*SQR(R):1:4);
```

When this program segment is run at a terminal, the following dialogue appears (computer-typed items underlined):

    RADIUS

    ? 2

    AREA = 12.5664

The programmer may be tempted to use WRITE instead of WRITELN so that input will be on the same line as the request. Unfortunately, on some interactive systems it is difficult to guarantee that all the requesting message is printed before the input is requested if WRITE is used.

1.7   THE IF STATEMENT AND SEMICOLONS

The two forms of the IF statement are

    IF condition THEN statement

and

    IF condition THEN statement ELSE statement

Execution of the IF statement proceeds as follows: the "condition" is evaluated to "true" or "false." If true, the statement following THEN is executed. If false and there is an ELSE part, its statement is executed. In any case, execution then continues at the statement following the IF statement.

The simplest form of a condition is

expression relation expression

Allowable relations are

=	equal
<>	not equal
<	less than
>	greater than
<=	less than or equal to
>=	greater than or equal to

The statements can be any Pascal statement: assignment, I/O, loop (not introduced yet), or even other IF statements. (See Section 1.16 for a preliminary list of Pascal statements.)

EXAMPLE 1.7.1   Set X equal to the larger of A and B.

Solution 1

```
IF (A < B) THEN X := B
ELSE X := A
```

(Note that there is no semicolon after X := B. Semicolons come *between* the end of one statement and the beginning of another, and ELSE does not begin a statement.) Another method, which generalizes, is contained in

Solution 2

```
X := A;
IF (X < B) THEN X :=B
```

EXAMPLE 1.7.2   Set X equal to the largest of A, B, and C.

Solution 1

```
IF (A < B) THEN
    IF (B < C) THEN X := C
    ELSE X := B
ELSE (* A >= B *)
    IF (A < C) THEN X := C
    ELSE X := A
```

As you can see, IF statements can contain other IF statements.

Solution 2

```
X := A;
IF (X < B) THEN X := B;
IF (X < C) THEN X := C
```

EXAMPLE 1.7.3   At one time (it is difficult to keep up), Social
Security tax was 5.85% of the first $14,100 earned each year. Write a
program segment to READ previous year-to-date income (on which tax
has already been paid) and current salary, and then print out the tax on
current salary. Note that the tax may be levied on all, part, or none of
the current salary payment, depending on previous income.

Solution 1

```
WRITELN('PREVIOUS YEAR-TO-DATE INCOME'); READ (PYTDI);
WRITELN('CURRENT SALARY'); READ(CURSAL);
IF (PYTDI >= 14100) THEN TAX := 0
ELSE
    IF (PYTDI + CURSAL > 14100) THEN TAX := 0.0585*(14100–PYTDI)
    ELSE TAX := 0.0585*CURSAL;
WRITELN('TAX = $', TAX:1:2)
```

Note the use of variable names suggestive of what the variables contain,
as opposed to A, B, C, and so on. This practice is highly recommended.

One problem with the preceding solution is that it breaks one of
the cardinal rules of programming: a program should have no *magic
numbers*. In this program, the magic numbers are 14100 and 0.0585.
They are unexplained and subject to change (in fact, they have changed
at least twice since these particular numbers were valid). Asking someone to search through a program and figure out which magic numbers
mean what and to change the appropriate ones is asking for trouble.
Therefore, we promulgate

The HOUDINI Principle

Don't use magic numbers!

Pascal makes it particularly easy to follow this principle by allowing
you to declare symbolic names for literals, called *constants*. These look
and work like ordinary variables except that their values cannot be
changed. They are declared at the beginning of your program, immediately after the PROGRAM statement. Use the keyword CONST followed by constant definitions of the form

                         name = literal;

Note there is no : before the =.

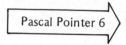

Pascal Pointer 6

Use = for permanent assignments in declarations; use := for (possibly) temporary assignments in executable code.

(And just to simplify things, you must still use : alone in VAR declarations.) Each constant (and each variable) declared should also be clearly identified by comments. A complete version of the example program is as follows

Solution 2

```
(* EXAMPLE 1.7.3: SOCIAL       *)
(* SOCIAL SECURITY TAX CALC  *)

PROGRAM SOCIAL(INPUT, OUTPUT);

CONST  MAXPERYR = 14100;  (* MAXIMUM YEARLY TAXABLE INCOME *)
       RATE = 0.0585;     (* TAX RATE *)

VAR    PYTDI,             (* PREVIOUS YEAR-TO-DATE'S INCOME  *)
       CURSAL,            (* CURRENT MONTH'S SALARY          *)
       TAX: REAL;         (* TAX COMPUTED                    *)

BEGIN (* SOCIAL *)
   WRITELN('PREVIOUS YEAR-TO-DATE INCOME'); READ(PYTDI);
   WRITELN('CURRENT SALARY'); READ(CURSAL);
   IF (PYTDI > MAXPERYR) THEN TAX := 0
   ELSE
       IF (PYTDI + CURSAL > MAXPERYR) THEN
           TAX := RATE * (MAXPERYR - PYTDI)
       ELSE TAX := RATE * CURSAL;
   WRITELN('TAX = $', TAX:1:2)
END.  (* SOCIAL *)
```

EXAMPLE 1.7.4 This example is somewhat contrived, but it is important to make the points it contains. Write a program segment which sets R to 0 and adds 1 to S if A > B, and otherwise adds 1 to R and sets S to 0. We appear to have a problem as the "statement" part(s) of an IF statement can be only one statement. Pascal comes to the rescue (as all languages should) by allowing us to combine any number of statements into a single statement by enclosing them in statement parentheses, the keywords BEGIN and END. Thus we can give the following solution:

```
IF (A > B) THEN
    BEGIN     (* DO BOTH OR NEITHER OF THESE *)
```

```
        R := 0;            (* NOTE:  ;  REQUIRED *)
        S := S + 1         (* NOTE:  ;  OPTIONAL *)
    END                    (* NOTE:  ;  NOT ALLOWED *)
ELSE
    BEGIN
        R := R + 1;
        S := 0
    END
```

This example points up a problem common to many ALGOL-like languages such as Pascal, that is, where to put the semicolons. A useful rule of thumb is

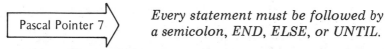

Every statement must be followed by a semicolon, END, ELSE, or UNTIL.

(UNTIL is part of the REPEAT statement, to be introduced in Section 1.8.) In the case of a statement followed by END, a semicolon between the statement and END is optional (remember the empty statement).

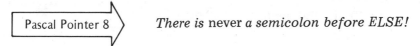

There is never *a semicolon before ELSE!*

This is because the semicolon in

IF . . . THEN X := 14; ELSE . . . (* ILLEGAL!! *)

would have the effect of ending the IF statement. Since no legal statement starts with ELSE, this would be an error. (Why the semicolon is not at least optional here is beyond me.)

EXAMPLE 1.7.5   If PROB < 0 or PROB > 1, write the message 'INVALID PROBABILITY'. This could be done with two IF statements, but that would require repeating the WRITELN statement. Instead we can use the logical operators AND, OR, and NOT, defined as follows:

    condition1 AND condition2
                is true when *both* conditions are
    condition1 OR condition2
                is true when *either* or *both* conditions are
    NOT condition
                is true when condition is false

Parentheses may be used to fix the order of evaluation of AND, OR, and NOT. (There is a standard order, but who can remember it?) A solution to the problem would be

```
IF (PROB < 0) OR (PROB > 1) THEN
    WRITELN('INVALID PROBABILITY')
```

Conditions which are relations must always be enclosed in parentheses when using AND and OR, as in the preceding. This is because in Pascal, wrongly, relations have lower precedence than AND and OR; as a result, if you write

```
IF PROB < 0 OR PROB > 1 THEN . . . (* ILLEGAL!! *)
```

the computer would try to evaluate "0 OR PROB" first, which is meaningless. So that we will not forget these parentheses, I suggest

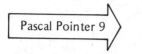 Pascal Pointer 9   Always *enclose relations in parentheses.*

Finally, let us consider the seemingly ambiguous statement

```
IF . . . THEN IF . . . THEN . . . ELSE . . .
```

The problem is that the ELSE could conceivably go with either IF. In Pascal, the ELSE always is attached to the nearest unELSEd IF. In this case, the IF statement is interpreted as

```
IF . . . THEN
    IF . . . THEN . . .
    ELSE . . .
```

If it is desired to attach the ELSE to the first IF, BEGIN-END brackets must be used, as in

```
IF . . . THEN
    BEGIN
        IF . . . THEN . . .
    END
ELSE . . .
```

Exercises 1.7 a

1. Assume you are amidst a program in which A has been set in some way. Write the necessary statements (we call it a program segment) to test A and, if A is less than 0, to set A to 0. Otherwise do nothing.

2. Write a program segment to set S equal to the largest of A, B, C, or D.

3. Write a complete program which asks the user for a minimum balance, MBAL, and computes and prints the service charge as $2.00 if MBAL is less than $100, and $1.00 otherwise. Arrange your program so that it does not contain magic numbers.

4. Write a program segment to test whether a real variable X has a whole-number value or not and print 'X IS AN INTEGER' or 'X IS NOT AN INTEGER'

accordingly. *Hint:* Does X = TRUNC(X)? (We are assuming that –MAXINT ⩽ X ⩽ MAXINT.)

5. A more useful function than TRUNC(X) is floor (X), the greatest integer less than or equal to *X* (floor(-2.1) = –3; TRUNC(-2.1) = –2; floor (X) = TRUNC(X) for X ⩾ 0). Pascal does not have a built-in floor function, so write an IF statement which sets N equal to floor(X). (Note that the ROUND function can be computed easily from floor, but *not* easily from TRUNC. This has gotten the author in trouble at least once.)

6. Write a program segment which adds 1 to COUNTER if it is less than 100 and otherwise sets COUNTER to 0 and writes the message 'COUNTER RESET'.

De Morgan's rules for AND, OR, and NOT are often useful in manipulating and understanding logical expressions. They are

NOT (a AND b) = (NOT a) OR (NOT b)

and

NOT (a OR b) = (NOT a) AND (NOT b)

Thus

NOT ((A > 0) AND (B = 7))

is equivalent to

(A <= 0) OR (B <> 7)

and

NOT ((A >= X–1) OR (B*B < 2))

is equivalent to

(A < X–1) AND (B*B >= 2)

Exercises 1.7 b

7. Simplify the following logical expressions:

NOT ((X < 0) AND (Y > Z))
NOT ((R <> 5) OR (T <= EPS))
NOT ((M >= N) AND ((X = 0) OR (Y < Z)))

1.8   LOOPS

Looping is the most important and difficult part of programming. Pascal has two general looping statements, which are

```
WHILE condition DO        REPEAT
    statement                     statement1; . . .; statementn
                           UNTIL condition
```

Execution of the WHILE statement is as follows:

```
start-of-loop:
    IF condition is false THEN jump to end-of-loop;
    execute 'statement';
    jump back to start-of-loop;
end-of-loop:
```

Note that "condition" is tested only at the beginning of the loop. If it becomes false in the middle of 'statement', 'statement' will nonetheless continue executing until the program goes back to the beginning of the loop for the condition test. Note also that most WHILE loops will have bodies with more than one statement. This list of statements must then be enclosed in BEGIN-END brackets.

Execution of the REPEAT statement is as follows:

```
start-of-loop:
    statement1;
        .
        .
        .
    statementn;
    IF condition is false THEN jump back to start-of-loop;
end-of-loop;
```

Note that REPEAT and UNTIL act like BEGIN-END brackets, and a separate BEGIN-END is not needed. Note also that WHILE executes its body as long as "condition" is *true*, and REPEAT executes its body as long as "condition" is *false*. Other than this, the main difference is that REPEAT always executes its body at least once, and WHILE may not execute its body at all. In fact, each statement can be rewritten in terms of the other. For instance,

```
WHILE c DO s
```

can be rewritten

```
IF c THEN
    REPEAT
        s
    UNTIL NOT c
```

while

```
REPEAT s1; . . .; sn UNTIL c
```

can be rewritten

```
s1; . . .; sn;
WHILE NOT c DO
    BEGIN s1; . . .; sn END
```

Finally, it is worth pointing out that "WHILE c DO s" and "REPEAT s1; . . . ; sn UNTIL c" are considered to be single statements even though they contain whole statements as parts. This is similar to a sentence which contains a sentence, as this sentence does.

EXAMPLE 1.8.1 Read in and add up an arbitrarily long list of numbers, terminated by the number –99. Such a special number used to terminate a list is called a *sentinel*. Of course, by the Houdini Principle, the value of the sentinel should be a CONST.

Solution

```
(* EXAMPLE 1.8.1:  SUMMER        *)
(* READ NUMBERS TERMINATED BY *)
(* SENTINEL AND PRINT SUM       *)

PROGRAM SUMMER (INPUT, OUTPUT);

CONST SENTINEL = -99;  (* INPUT TERMINATING NUMBER *)

VAR    X,              (* INPUT NUMBER            *)
       SUM: REAL;      (* SUM OF INPUT NUMBERS *)

BEGIN (* SUMMER *)
    SUM := 0;
    WRITELN('TYPE IN NUMBERS TERMINATED BY ', SENTINEL:1);
    READ(X);
    WHILE (X <> SENTINEL) DO
        BEGIN
            SUM := SUM + X;
            READ(X)
        END;
    WRITELN('SUM =',SUM:1:3)
END.  (* SUMMER *)
```

If this program is executed interactively, we set

```
TYPE IN NUMBERS TERMINATED BY -99
?  2   3   5
?  -1  -99
SUM = 9.000
```

Note the "extra" READ outside the WHILE loop. This is necessary, roughly, because we are going to READ one more *X* than we are going to sum. This general form comes up so often that it is worth designating as a Model Program:

Model Program 1: Read and process numbers, terminating on a sentinel.

```
CONST SENTINEL = ...
       .
       .
       .
READ(X)
WHILE (X <> SENTINEL) DO
    BEGIN
        process X;
        READ(X)
    END
```

It is more awkward to use REPEAT instead of WHILE in this application, as we would have to say

```
REPEAT
    READ(X);
    IF (X <> SENTINEL) THEN
        process X
UNTIL  (X = SENTINEL)
```

Exercises 1.8 a

1. For $X \geqslant 1$, TRUNC($\log_2(X)$) is the largest integer N such that $2 ** N$ is $\leqslant X$. Write a WHILE loop to compute this N. ($\log_2(X)$ is the log to the base 2 of X.)

2. Write a program segment to set P equal to $X ** N$, N an integer, by performing repeated multiplication.

3. Write a program segment to print out a table of X and SQRT(X) for $X = 0.01, 0.02, \ldots, 1.00$.

4. The first few Fibonacci numbers are $1, 1, 2, 3, 5, 8, 13, \ldots$. After the first two, each succeeding number is the sum of the two previous ones (e.g., $13 = 5 + 8$). Write a program which reads a number and finds and prints the smallest Fibonacci number which is greater than or equal to it.

5. (See the discussion of De Morgan's laws before Exercise 1.7.7.) When the loop WHILE condition DO . . . terminates, we know that 'condition' is false. Give a simplified condition that is true after each of the following WHILE loops is terminated:

```
WHILE (X <> -99) AND (I < N) DO . . .
WHILE (X >= EPS) OR (Y = W) DO . . .
```

During the execution of the loop REPEAT . . . UNTIL condition, its 'condition' is false (at least after the first execution). Give a simplified condition which is true during each execution of the following loops after the first:

```
REPEAT . . . UNTIL (X < 0) OR (Y = 5)
REPEAT . . . UNTIL (X <> W) AND (Y <= 0)
```

Using De Morgan's rules, convert the following REPEAT loop to a WHILE loop:

```
REPEAT s UNTIL (A < B) OR ((C = D) AND (X <> Y – 1))
```

The FOR statement offers a more specialized looping statement, with built-in counting. It comes in two forms:

```
FOR intvar : = lolim TO hilim DO statement
```

and

```
FOR intvar : = hilim DOWNTO lolim DO statement
```

where "intvar" is an integer variable and "lolim" and "hilim" are integer expressions. Execution of the TO ⌐ ¬m is equivalent to

```
intvar := lolim; TEMP := hilim;
WHILE (intvar <= TEMP) DO
    BEGIN statement; intvar := intvar + 1 END
```

and the DOWNTO form is equivalent to

```
intvar := hilim; TEMP := lolim;
WHILE (intvar >= TEMP) DO
    BEGIN statement; intvar := intvar – 1 END
```

In either case, if hilim < lolim, the loop body statement is not executed at all. If you wish to program a loop like this with an increment of other than plus or minus 1, you must do it manually.

EXAMPLE 1.8.2   Write a program to read a number SIZE and print a triangle of asterisks with base and height SIZE. FOR is used as a counter.

```
(* EXAMPLE 1.8.2: TRIANGLE        *)
(* READ SIZE AND PRINT A TRIANGLE *)
(* WITH BASE AND HEIGHT SIZE      *)

PROGRAM TRIANGLE(INPUT, OUTPUT);
CONST PRINTCHAR = ' * ';      (* WHAT TRIANGLE IS PRINTED WITH *)

VAR   SIZE,            (* BASE, HEIGHT OF TRIANGLE      *)
      LEN,            (* NO OF PRINTCHARS IN CUR LINE  *)
      I: INTEGER;      (* INDEX WITHIN LINE             *)

BEGIN (* TRIANGLE *)
    WRITELN('SIZE:'); READ(SIZE);
    FOR LEN := 1 TO SIZE DO
```

```
BEGIN
    WRITE(' ':SIZE-LEN+1); (* INDENTATION *)
    FOR I := 1 TO LEN DO
        WRITE(PRINTCHAR);
    WRITELN
END
END. (* TRIANGLE *)
```

An example run might be

```
SIZE:
? 5
          *
        *   *
      *   *   *
    *   *   *   *
  *   *   *   *   *
```

Note: The loop FOR I := . . . should NEVER contain any state-ment which alters I! In particular I := I + 1 is not valid or necessary in a FOR loop, and may well do something unexpected anyway.

One final word of warning: WHILE condition DO; does nothing (the empty statement) forever! (Note the semicolon!) FOR. . .DO; simply does nothing. An advanced student of mine and I once spent an embarrassing amount of time trying to find this bug in a program of hers.

Pascal Pointer 10   *Never put; after DO.*

Exercises 1.8 b

6. Write a PROGRAM to read a WIDTH and HEIGHT and print an American flag star pattern in those dimensions. For instance a WIDTH of 6 and HEIGHT of 9 produces

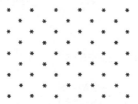

1.9   ARRAYS

One of the important ways in which a programming language can help a programmer is in making it possible to structure data in such a way that it resembles the "natural" structure of the problem that is being solved. One of the best features of Pascal is its rich repertoire of data-structuring methods. The simplest method is the array (a method which is available in most languages). We will introduce the array in its simplest form in this section and give more complete details in Section 1.11.

For example, suppose we have an inventory of 40 items, each with a given price, and we wish to store the price of each item. Since the principle involved here is that the program's representation of data should reflect its actual organization, consider this: we have the same kind of data concerning each of a large number of items. This suggests a data representation in two parts: (1) a single name for the data represented, and (2) a *selector* telling us which item we would like the datum for.

In Pascal arrays, the selector (or *subscript*) is enclosed in square brackets ([and]) (not ordinary parentheses). Thus, for example, we could let PRICE be the name of the array of prices, PRICE[1] = the price of the first item, PRICE[12] the price of the twelfth item, and in general, PRICE[I] the price of the Ith item, whatever I may be at the time.

A simple array declaration is of the form

VAR name: ARRAY [losub..hisub] OF type;

where "losub" and "hisub" are the lower and upper limits of its subscript, and "type" is the data type of each of its values. Losub and hisub may be CONSTants or literals, but may not be expressions. The declaration of the PRICE array could be

VAR PRICE: ARRAY [1..40] OF REAL;

Arrays with two or more subscripts are also possible. For example, if we have a class of 100 students, each of whom has 5 grades, we might record these grades in an array declared by

VAR GRADE: ARRAY [1..5, 1..100] OF INTEGER;

where the third grade of the forty-first student would be GRADE[3, 41].

The lowest subscript in an array is 1 most of the time, but Pascal allows other lower limits, even negative ones!

A reminder: A statement such as PRICE[I] := 5.20 changes the Ith element of the PRICE array, but does *not* alter I. Thus, if I = 16 before the preceding statement is executed, then, after it is executed, PRICE[16] = 5.20 but I still is 16.

Loops are intimately involved in processing arrays. In the remainder of this section, we will discuss two fundamental models for this. The first is

---

Model Program 2:   Perform some process on each
of A[1 .. N].

```
FOR I := 1 to N DO
    BEGIN
        process A[I]
    END
```

One of the most common applications of this model is to summing,
say, A[1 .. N]:

```
SUM := 0;
FOR I := 1 TO N DO
    SUM := SUM + A[I]
```

More subtle is the problem of reading items up to a sentinel and
storing them in an array. This of course is a special case of our model
program to read and process items up to a sentinel:

Model Program 3:   Read items, ended by a sentinel,
and store them in an array A[1 . . TOP], TOP a
constant. Set N equal to the number of items in the
array (less the sentinel).

```
N := 0; READ(TEMP);
WHILE (TEMP <> SENTINEL) AND
        (N < TOP) DO
    BEGIN
        N := N + 1; A[N] := TEMP;
        READ(TEMP)
    END
```

The N < TOP condition was added to avoid overflowing the array.
(Pascal does check for legal subscripts, but when it dies on an illegal
subscript, it tends to give an error message which is not very useful to
anyone except the person who wrote the program.)

We could not have written the program using a FOR loop,

```
FOR I := 1 TO TOP DO
    whatever
```

since we may not wish to read TOP items. In general, a *FOR loop
should be used only when the limits are known in advance.*

Many programmers hate to use "extra" variables, especially in a language like Pascal where they have to be declared. The following program *appears* to avoid the TEMP location:

```
N := 0; READ(A[N+1]);
WHILE (A[N+1] <> SENTINEL) AND (N < TOP) DO
    BEGIN
        N := N + 1;
        READ(A[N+1])
    END
```

The problem here is that if N = TOP we will have read into A[N+1] = A[TOP+1], so the program will abort unless A is given an extra unused location! Not only that, as I can attest from years of trying to explain this to students, this is a much more mysterious and error-prone place to waste a memory location than using TEMP.

To avoid using N+1 in a program like the preceding, you might be tempted to write

```
N := 1; READ(A[N]);
WHILE (A[N] <> SENTINEL) AND (N < TOP) DO
    BEGIN
        N := N + 1;
        READ(A[N])
    END;
N := N - 1    (* !!!!!!!!! *)
```

This is also an error-prone form, as you tend to forget the last statement, with the result that N is one too big! This problem is caused by the fact that you are using N to mean two different things: at first, the number of items *read*, and then at the end, the number actually *used*.

Exercises 1.9

1. Write a Pascal program segment to set BIGGEST equal to the largest item in the array $A[1 .. 100]$.

2. A polynomial $A[0] + A[1] * X + \cdots + A[20] * X ** 20$ is defined by its array of coefficients.

    (a) Give the VAR declaration for this array.

    (b) Write a Pascal program segment to set VAL equal to the value of the polynomial. Use an auxiliary variable XPOW to accumulate the powers of X as you go (and do not use EXP and LN to find powers).

    (c) Write a Pascal program segment to set VAL equal to the value of the polynomial using Horner's method:

$$VAL = (\ldots (((A[20] * X + A[19]) * X + A[18]) * X + \ldots) * X + A[0]$$

    (d) The *degree* of the polynomial is the largest N for which A[N] is not zero. Write a program segment to set N to the degree of this polynomial (and to −1 if all of the A's are zero).

1.10 BOOLEAN AND CHAR DATA TYPES

Boolean data are logical values; Boolean literals are the two words
TRUE and FALSE. The operations on Boolean data are AND, OR,
and NOT. All "conditions" as previously discussed are simply expressions with Boolean values. Relations, as in Section 1.7, are used to
convert from numeric to Boolean data. Thus

```
VAR X, Y, Z: BOOLEAN;
        .
        .
        .
X   := (5 < 3);          (* SETS X TO FALSE *)
Y   := (8 <= 10);        (* SETS Y TO TRUE *)
Z   := Y AND (NOT X);    (* SETS Z TO TRUE *)
IF Z THEN . . .          (* THEN PART WILL BE EXECUTED *)
```

The built-in function ORD can be used to convert Boolean data
to integer:

$$ORD(FALSE) = 0, \quad ORD(TRUE) = 1$$

EXAMPLE 1.10.1   Set S = 1 if A $>$ 0, S = 0 if A = 0, S = -1 if
A $<$ 0.

Solution 1:

```
IF (A > 0) THEN S := 1
ELSE
    IF (A < 0) THEN S := -1
    ELSE S := 0
```

Solution 2

```
S := ORD(A > 0) - ORD(A < 0)
```

This is the sort of formula beloved by APL programmers, but I
find it somewhat suspect as it violates

```
┌─────────────────────────────────────┐
│      The SHIRLEY TEMPLE Principle    │
│         Don't get too cute!          │
└─────────────────────────────────────┘
```

(which may be self-violating). Cute code has a way of outsmarting us.
It seems that everytime something goes wrong with the program, it is
in the area of the cute code, and even if the cute code itself is valid, it
must be reunderstood.

The CHAR data type is used to represent single characters. Literals are of the form 'character', (for example, 'A' and ':'). Any "printable" character in the computer's character set can be used. The single quote is represented by ''''(four single quotes). Characters can be compared for order, and it is always the case that

$$'A' < 'B' < 'C' < \ldots < 'Y' < 'Z'$$
$$'0' < '1' < \ldots < '9'$$

Note that there is a difference between say, '5' and 5. '5' cannot be used in arithmetic. The built-in function ORD can be used to convert CHARs to integers [actually, to the internal numeric representation of the character; if the ASCII character set is used, ORD('A') is the ASCII representation of 'A', the number 65]. The built-in function CHR is the inverse function of ORD:

$$\text{CHR(ORD(C))} = \text{C for all CHARs C}$$

ORD('5') is usually not 5, no matter what character set is used. However, there is a useful relationship between digit characters and their ORDs:

$$\text{CHR(ORD('0')} + 1) = '1'$$
$$\cdot \qquad \cdot$$
$$\cdot \qquad \cdot$$
$$\cdot$$
$$\text{CHR(ORD('0')} + 9) = '9'$$

EXAMPLE 1.10.2   Write a program to read a number with embedded commas, as in 1,234,567, and print its value. The number is assumed to terminate on the first nondigit, noncomma. Don't check for validity (i.e., 1,,234, would produce the result 1234). Note that this program is an example of reading and processing until a sentinel occurs, in this case a nondigit noncomma character.

```
(* EXAMPLE 1.10.2:  COMMAS          *)
(* READ A NUMBER WITH EMBEDDED *)
(* COMMAS AND PRINT IT          *)

PROGRAM COMMAS(INPUT, OUTPUT);

CONST SEP = ',';     (* DIGIT SEPARATER *)

VAR   C: CHAR;     (* THE CHARACTER READ *)
      VAL: REAL; (* ACCUMULATED VALUE OF NUMBER *)

BEGIN (* COMMAS *)
    VAL := 0;
    WRITELN('TYPE IN NUMBER WITH ',SEP, '''S');
```

```
        READ(C);
        WHILE ((C >= '0') AND (C <= '9')) OR (C = SEP) DO
            BEGIN
                IF (C <> SEP) THEN
                    VAL := VAL * 10 + ORD(C) – ORD('0');
                READ(C)
            END;
        WRITELN('VALUE =', VAL:1:1)
    END.    (* COMMAS *)
```

A run of this program produces

```
TYPE IN NUMBER WITH  ,'S
? 1,234,567
VALUE = 1234567.0
```

Note that in terms of magic numbers I made the comma a constant so that it could be easily changed (to a blank, for instance), and that I did not call it COMMA! It seems to me to be a waste of time to make a constant whose name tells what its value is, not what it is used for. For this reason, '0' and '9' were not defined as constants. There seems to me to be no point in calling them, say ZERODIGIT and NINEDIGIT, particularly since to change them would change the whole sense of the program. (But then again, suppose one wanted to read octal (base 8) numbers.)

The situation with letters is not as nice as with digits. There are three main character sets in use for Pascal: EBCDIC (IBM), BCD (CDC), and ASCII (most others). In BCD and ASCII the letters are contiguous; that is,

$$ORD('Z') = ORD('A') + 25$$

but this is false in EBCDIC! However, even in EBCDIC there are no *meaningful* (printing) characters between 'A' and 'Z', other than letters. Thus a CHAR variable C assumed to be a legitimate character is a letter if and only if $'A' \leqslant C \leqslant 'Z'$.

Strings of characters are represented (very primitively) as an *array* of values of type CHAR. To save memory space and make some operations easier internally, CHARacters may be packed several per storage unit (10 per word on large CDC computers) by declaring them a PACKED ARRAY. Thus

```
    VAR NAME: PACKED ARRAY [1 . . 24] OF CHAR;
```

Individual characters may be accessed in NAME in the usual manner, for example, NAME[3], or all of NAME may be assigned to or written (but not read in some systems). Thus

NAME :='PASCAL

Notice that the literal character string must contain exactly the same number of characters as NAME.

Whole packed arrays of characters may also be compared if they are the same length. If for instance WORD and DROW are both packed arrays of dimension [1 . . 15], then WORD < DROW means that for some I, all characters of WORD before character I equal the corresponding ones of DROW, and WORD[I] < DROW[I]. For letters, this ordering is more or less alphabetical (but note that in a character set like BCD in which the blank follows letters of the alphabet, 'RED   ' follows 'REDHEAD').

Some implementations of Pascal include a predefined data type ALFA which is equivalent to PACKED ARRAY [1 . . 10] (or sometimes [1 . . 8]) OF CHAR.

Pascal Pointer 11   *ALFA is spelled with an F, not PH!*

Exercises 1.10

1. How would you convert the value of a variable X equal to 0 or 1 back to FALSE or TRUE?

2. (a) Using ORD, write an expression which is 0 if $X \leqslant 0$, 1 if $0 < X < 10$, and 2 if $X \geqslant 10$.

(b) The built-in function ABS(X) has as its value X without its sign; that is, if $X \geqslant 0$, ABS(X) = X and if $X < 0$, ABS(X) = -X. Write an expression for ABS(X) using ORD instead of ABS.

3. What are ORD('7') - ORD('0') and CHR(ORD('3')+2)?

4. Let C be a variable of type CHAR. Write an IF statement which prints 'NOT ALPHABETIC' if C is not a letter of the alphabet.

5. Let C be a character variable which is a digit. Write an assignment statement which sets N equal to the numeric value of C.

6. In both ASCII and EBCDIC, there is a constant difference between the ORDs of corresponding upper- and lowercase letters; that is, ORD('A') - ORD('a') = ORD('B') - ORD('b') = ... Write a program segment which checks to see if the CHAR variable C is a lowercase letter and, if so, converts it to the corresponding uppercase letter. You may assume that C is a meaningful character.

7. Assuming that A and B are Boolean variables, simplify the following statement:

IF A = TRUE THEN B := TRUE ELSE B := FALSE

1.11   MORE ON DATA TYPES

Data types play a much more prominent role in Pascal than they do in most other languages. In this section I want to give an orderly treatment of the class of variables having a single value and to arrays. We will also see how new data types can be created.

The following is a list of all single-valued data types (which are precisely the data types that can be the value of a function; see Section 2.3). I also list the section where each type is introduced and two important subclassifications: *scalar* types, in which there is a meaningful ordering of values, and *subscript* types, which are the types that can be used as subscripts for arrays:

1. REAL (1.1)
2. INTEGER (1.1)
3. CHAR (1.10)
4. BOOLEAN (1.10)   Subscript   Scalar types
5. enumerated (1.11)   types
6. subrange (1.11)
7. pointer (5.1).

Types 5 and 6 are created by the programmer, so before discussing them we need a little information on how this is done. Pascal is an *extensible language* in the sense that programmers can create and name their own data types. These names are then used just like the built-in type names REAL, INTEGER, and so on. For example, instead of saying

```
VAR X: ARRAY [1 .. 10] OF REAL;
```

the programmer can declare

```
TYPE TENAR = ARRAY [1 .. 10] OF REAL;
        .
        .
        .
VAR X: TENAR;
```

The general form of the TYPE statement is

```
TYPE name1 = definition1;
     name2 = definition2;
            .
            .
            .
     nameN = definitionN;
```

The TYPE statement goes *between* the CONST and VAR statements. This is easy to remember as TYPEs can use CONSTs (for example, as array limits), and VARs can use TYPEs, and almost everything must be

defined before it can be used in Pascal. Note also that TYPE obeys
Pascal Pointer 6 in using =.

It is easy to confuse TYPE names with variable names. To help
avoid this confusion, you might want to include the word 'TYPE' in
all your type names. Also remember

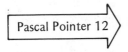

Pascal Pointer 12

Never *use TYPE names in an executable part of your program, that is,
between BEGIN and END.*

Now we can finish up scalar types. *Enumerated* types are used in
situations where we have data with no particular numeric content. An
example might be a person's marital status — SINGLE, MARRIED,
WIDOWED, DIVORCED — or a kind of store transaction — CASH,
CHARGE, EXCHANGE. In traditional languages we would assign a
number or perhaps a letter to each possibility, but this tends to make
programs difficult to read. Even if the CONST feature of Pascal is used,
it would be possible to (erroneously) do arithmetic on such items, with
possibly disastrous results. Instead, Pascal allows us to define our own
nonnumeric data types to cover these situations. For example, we
could write

```
TYPE MARSTAT = (SINGLE, MARRIED, WIDOWED, DIVORCED);
     TRANSKIND = (CASH, CHARGE, EXCHANGE);
         .
         .
         .
     VAR T: TRANSKIND; M: MARSTAT;
```

or

```
VAR T: (CASH, CHARGE, EXCHANGE);
    M: (SINGLE, MARRIED, WIDOWED, DIVORCED);
```

or a combination of the two. The literal values for the variable T would
be CASH, CHARGE, and EXCHANGE, and Pascal would check to
see that only these values are given to T. We can write statements like

```
T := CASH
```

or

```
IF (T = EXCHANGE) THEN . . .
```

The literal values of enumerated types are ordered according to the
order in which they are defined: SINGLE < MARRIED < WIDOWED
< DIVORCED. In fact, these four values are stored internally as 0,
1, 2, and 3, respectively, and the program does numeric comparisons.

The ORD function also applies to enumerated types, and its value is just this internal representation.

One can think of BOOLEAN as being a predefined enumerated type:

```
TYPE BOOLEAN = (FALSE, TRUE);
```

But this ignores that BOOLEANS have very special properties in relations and conditions.

One serious disadvantage of enumerated types is that they can only be used internally; in most Pascals, there is no direct way of reading or writing them. To get around this, we might for instance suppose that a CHARacter C indicates transaction kind: 'S' for CASH, 'R' for CHARGE, and 'X' for EXCHANGE, and convert to the enumerated type by writing

```
IF (C = 'S') THEN T := CASH
ELSE IF (C = 'R') THEN T := CHARGE
    ELSE IF (C = 'X') THEN T := EXCHANGE
        ELSE WRITELN('WRONG TRANSACTION KIND')
```

We will see other ways to convert later, but in fact enumerated types are not very satisfactory except for purely internal use (see Example 1.11.2).

The final new type to be discussed here is the *subrange* type. Variables of this type take on part of the range of values of INTEGER, CHAR, or an enumerated type. Its definition in TYPE or VAR statement is

lolim . . hilim

For example,

```
TYPE TESTSCORE = 0 . . 100;
     CLASSGRADE = 'A' . . 'F';
     MARSTAT = (SINGLE, MARRIED, WIDOWED, DIVORCED);
     WASMARTYPE = MARRIED . . DIVORCED;
```

If a variable were declared, say, as a TESTSCORE, then Pascal would check that any integer assigned to that variable is in the range 0 to 100.

As you have probably noticed, our previous use of lolim . . hilim in ARRAY declarations was a special case of subrange. For instance, we could have declared

```
TYPE ITEMRANGE = 1 . . 40;
```

```
VAR  PRICE: ARRAY [ITEMRANGE] OF INTEGER;
```

In fact, any of the types BOOLEAN, CHAR, enumerated, or subrange can be used as a subscript type, and in an array with multiple subscripts the types can be mixed arbitrarily.

EXAMPLE 1.11.1 Print out the value of the VAR T: TRANS-KIND in legible form. One simple solution is to define an array TPRINT whose subscripts are the possible values of T and whose values are strings of characters describing these values. The relevant parts of the program are

```
TYPE TRANSKIND = (CASH, CHARGE, EXCHANGE);
     TVAL = PACKED ARRAY [1 .. 11] OF CHAR;

VAR  TPRINT: ARRAY [TRANSKIND] OF TVAL;
     T: TRANSKIND;
        .
        .
        .
     (* INITIALIZE TPRINT *)
     TPRINT[CASH]  := 'CASH SALE    ';
     TPRINT[CHARGE] := 'CHARGE SALE';
     TPRINT[EXCHANGE] := 'EXCHANGE    ';
        .
        .
        .
     (* PRINT T'S VALUE *)
     WRITELN(TPRINT[T])
```

An interesting and characteristic use of enumerated types and arrays is given in Example 1.11.2, which also uses the fact that the index of a FOR loop need not be an integer: it can be any of the types INTEGER, CHAR, BOOLEAN, enumerated, or subrange. The body statement of the loop is executed with index variable set to each of the specified values, in order.

EXAMPLE 1.11.2 Write a program to read a line of input and determine whether or not it is a palindrome. A palindrome is a sentence which, when all letters are converted to the same case and all blanks and punctuation are removed, reads the same forward and backward. Examples are "Able was I ere I saw Elba" (attributed to Napoleon, and in English), "Yreka Bakery," and "A man, a plan, a canal: Panama."

To find the end of the input line, we anticipate Section 1.13 and use the built-in function EOLN (no arguments in this case), which becomes TRUE immediately after the last character on the line is read.

It is necessary to pick a character set (so we know the largest and smallest character), and I have assumed ASCII.

```
          (* EXAMPLE 1.11.2: PAL          *)
          (* READ A LINE OF INPUT AND DE- *)
          (* TERMINE IF IT'S A PALINDROME *)


    PROGRAM PAL(INPUT, OUTPUT);


    CONST LOWORD = 0;           (* ORD OF SMALLEST ASCII CHAR *)
          HIGHORD = 127;        (* ORD OF LARGEST ASCII CHAR *)


    TYPE   CHARTYPE = (THROWOUT, UCLETTER, LCLETTER);


    VAR    CLASS: ARRAY [CHAR] OF CHARTYPE; (* GIVES LETTER CLASS *)
           C: CHAR;                (* CONTAINS CHARACTERS AS READ *)
           LINE: PACKED ARRAY [0 . . 80] OF CHAR; (* POSSIBLE PALINDROME *)
           N,                     (* NUMBER OF CHARACTERS IN LINE *)
           I,J: INTEGER;          (* RUNNING INDICES IN LINE *)

    BEGIN (* PAL *)
       (* INITIALIZE CLASS ARRAY *)
       FOR C := CHR(LOWORD) TO CHR(HIGHORD) DO
           CLASS[C] := THROWOUT;
       FOR C := 'A' TO 'Z' DO CLASS[C] := UCLETTER;
       FOR C := 'a' TO 'z' DO CLASS[C] := LCLETTER;


       WRITELN('ENTER TEST SENTENCE');


       N := 0; (* USING MODEL PROGRAM 3 TO READ INTO ARRAY *)
       WHILE NOT EOLN DO
           BEGIN
               READ(C); (* HERE, CAN TEST 'SENTINEL' EOLN BEFORE READ *)
               IF (CLASS[C] = LCLETTER) THEN
                   C := CHR(ORD(C) + ORD('A') - ORD ('a'));
                       (* LOWER TO UPPER CASE CONVERSION *)
               IF (CLASS[C] <> THROWOUT) THEN
                   BEGIN
                       N := N + 1; LINE[N] := C
                   END
           END;


       (* NOW TEST LINE FOR PALINDROME *)
       I := 1; J := N;
       WHILE (I < J) AND (LINE[I] = LINE[J]) DO
           BEGIN
               I := I + 1; J := J - 1
           END;


       IF (I < J) THEN WRITELN('NOT A PALINDROME')
       ELSE WRITELN('IT''S A PALINDROME')
    END. (*PAL *)
```

Notes

1. Modifying programs like this to handle more than one line of input is tricky and will be discussed in Section 1.13.

2. The lower limit of LINE is 0 instead of 1 to take care of the case when N is 0, as otherwise on the first loop test we would try to look at LINE[J] when $J = 0$ and the program would abort. It is always advisable to allow for bad input.

3. J was not really necessary (N could have been used instead), but I think the nice symmetric feeling it gives is worth the slight price.

4. The experienced Pascal user may wonder why I did not use SETs instead of the CLASS array. This is because most Pascals do not allow SETs large enough to contain all CHARs, which in my opinion makes sets of CHARs next to worthless. Though very useful in other contexts, SETs will not be used in this book. For those who know about them, it is still worth mentioning that

Pascal Pointer 13   *SETs of CHARs probably will not work.*

Since Pascal is very serious about its data typing and does practically no automatic conversion between types, it is worth closing out this section with Figure 1.1, showing the conversion facilities that are built in.

Type Conversion Facilities

From \ To →	INTEGER	REAL	CHAR	BOOLEAN
INTEGER	/////	automatic	CHR	<
				=
REAL	ROUND TRUNC	/////	none	>
CHAR			/////	<=
	ORD		/////	>=
enumerated (and BOOLEAN)		none		<>

FIGURE 1.1   Type Conversion Facilities

Exercises 1.11

1. Suppose we have defined

```
TYPE ANS = PACKED ARRAY [1 . . 3] OF CHAR;

VAR  PRANS: ARRAY [BOOLEAN] OF ANS;
        .
        .
        .
PRANS[FALSE] := 'NO  '; PRANS[TRUE] := 'YES';
```

What is printed by

```
WRITELN(PRANS[5 < 8] , '  ', PRANS['A' > 'Z'] )
```

2. (a) Declare an array LCTOUC with all possible CHARacters both as subscripts and as values.

(b) Write code to initialize LCTOUC so that, if C is any meaningful printing character, then LCTOUC[C] is C if C is not a lowercase letter and is the corresponding uppercase version of C if C is a lowercase letter.

1.12   THE CASE STATEMENT

Occasionally it is useful to have a more general choice statement than the IF statement. In Pascal, this is the CASE statement, which has the form

```
CASE expression OF
    value1: statement1;
        .
        .
        .
    valueN: statementN
END
```

the effect of which is like

```
IF expression = value1 THEN statement1
ELSE IF expression = value2 THEN statement2
ELSE . . .
ELSE IF expression = valueN THEN statementN
ELSE something unpredictable will happen
```

The data type of "expression" can be any of the types that can be used for a subrange: INTEGER, BOOLEAN, CHAR, or enumerated. In fact, the IF statement can be considered to be a special case of the CASE statement:

IF condition THEN statement1 ELSE statement2

is equivalent to

```
CASE condition OF
    TRUE: statement1;
    FALSE: statement2
END
```

It is difficult to give simple examples using the CASE statement which cannot be done better using arrays, but I will force a few.

EXAMPLE 1.12.1 Write a program segment which converts CHARacter letter grades 'A', 'B', 'C', 'D', 'F' to their numeric equivalents 4, 3, 2, 1, and 0, respectively. The input character will be C and the output number N.

```
CASE C OF
    'A': N := 4;
    'B': N := 3;
    'C': N := 2;
    'D': N := 1;
    'F': N := 0
END
```

EXAMPLE 1.12.2 Suppose we have defined the enumerated type

```
TYPE MOTYPE=(JAN,FEB,MAR,APR,MAY,JUN,JUL,AUG,SEP,OCT,NOV,DEC);
```

and we wish to construct a program segment which takes a variable MONTH of this type and produces the integer NDAYS, which is the number of days in the month in a non-leap year. We use the fact that a single statement in a CASE can be labeled with several values, separated by commas. The solution is

```
CASE MONTH OF
    JAN,MAR,MAY,JUL,AUG,OCT,DEC: NDAYS := 31;
              APR,JUN,SEP,NOV: NDAYS := 30;
                          FEB: NDAYS := 28
END
```

Exercises 1.12

1. Redo Example 1.11.1 using a CASE statement.

2. Write a CASE statement which takes as input an integer SCHOOLYEAR in the range 1 . . . 8 and writes FRESHMAN if it is 1, SOPHOMORE if 2, JUNIOR if 3, SENIOR if 4, and GRADUATE STUDENT if in the range 5 to 8.

1.13   READ AND READLN

This section is rather technical and might best be skimmed or omitted entirely on first reading. Return to it when you have I/O problems. (You will!) Some details on specific implementations can be found in Appendix B.

The original implementation of Pascal on large CDC computers was hampered by the operating system, and, instead of concealing its limitations, Pascal magnifies them. As a result, input in Pascal is extremely tricky and rather inflexible. When interactive I/O (for which Pascal was not designed) is used, as we will, the situation becomes almost intolerable. An attempt will be made here to give you enough of an understanding of how Pascal I/O works that you will be able to figure out the mysterious things which will inevitably happen to you. There is a summary of things to remember at the end of the section.

1.13.1   The Current-Position Pointer

The READ command maintains a pointer to the current position in the input file. Suppose the situation were the following:

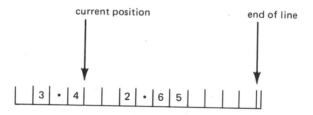

and a READ(X) instruction occurs at this point, X a numeric variable; blanks will be skipped until a number is found, the value of the number will be read, stopping at the first character which is not valid as part of the number, here, the blank after the 5, and X will be given the value 2.65, and current position will be set to just beyond the 5:

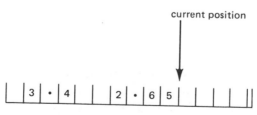

If Pascal encounters a bad character (such as a comma) before it finds a number, this is a fatal error. Thus if you wish to separate your

numbers by something other than blanks, you must get rid of the separators yourself, probably by reading them into a CHARacter variable.

1.13.2   EOLN

When (through further READing) the current-position pointer
reaches the point where it is about to fall off the end of the line,

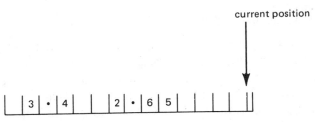

current position

the built-in function EOLN becomes TRUE and the next single character supplied is a (fictitious) blank. The current-position pointer is then
advanced to the beginning of the next line. In interactive situations,
this may cause the terminal to request input with a prompting "?". The
end of line blank has the effect of ending any number in progress, so
numbers may not be broken between two lines of input.

In CDC implementations, a pseudorandom number of blanks is
attached to or removed from the end of each line. The simplest way to
skip over any unwanted garbage at the end of a line, such as these
blanks, is to use the READLN statement. READLN should be equivalent, for C a character variable, to

```
WHILE NOT EOLN DO
    READ(C); (* GETS TO END OF CURRENT LINE *)
READ(C); (* SKIPS OVER PSEUDO BLANK AT END OF LINE *)
```

1.13.3   EOF

The built-in Boolean function EOF becomes TRUE when the program has read to the end of the INPUT file. In many interactive systems, there is no way to signal EOF from a terminal, but on CDC
interactive systems this occurs when the user responds to the prompt
with an immediate carriage return:

```
?  3.4  2.65<CR>
? <CR>
```

We could represent the preceding input internally as

EOF is tricky, too. If asked to write a program to READ and sum numbers until EOF occurs, the user might produce

```
SUM := 0;
WHILE NOT EOF DO
   BEGIN
      READ(X);
      SUM := SUM + X
   END;
WRITELN('SUM =', SUM)
```

Unfortunately, given the preceding input, after 3.4 and 2.65 have been read, the current position will be just after the 5 and the EOF will not be "seen." On the next execution of the loop an attempt will be made to read another X. Various things can happen here, all of them bad. The original implementation on CDC machines gives you the last X twice and then finds the end of file.

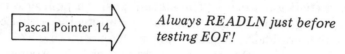

Always READLN just before testing EOF!

An acceptable version of the preceding program, which now requires that the input numbers be on separate lines, is

```
SUM := 0;
WHILE NOT EOF DO
   BEGIN
      READ(X); READLN; SUM := SUM + X
   END;
WRITELN('SUM =', SUM)
```

The sequence READ(X); READLN can be replaced by the equivalent READLN(X).

All in all, though

Sentinels are safer than EOF!

1.13.4   READing CHARacter Arrays

One often wants to read a whole line of characters into an array. This cannot be done without a loop in standard Pascal, but many Pascals have been extended in a fairly consistent way to allow for this. We will assume such an extension, as follows: If A has been declared

```
VAR A: PACKED ARRAY [1 . .N] OF CHAR;
```

and we perform the statement READ(A), the following occurs. Characters are read from the standard input file and stored successively in A[1], A[2], . . . until either (1) EOLN occurs or (2) N characters have been read. In case 1, the remainder of A is filled with blanks (and EOLN remains TRUE). If we were to do a READ(B) immediately after case 1 had occurred, B would be all blanks since EOLN would already be TRUE.

I am using this extended READ to make the sample programs here easier to read (and also, in a modest way, to encourage a rational extension of the language). If your Pascal is not so equipped, the code to do this can be written out in full using

```
Model Program 4:  Read a line of characters with
blank fill.

    CONST N = . . .

    VAR A: ARRAY [1 . . N] OF CHAR;
        I:  INTEGER;
        .

        .

    I := 0;
    WHILE (I < N) AND NOT EOLN DO
        BEGIN
            I := I + 1; READ(A[I])
        END;
    FOR I := I+1 TO N DO A[I] := ' '
```

1.13.5   Interactive I/O

EXAMPLE 1.13.1 The following program is an example of what happens with standard Pascal in a CDC interactive system:

```
(* EXAMPLE 1.13.1: TESTRD1       *)
(* DEMONSTRATE THE FOIBLES OF *)
(* INTERACTIVE PASCAL I/O         *)

PROGRAM TESTRD1(INPUT, OUTPUT);

VAR   B, C: ARRAY[1 . . 100] OF CHAR; (* SAVE FOR OUTPUT *)
      I, J: INTEGER; (* INDICES *)
      TR: ARRAY [BOOLEAN] OF CHAR; (* TRANSLATE BOOL TO CHAR *)

BEGIN (* TESTRD1 *)
    WRITELN('TYPE IN LINES OF INPUT:');
    TR[FALSE] := ' '; TR[TRUE] := ''''; (* INITIALIZE TR *)
```

```
        I := 0;
    WHILE (NOT EOF) DO
        BEGIN
            I:= I + 1;
            B[I] := TR[EOLN];
            READ (C[I])
        END;
    FOR J := 1 TO I DO WRITE(B[J]);
    WRITELN('#'); (* INDICATES EOF *)
    FOR J := 1 TO I DO WRITE(C[J]);
    WRITELN
END.    (* TESTRD1 *)
```

Execution gives

```
?  ABCDEFGH
TYPE IN LINES OF INPUT:
?  IJK
?
                    '       '#
ABCDEFGH   IJK
```

Notes

1. The message 'TYPE IN LINES . . .' requesting input appears *after* you have typed in the first input line.

2. EOLN and EOF become true just *before* their corresponding condition is encountered (instead of after, as in some languages).

3. An extra blank was tacked on at the end of the second input line by this particular operating system. (This is beyond Pascal's control.)

The reason for items 1 and 2 is that Pascal secretly reads one character ahead. To start off doing this properly, it must read the first character before the program even starts executing, which, in interactive situations, means it must read the whole first line of input before any code is executed as none of the line is finalized until carriage return is hit.

I know of two main methods to solve this problem, and unfortunately a program written for one method often develops mysterious problems when run under the other method. Method B seems to me to be the better, and is the one we will assume here.

Method A: Keep reading ahead, but avoid reading the initial line before execution begins by supplying a fictitious empty line at the beginning of the program. On the particular CDC implementation I use,

this is indicated by following the file INPUT in the PROGRAM statement with a '/'. The output resulting from Example 1.13.1 then
becomes

```
TYPE IN LINES OF INPUT:
?  ABCDEFGH
?  IJK
?
'                      '#
   ABCDEFGH  IJK
```

(Note the extra EOLN and blank at the beginning of the output.)

Processing lines of input in this method involves repetition of the
pair "READLN; READ and process line." The initial READLN serves
to skip over the fake empty line. If the system has EOF and you want
to stop on it, you need something like

```
READLN;
WHILE NOT EOF DO
    BEGIN
        READ and process line;
        READLN
    END
```

If you want to stop when a line of a certain type is read, you
should *not* end the loop with a READLN. Do something like

```
READ(LINE); (* LINE IS AN ARRAY OF CHARS *)
WHILE (LINE <> 'STOP              ') DO
    BEGIN
        process LINE;
        READLN;
        READ(LINE)
    END
```

To stop this program, type

```
STOP<CR>
```

If we had erroneously written

```
READLN(LINE);
WHILE (LINE <> 'STOP              ') DO
    BEGIN
        process LINE;
        READLN(LINE)
    END
```

then, to stop the program, we must type

```
STOP<CR>
<CR>
```

Method B: "Lazy" input (see the paper by Saxe and Hisgen listed in the Bibliography for more details). In this method, the next character of interactive input is not read until needed, that is, when a READ occurs or EOLN or EOF is tested. Thus READLN eats up the current line but does not require a new line to be typed until it is referenced. Input processing in this method consists of a repetition of the pair "READ and process line; READLN." we can read and process until a specific line occurs using

```
READLN(LINE);
WHILE (LINE <> 'STOP              ') DO
   BEGIN
      process LINE;
      READLN(LINE)
   END
```

which is stopped by typing

```
STOP<CR>
```

You should not start such a program with READLN (alone) as this will throw away the first real line of input!

EXAMPLE 1.13.2 Rewrite Example 1.13.1 for a Pascal with lazy input and no EOF on interactive input. Use the character '$' to indicate end of input. The first part of the progam will be the same, except that it will be called TESTRD2. From the WHILE statement on, it becomes

```
REPEAT
   I := I + 1; B[I] := TR[EOLN] ; READ(C[I] )
UNTIL (C[I] = '$');
FOR J := 1 TO I DO WRITE(B[J] ); WRITELN;
FOR J := 1 TO I DO WRITE(C[J] ); WRITELN
END.  (* TESTRD2 *)
```

A test run of this program produced

```
TYPE IN LINES OF INPUT
?  ABCDEFGH<CR>              (carriage return shown explicitly here)
?  <CR>                      (empty line)
?  IJK<CR>
?  $<CR>
                  ' '      '
ABCDEFGH    IJK  $
```

A common moral to be drawn from both of these methods is

Pascal Pointer 16

(Incorrect) Pascal programs often require more input than they appear to.

See also Pointer 5.

One simple debugging technique which is useful in uncovering such problems (as well as others) is *echoing* the input back to the user while you are debugging; for example

```
READ (A[I]);
WRITELN('A[', I:1, ']=', A[I]); (* REMOVE LATER!!! *)
```

which, if I is 14, would give an interchange like

```
?  2.345<CR>
A[14] =     0.23450000000000E+01
```

READ Summary

1. A pointer is kept to the current next character of input. At the end of a line, the next character is an extra supplied blank, and just before it is read the function EOLN is TRUE.

2. On some systems, blanks may be added or removed from the end of an input line.

3. In Method A interactive systems, when the phony EOLN blank is read, execution of the program ceases until the next whole line of input can be read. Start input with a READLN to skip over the initial fake line. End with READLN if terminating on end of file; do *not* end with READLN if not terminating on end of file.

4. In Method B interactive systems, do *not* start with READLN. End with READLN if ending on EOF; otherwise, ending with READLN is optional.

Exercises 1.13

1. Rewrite the following segment for a Pascal system which doesn't allow you to read a whole line of characters with a single READ statement:

```
READLN(LINE);
WHILE (LINE <> 'STOP                      ') DO
    BEGIN
        WRITELN(LINE); READLN(LINE)
    END
```

2. Rewrite the palindrome program of Example 1.11.2 so that it accepts and processes arbitrarily many potential palindromes on separate lines, stopping when the line 'STOP' is entered. Use the interactive method of your Pascal system or Method B.

1.14   ERROR EXITS AND THE GOTO STATEMENT

The GOTO statement will not be used in this book (for some reasons, see Chapter 2). Instead I will assume the availability of a built-in (non-standard) procedure HALT('message') which prints the message and stops the program. For example,

    HALT('BAD INPUT DATA')

If your system does not have this or a similar statement (see Appendix B), the GOTO statement is probably the best choice as a substitute. It is of the form

    GOTO label

 *GOTO is one word!*

Labels are from one to four digits. All labels must be declared at the beginning of the program between PROGRAM and CONST. The declaration is of the form

    LABEL label1, label2, . . .;

For example, the preceding HALT statement can be written in standard form as

    LABEL 9999;
       . . .
       BEGIN (* HALT *)
          WRITELN('BAD INPUT DATA');
          GOTO 9999
       END
       . . .
    9999: END.

When the label is used it is followed by a colon, and the statement before it, if any, must be terminated by a semicolon, as there is at least an empty statement after it. Thus the semicolon below is required:

       WRITELN;
    9999: END.

Use of HALT or this type of GOTO is preferable to IF-THEN-ELSE in situations where there are rarely occurring error stops. Such a program might have an actual structure like

       S1;
       S2;
       S3;

```
IF error 1 THEN HALT( . . . );
S4;
S5;
IF error 2 THEN HALT( . . . );
S6;
S7;
S8;
IF error 3 THEN HALT( . . . );
S9;
S10
```

Without HALT or this form of GOTO, the program assumes a very unnatural and awkward form:

```
S1;
S2;
S3;
IF error 1 THEN print message
ELSE
    BEGIN
        S4;
        S5;
        IF error 2 THEN print message
        ELSE
            BEGIN
                S6;
                S7;
                S8;
                IF error 3 THEN print message
                ELSE
                    BEGIN
                        S9;
                        S10;
                    END
            END
    END
```

1.15 FORMATING PASCAL PROGRAMS

As the reader has no doubt noticed, we have been formating our program texts in a way related to the programming statements used. This is very important as far as making programs easier to read and debug. (However, remember that Pascal ignores the formating so you can confuse yourself if the formating does not correspond to the program.) There are many sets of rules for formating programs; the following set will be used in this book:

1. Put statements and BEGIN and END on separate lines unless they are related and all short.

2. When a statement is too long for one line, continue it on the next line, indented three spaces.

3. BEGIN and its corresponding END are indented the same amount. The statements enclosed by BEGIN and END are indented three spaces more than BEGIN and END are:

```
BEGIN
    statement;
    statement;
    statement
END
```

4. IF condition THEN is placed on one line with its statement on the next line, indented three spaces. If there is an ELSE clause, ELSE is on a separate line, indented the same amount as its IF, and its statement is on the next line, indented three from ELSE. If either statement is short, it can be on the same line as THEN or ELSE:

```
IF condition THEN
    statement
ELSE
    statement
```

5. WHILE condition DO or FOR . . . DO is placed on one line, with the loop body statement on the next line(s) indented three spaces unless it is short; for example,

```
WHILE condition DO
    statement
```

6. The REPEAT statement is formated with REPEAT and UNTIL aligned and the statements of the loop indented three spaces:

```
REPEAT
    statement1;
        . . .
    statementn
UNTIL condition
```

7. The CASE statement is the most difficult to format satisfactorily. I line up CASE with its corresponding END and line up the :'s of the CASE labels, indented with respect to CASE. For example,

```
CASE I OF
    2, 5: statement1;
       3: statement1;
 1, 4, 6: statement3
END
```

These rules will be interpreted loosely occasionally, as their purpose is to help rather than hinder us. As we introduce other Pascal statements, formating rules for them will become evident.

1.16 SUMMARY

In this section I will summarize the topics introduced in this chapter, giving the section numbers where they are discussed.

The six scalar data types were introduced: REAL (1.1, 1.2), INTEGER (1.1, 1.2), BOOLEAN (1.10), CHAR (1.10), enumerated (1.11), and subrange (1.11), as well as the compound data type ARRAY (1.9, 1.11).

Four types of declaration were introduced: LABEL (1.14), CONST (1.7), TYPE (1.11), and VAR (1.5), which may appear at most once, in this order, in each program.

Five types of statements were introduced:

1. Assignment statements (1.3).

2. I/O statements: READ, READLN, WRITE, and WRITELN (1.4, 1.6, 1.13).

3. Two types of choice statements, the IF statement (1.7) and the CASE statement (1.12).

4. Compound statements (1.7).

5. Three looping statements: WHILE, FOR, and REPEAT (1.8).

The built-in functions ABS (1.10), CHR (1.10), EOF (1.13), EOLN (1.13), EXP (1.2), LN (1.2), ORD (1.10), ROUND (1.2), and TRUNC (1.2) were discussed.

Finally, we also discussed at length the pesky ";" (1.7) and READ problems (1.13).

Programming Problems

1.1 Write a program to compute the mean (average) and standard deviation (a measure of how much the data vary from the average) of up to 100 data points. The program should read the data into an array X, stopping when –99 is read. N will be the number of data points (not including the terminating –99 of course). Then

$$\text{mean} = (X[1] + X[2] + \cdots + X[N])/N$$
$$\text{variance} = ((X[1] - \text{mean})**2 + \cdots + (X[N] - \text{mean})**2)/(N - 1)$$
$$\text{standard deviation} = \text{SQRT(variance)}$$

The output from your program should be

MEAN = whatever; STANDARD DEVIATION = whatever

Hint: To improve efficiency, compute the sum used to find the mean at the same time you are READing Xs.

Test your program with the data 1, 2, 3, 4, 5, 6, 7, 8, 9, 10, -99, which should produce a mean of 5.5 and a standard deviation of about 3.02765.

1.2 Write a program which reads an integer N > 1 and prints out the prime factorization of N. A prime is a number greater than 1 which is divisible only by 1 and itself. Every N > 1 can be written in essentially one way as a product of primes (this is called the fundamental theorem of arithmetic). Input of 24 to your program should produce

24 = 2 * 2 * 2 * 3

and input of 77 should produce

77 = 7 * 11

Hints: Start with POSFACT = 2. Keep dividing N by POSFACT and printing "* POSFACT" as long as POSFACT divides N evenly. Then add 1 to POSFACT and continue until N = 1. To avoid printing * as many times as POSFACT, use a three-character array, say INTER. Initialize it to ' = ' and each time POSFACT is to be printed, execute WRITE(INTER, POSFACT:1); INTER := ' * '.

1.3 Write a program to read a name in the form "first middle(s) last" and print the name in the form "last, first middle(s)." The name will be entirely on one line. Thus input of

JOHN SMITH

produces output of

SMITH, JOHN

and input of

ALPHA BETA GAMMA DELTA

produces

DELTA, ALPHA BETA GAMMA

Don't worry about JR., ESQ., III., and the like.

chapter 2

structured
programming
and all that

You may have noticed that the GOTO statement (mentioned in Section 1.14) seems to have been designed to be unpleasant to use. This is a *good thing!* It has been generally recognized that GOTOs are bad for programming, at least since the celebrated letter of E. W. Dijkstra (see Bibliography). This has led to the rise and widespread use of the concept of *structured programming*. I believe that structured programming is an extremely important concept, but that it has been widely misunderstood and applied much too rigidly.

First, we need to say what structured programming is. Some would say that it is programming without GOTOs. Others (with perhaps a vested interest in a language that requires GOTOs) seem to say that it is writing in pseudolanguages without GOTOs and then handtranslating into real programs with GOTOs. It is my view that the lack of GOTOs is the *result* rather than the cause of structured programming, but that true structured programming is not possible in languages requiring them.

My own (totally unrigorous) definition is that a structured program is a *program in which the structure of the problem solution is made clearly visible in the structure of the program.* Structured programs are usually the result of the *process* of *structured programming*, which is usually taken to mean top-down design. We will discuss this topic in Section 2.2.

In spite of the vagueness of the preceding definition, we can make the following assertions:

1. There are algorithms which cannot be programmed in a structured way in any known language *without* GOTOs; that is, though such a program can be written without GOTOs, it will be badly structured (see Section 1.14).

2. A structured program will tend to have few or no GOTO statements.

It can be proved theoretically that any program can be written using only the usual simple statements (assignment, I/O, etc.) and the ruling triumvirate of structured programming, which in Pascal are BEGIN-END brackets, IF-THEN-ELSE, and WHILE-DO. It can also be shown that this may require a substantial amount of additional storage and/or execution time. In addition, as mentioned in assertion 1, it may produce a poor program. For this reason, it does not pay to be doctrinaire about the eradication of GOTOs.

Properly structured programs seem to be somewhat harder to write (more advance planning is required) and slightly less efficient, but also seem to be easier to read, debug, and modify, and are more reliable. It seems to be the case that the overall programming process is more efficient when structured programming methods are used.

For most programmers, giving up the GOTO is a trauma on the same level as giving up smoking, so this book is going to do it "cold turkey." We will not use the Pascal GOTO facility at all, not because it should never be used but because you should get into the habit of using it as little as possible, and because the kinds of problems we will treat here are best handled without it.

2.1 AN EXAMPLE: LINEAR SEARCHING

Given the array A[1 . . N], and an item X of the same type, we want to find the first I for which A[I] = X. Set I to 0 if, for all I, X <> A[I]. This problem occurs frequently in programming. We will use the method of linear search, in which we start at the beginning of the array and look at it item by item.

Solution 1: The programmer who is used to FORTRAN or BASIC might code this as follows:

```
FOR I := 1 TO N DO
    IF (X = A[I]) THEN GOTO 10;
 I := 0;
10:
```

Although it is difficult to make a program this small really un-readable, this one does have a loop which is terminated in two different places, something which can get quite confusing if the places are physically more separate in the program. Therefore, if the reader will indulge me, let's see if we can get the loop test exit all in one place and, in the process, rid the program of its GOTO.

Solution 2

```
I := 1;
WHILE (I <= N) AND (A[I] <> X) DO
    I := I + 1;
IF (I > N) THEN I := 0
```

While this program would work in many languages similar to Pascal, it does not work properly in Pascal for a combination of two reasons:

1. Most Pascals evaluate all parts of a condition even if it could be determined part-way through that the whole condition is TRUE or FALSE. In the preceding program, it would be known that the condition was FALSE when it was known that I <= N is false, but Pascal would go ahead and check A[I] <> X. In most languages, this might not matter.

2. However, in Pascal, subscripts are checked for valid values and an invalid subscript causes a fatal error and termination of execution.

Thus if X is not found in the A array, the program will terminate with a fatal error if A's top dimension is N. A standard way to get around this problem in this and other such situations is to introduce an auxiliary Boolean variable, called, say, FOUND. We then have

Solution 3

```
FOUND := FALSE; I := 1;
WHILE (I <= N) AND NOT FOUND DO
    IF (X = A[I]) THEN FOUND := TRUE
    ELSE I := I + 1;
IF NOT FOUND THEN I := 0
```

This may well seem more complicated and less natural than the solution with GOTO. However, with a clever change we can improve this solution considerably. All the solutions so far have the property that *two* tests are performed each time through the loop (even in Solution 1, one test is hidden in the FOR statement). We could reduce this to one test, A[I] <> X, if we were sure that some A[I] = X would stop the search every time. The solution to this is to *force* this to happen by enlarging the A array to include A[N+1] if necessary, and arranging it so that this is X before the search takes place. A[N+1] is called a sentinel, now signaling the end of an array.

Solution 4

```
A[N+1] := X; I := 1;
WHILE (A[I] <> X) DO I := I + 1;
IF (I > N) THEN I := 0
```

This solution is a program which is shorter, simpler, almost twice as fast as solution 1, and contains no GOTOs! The reader may quibble that solution 4 only works because we enlarged the A array and that solution 2 would have also worked if the A array had been enlarged. However, solution 4 is much more efficient than solution 2.

If all the A[I]s are different, or it does not matter whether we get the first or last A[I] equal to X, there is an even simpler program using subscript 0 to contain the sentinel:

Solution 5

> **Model Program 5:**   Linear search for X in A[1 .. N] ;
> I = 0 or A[I] = X when done.
>
> ```
>     A[0] := X; I := N;
>     WHILE (A[I] <> X) DO I := I - 1
> ```

An aside on programming style: There is a particularly poor way of writing loops like that in solution 3, which in this case is

```
WHILE (I <= N) AND NOT FOUND DO
   IF (A[I] = X) THEN
      BEGIN
         FOUND := TRUE;
         do whatever you do when found (* BAD CODE!!!! *)
      END
   ELSE I := I + 1
```

I guess that the programmer's natural parsimony requires that the most possible use be made from the test. This however violates

> ### The INSIDE-OUT Principle
>
> Things which are done only once should be done OUTSIDE loops as much as possible.

The philosophy behind this principle is that what *appears* to be part of the loop should be an essential part of it, and conversely. (The FOUND := TRUE is done only once but it must remain inside to get you outside.)

In the example given here there is a positive danger of doing the "found" processing inside the loop because you may forget that you must still test for "not found" outside the loop, and thus *always* do the "not found" processing.

2.2   TOP-DOWN DESIGN

As indicated previously, there is no really rigorous definition of structured programming. Generally, it is thought of as a process, *top-down design*, rather than an end result. Once again though, top-down design is neither necessary nor sufficient for writing well-structured programs.

In top-down design, the programmer works like a good painter, roughing out the program in a few broad strokes, and then successively refining all parts of it more or less at once to arrive finally at the completely detailed program. A bottom-up approach would be to write individual units and piece them together into a program. An example of the possible ill effects of bottom-up design is the humorous version of IBM's famous THINK sign (Figure 2.1).

FIGURE 2.1

In discussing top-down design, it is useful to think geometrically. Statements of actions to be performed will be represented as boxes, rather like flowchart boxes, but we will not actually write the statements in the boxes. The statements can be anything from vague general ones bearing no relationship to an actual programming language to actual programming language statements. The goal is to start with the former and get to the latter.

We start with a single box (statement), which is a statement of what the program is to do (Figure 2.2). Then, and at any later time in the process, any such box can be *refined*, that is, replaced by one of three more detailed constructs.

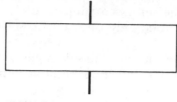

FIGURE 2.2

1. A list of boxes (Pascal BEGIN-END statement compounding), Figure 2.3.

2. A choice of two boxes (Pascal IF statement), Figure 2.4.

3. A loop (Pascal WHILE statement), Figure 2.5.

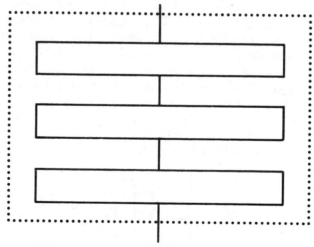

FIGURE 2.3

Note that the Pascal FOR, REPEAT, and CASE statements can be built up from these. This process of refinement continues (in principle) until each box corresponds to an actual statement in the programming language used.

In theory, if we know that a box does the correct thing in a program and that the refinement does the same thing, then the refinement is also correct. This should allow us to consider relatively small pieces of a program independently of the rest when determining

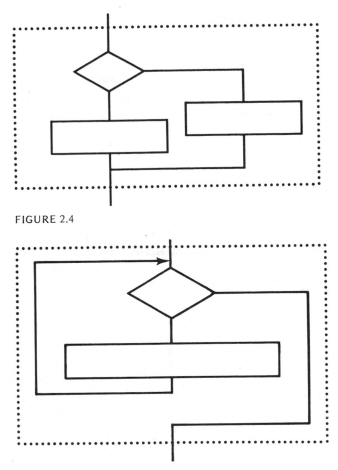

FIGURE 2.4

FIGURE 2.5

whether or not a program is correct. Of course, it is not always that simple, but the top-down approach does seem to help in this way.

One of the simplifying features of the top-down process is that each box has only one entry point and one exit point, and that the three methods of refinement all preserve this feature. If GOTOs were allowed, this would not be the case.

Note also that the existence of statement parentheses, BEGIN-END in Pascal, is crucial to this process. To refine refinements repeatedly, there must be some way of blocking lists of statements into the proper places. This fact seems strangely to have escaped most language designers associated with FORTRAN, BASIC, and COBOL.

Of the three methods of refinement discussed, loops are by far the most important and powerful, and are the hardest to understand. All programs are (or should be) organized in terms of a *fundamental loop*, which may, in turn, contain other (less) fundamental loops. This leads to

---

The COWBOY Principle

Look for fundamental loops.

The standard form for loops is

```
initialization;
WHILE condition DO
     body;
cleanup
```

To demonstrate the top-down approach, we give three examples. (Note that we do not actually draw the boxes. The statements corresponding to the boxes are used instead.) The third example also demonstrates what will be a constant theme: the tradeoff between speed and storage.

EXAMPLE 2.2.1 Write a program to read a string of numbers terminated by -999 and print out their median. For an odd number of numbers, the median is the middle item of the numbers in order, and for an even number, it is the average of the two middle numbers.

We will take a rather simple-minded approach, arranging the numbers in ascending order by a rather brute-force method. (For a more sophisticated method, see Programming Problem 6.3.) We start with a single statement expressing the purpose of the program:

read data and print median

and refine this first into three steps:

read the data
order it
print median

The first two of these are each realized by a fundamental loop. The first we have seen before (it is Model Program 3) and the "print median" step is essentially trival, so we will concentrate on the middle statement. Our program to do it is based on the following ideas:

```
FOR I := 1 TO N – 1 DO
    IF (A[I] > A[I+1]) THEN
        exchange A[I] and A[I+1]
```

Unfortunately, this is not sufficient to order the A's properly, as the following simple example shows:

A[1]   A[7]

8	5	12	3	7	4	6

Tracing one execution of the loop,

I	A[1]					A[7]
1	8←→5					
2	5	8	12			
3			12←→3			
4		3	12←→7			
5			7	12←→4		
6				4	12←→6	
final	5	8	3	7	4	6	12

Repeated executions of this loop produce

5	3	7	4	6	8	12
3	5	4	6	7	8	12

and

3	4	5	6	7	8	12

which is in order.

This suggests that we can refine "order it" to the fundamental loop

```
WHILE not in order DO
    reorder loop
```

where "reorder loop" is based on the FOR loop just discussed. To be precise, we use a Boolean variable INORDER to control the loop, and the refinement of "order it" becomes

```
INORDER := FALSE;          (* initialize *)
WHILE NOT INORDER DO       (* loop *)
    reorder and recompute INORDER;
                           (* no cleanup *)
```

"reorder and recompute INORDER" consists of the (less) fundamental loop

```
INORDER := TRUE;           (*initialize *)
FOR I := 1 TO N - 1 DO     (* loop *)
    IF A[I] , A[I+1] out of order THEN
        exchange them and set INORDER := FALSE
                           (* again, no cleanup *)
```

We refine "IF A[I], . . ." by

```
IF (A[I] > A[I+1]) THEN
    BEGIN
        exchange A[I] and A[I+1];
        INORDER := FALSE
    END
```

At this point all remaining refinements are straightforward, so we can write the program.

```
             (* EXAMPLE 2.2.1: MEDIAN       *)
             (* READ NUMBERS TERMINATED *)
             (* BY -999 AND PRINT MEDIAN    *)

          PROGRAM MEDIAN(INPUT, OUTPUT);

          CONST SENTINEL = -999;      (* END OF INPUT *)
                MAX = 100;    (* MAXIMUM NUM OF ITEMS CONSIDERED *)

          VAR   A: ARRAY [1 .. MAX] OF REAL; (* DATA ITEMS *)
                TEMP: REAL; (* FOR READ AND EXCHANGE *)
                N,            (* NUMBER OF DATA ITEMS *)
                I: INTEGER;  (* ARRAY INDEX FOR ORDERING *)
                INORDER: BOOLEAN; (* LOOP TERMINATOR *)

          BEGIN (* MEDIAN *)
                (* READ DATA *)
              N := 0; READ(TEMP);
              WHILE (TEMP <> SENTINEL) AND (N < MAX) DO
                  BEGIN
                      N := N + 1; A[N] := TEMP;
                      READ(TEMP)
                  END;

                  (* REORDER IT *)
              INORDER := FALSE;
              WHILE NOT INORDER DO
                  BEGIN
                      INORDER := TRUE;
                      FOR I := 1 TO N - 1 DO
                          IF (A[I] > A[I+1]) THEN
                              BEGIN
                                  TEMP := A[I]; (* A[I] <-> A[I+1] *)
                                  A[I] := A[I+1];
                                  A[I+1] := TEMP;
                                  INORDER := FALSE
                              END
                  END;
```

```
            (* PRINT MEDIAN *)
    WRITE('MEDIAN  =');  I := (N + 1) DIV 2;
    IF ODD(N) THEN WRITELN(A[I]:1:3)
    ELSE WRITELN(0.5*(A[I] + A[I+1]):1:3)
END.  (* MEDIAN *)
```

Notes

1. The ordering loop demonstrates that the condition test (IN-ORDER) happens only at the head of the loop; not continuously during its execution.

2. ODD is a built-in Boolean function which is true if its integer argument is odd, and false if it is even.

3. The second WHILE loop can be rewritten more simply as a REPEAT loop:

```
REPEAT
    INORDER := TRUE;
    FOR I := 1 TO N - 1 DO
        IF (A[I] > A[I+1]) THEN
            BEGIN
                exchange A[I] and A[I+1];
                INORDER := FALSE
            END
UNTIL INORDER
```

4. A refined form of this sorting method (see Exercise 2.2.1) is called the *bubble sort*, presumably because if the array is written vertically with large indices at the top, data items appear to "bubble up" to their proper position. This method is often given as the method of choice for sorting small files. As we will see in Sections 3.5 and 7.2, there are much simpler methods, which are also faster. As Donald Knuth says, "In short, the bubble sort seems to have nothing to recommend it, except a catchy name and the fact that it leads to some interesting theoretical problems" (*Sorting and Searching*, page 111).

EXAMPLE 2.2.2 Write a complete program to read a number and print it out in hexadecimal (base 16, often called hex). The method is as follows: divide by 16; the remainder is the last digit of the hexadecimal representation (10 is represented by A, 11 by B, etc.). Replacing the number by the quotient, repeat the process to set the next-to-last digit. The process stops when the quotient is zero. For example, let's convert 1463 to hex:

$$1463 \text{ DIV } 16 = 91 \qquad 1463 \text{ MOD } 16 = 7$$

So the last digit is 7 and we continue:

$$91 \text{ DIV } 16 = 5 \qquad 91 \text{ MOD } 16 = 11$$

So the next-to-last digit is B.

$$5 \text{ DIV } 16 = 0 \qquad 5 \text{ MOD } 16 = 5$$

So the first digit is 5 and the result is $1463 = 5B7(16)$.
The fundamental loop of the program is

```
read N;              (* initialize *)
compute digits;      (* loop *)
write out result     (* cleanup *)
```

"Read N" is not so self-evident as it appears. On some machines negative input might produce erroneous results or even an infinite loop. To avoid such situations we should follow

---

The PLAID Principle

Always check input for validity.

The "compute digits" loop becomes

```
WHILE (N <> 0) DO
    generate a digit and reduce N
```

We refine "generate a digit and reduce N" to

```
QUOT := N DIV 16;
REM := N MOD 16;
save character corresponding to REM;
N := QUOT
```

A little thought here shows us we can simplify slightly to

```
REM := N MOD 16;
N := N DIV 16;
save character corresponding to REM
```

To do the character saving, we will keep an array DIGIT of the digit CHARs. To convert from numeric value to character value of digits, the method which usually occurs first to inexperienced programmers is a linear search. A somewhat more sophisticated method uses the order properties of characters:

```
IF (REM < 10) THEN char version := CHR(ORD('0') + REM)
ELSE char version := CHR(ORD('A') + REM – 10)
```

(This even works in EBCDIC.) An even simpler method is possible. We define CHDIGITS as the character string '0123456789ABCDEF' indexed 0 . . 15 and "save character corresponding to REM" becomes

```
I := I + 1;
DIGIT[I] := CHDIGITS[REM]
```

The initialization of the CHDIGITS array and of I will have to be added to the initialization part of the loop. As the cleanup part of the program is fairly self-evident, we can now collect what we have done as a complete program. To avoid violating the Houdini principle, we make the base (16) and CHDIGIT initializer constants.

```
(* EXAMPLE 2.2.1: HEX        *)
(* CONVERT DECIMAL NUMBER *)
(* TO HEXADECIMAL           *)

PROGRAM HEX(INPUT, OUTPUT);

CONST BASE = 16;       (* BASE TO CONVERT TO *)
      BASEM1 = 15;     (* BASE – 1 *)
      DIGCHARS = '0123456789ABCDEF'; (* CHARACTER *)
             (* REPRESENTATION OF DIGITS 0 . . BASEM1 *)
      MAXDIGCT = 20; (* MAX NUMBER OF DIGITS OUTPUT *)

VAR    CHDIGITS: PACKED ARRAY [0 . . BASEM1] OF CHAR;
                    (* DECIMAL TO CHAR CONVERSION ARRAY *)
       N,               (* INPUT NUMBER *)
       NSAVE,           (* SAVED VERSION OF N FOR OUTPUT *)
       I,               (* NUMBER OF OUTPUT DIGITS COMPUTED *)
       J,               (* INDEX INTO OUTPUT DIGITS *)
       REM: INTEGER;  (*REMAINDER FROM DIV BY BASE *)
       DIGIT: ARRAY [1 . . MAXDIGCT] OF CHAR;
                    (* OUTPUT DIGITS *)

BEGIN (* HEX *)
    CHDIGITS := DIGCHARS;
    WRITELN('TYPE POSITIVE NUMBER:');READ(N);
    WHILE (N <= 0) DO (* INPUT VALIDITY CHECK *)
        BEGIN
            WRITELN('YOU CAN DO BETTER THAN THAT!');
            READ(N)
        END;
    I := 0; NSAVE := N;
    WHILE (N <> 0) DO (* COMPUTE DIGITS *)
```

```
BEGIN
    REM := N MOD BASE;
    N := N DIV BASE;
    I := I + 1;
    DIGIT[I] := CHDIGITS[REM]
END;
WRITE(NSAVE:1,' IN BASE ', BASE:1,' IS ');
FOR J := I DOWNTO 1 DO WRITE(DIGIT[J]);
WRITELN
END.    (* HEX *)
```

EXAMPLE 2.2.3 Write a program to read in a list of numbers, interpreting them as columns in which tab stops are to be set. Then read text in which one particular character, say \$, is interpreted as a tab which is to be replaced by the appropriate number of blanks to get to the next tab stop column. For simplicity we will read everything from the standard input file and write to the standard output file, even though in interactive situations this will result in mixing of input and output on the terminal screen. End of input will be indicated by a line starting with a ".". A sample terminal dialog might be

```
NUMBER OF TABS:
? 4
TAB COLUMNS:
? 8   12   16   35
ENTER TEXT:
? $DATA DIVISION.
        DATA DIVISION.
? $01$RECORD$PIC  X(29).
        01      RECORD              PIC X(29).
? .
```

We think of the program as a fundamental loop:

```
read in tab stops;     (* initialization *)
read a line;
WHILE first character <> '.' DO       (* loop *)
    BEGIN
        process and print text line;
        read next line
    END
                    (* no cleanup *)
```

We cannot determine how to read in tabs until we know how they will be stored, and this should be determined by the "process and print text line," box since presumably this will be executed much more often. The refinement for "process and print text line" uses a variable OUTCOL to keep track of the column position about to be printed in the output. Now we come to a bit of awkwardness. If we use the extended Pascal character READ feature, we need a fairly good sized array to hold long lines. This means that short lines will be padded with a lot of blanks, which slows down printing, and if a line contains tabs this blank padding may overflow onto the next line. Two possible solutions suggest themselves: (1) hand code the line reading part so we can keep track of how many "real" characters there were (to avoid repeating the code, a separate PROCEDURE could be used; see the next section), or (2) use a loop to strip off trailing blanks. Method 2 has the advantage that it also gets rid of "real" and operating system added trailing blanks, too, but it has the disadvantage that there is no place to put a sentinel when looking for a nonblank (as READ must read into a whole array); hence a loop with two tests is required.

We will in fact choose a third solution: blanks will be counted but not printed until a nonblank character occurs. Thus trailing blanks will not be printed. Tabs can also be handled by adding an appropriate number to this counter, which we call XTRABLANKS. The statement "process and print text line" becomes

```
OUTCOL :- 1; XTRABLANKS := 0;   (* initialization *)
FOR I := 1 TO line length DO       (* loop *)
    process LINE[I] ;
WRITELN                            (* cleanup *)
```

and "process LINE[I] " is

```
IF (LINE[I] = tab char) THEN
    process tab
ELSE
    BEGIN
        OUTCOL := OUTCOL + 1;
        IF (LINE[I] = ' ') THEN XTRABLANKS := XTRABLANKS + 1
        ELSE
            BEGIN
                write out XTRABLANKS blanks;
                WRITE(LINE[I])
            END
    END
```

We have finally come to the point where we must decide how tab stops are to be represented. The most obvious solution is to save them in an array, say TABSTOP, and linear search for the first one greater than OUTCOL. This necessitates a different type of sentinel:

```
TABSTOP[NTABS+1] := OUTCOL+1;  (* sentinel *)
I := 1;
WHILE (OUTCOL <= TABSTOP[I]) DO I := I + 1;
```

This method has the feature that if we tab when beyond the last tab stop we generate one space.

On the other hand, if we are willing to use more data storage we can make the tabbing process more efficient. This is a typical tradeoff. Also, as you will see, the process of initializing tab stops becomes more time consuming: there is no such thing as a free ride. The technique used here to dispense with a linear search for tab column is similar to that used in the last example to avoid having to search for digit to character conversions. Here we will keep an array NEXTTAB with one entry per column. NEXTTAB[I] will be the column to tab to from column I. Thus, given the data of the preceding example, the entries in the NEXTTAB array would be 8, 8, 8, 8, 8, 8, 8, 12, 12, 12, 12, 16, 16, 16, 16, 35, 35, . . ., and so on.

```
(* EXAMPLE 2.2.3: TABS              *)
(* REPLACE TAB CHAR WITH APPRO-     *)
(* PRIATE NUMBER OF BLANKS          *)


PROGRAM TABS (INPUT, OUTPUT);

CONST TABCHAR = '$';           (* INDICATES TAB *)
      STOPCHAR = '.';          (* THIS CHAR IN COL 1 STOPS INPUT *)
      LINELEN = 80;            (* MAX LEN OF LINE *)


VAR NEXTTAB: ARRAY [1 . . LINELEN] OF INTEGER;
        (* COL TO TAB TO GIVEN CURRENT COL *)
    LINE: PACKED ARRAY  [1 . . LINELEN] OF CHAR: (* INPUT LINE *)
    OUTCOL,                   (* POSITION IN OUTPUT LINE *)
    XTRABLANKS,               (* BLANKS NOT YET PRINTED *)
    NTABS,                    (* NUMBER OF TABS TO READ *)
    T,                        (* TAB COUNTER *)
    I: INTEGER;               (* INDEX USED SETTING NEXTTAB *)
    CH: CHAR;                 (* INPUT CHARACTER *)

BEGIN (* TABS *)
   WRITELN('NUMBER OF TABS:'); READ(NTABS);
   IF (NTABS <= 0) OR (NTABS > LINELEN) THEN
      HALT('BAD NUMBER OF TABS');
   OUTCOL := 1; (* COL OF NEXT TAB POS TO BE SET *)
   FOR T := 1 TO NTABS DO
      BEGIN
         READ(I);
         IF (I <= OUTCOL) OR (I > LINELEN) THEN
            HALT('BAD TAB');
         WHILE (OUTCOL < I) DO
            BEGIN
               NEXTTAB[OUTCOL] := I; OUTCOL := OUTCOL + 1
```

```
                    END
              END;
          FOR OUTCOL := OUTCOL TO LINELEN DO
              NEXTTAB[OUTCOL] := OUTCOL + 1;
          READLN(LINE);
          WHILE (LINE[1] <> STOPCHAR) DO
              BEGIN (* PROCESS AND PRINT TEXT LINE *)
                  OUTCOL := 1; XTRABLANKS := 0;
                  FOR I := 1 TO LINELEN DO
                      IF (LINE[I] = TABCHAR) THEN
                          BEGIN
                              XTRABLANKS := XTRABLANKS+NEXTTAB[OUTCOL]-
                                  OUTCOL;
                              OUTCOL := NEXTTAB[OUTCOL]
                          END
                      ELSE
                          BEGIN
                              OUTCOL := OUTCOL + 1;
                              IF (LINE[I] = ' ') THEN
                                  XTRABLANKS := XTRABLANKS + 1
                              ELSE
                                  BEGIN
                                      IF (XTRABLANKS > 0) THEN
                                          BEGIN
                                              WRITE(' ':XTRABLANKS);
                                              XTRABLANKS := 0
                                          END;
                                      WRITE(LINE[I])
                                  END
                          END;
                  WRITELN; READLN(LINE)
              END
          END.  (* TABS *)
```

Exercises 2.2

1. As you may have noticed in Example 2.2.1, if L is the last index I for which A[I] and A[I+1] were interchanged, then A[L .. N] are in their final position. Thus the next time through we need only do the loop FOR I := 1 TO L - 1 DO . . .. Also, if L is used, INORDER is no longer needed as INORDER is the condition (L > 1). Rewrite the reordering program using L. (This is called the bubble sort, as mentioned previously.)

2. Rewrite HEX so that it will take *two* numbers as input, N and BASE (1 < BASE < 36), and print out N in the given BASE.

2.3 PROCEDURES AND FUNCTIONS

An alternative to refining a pseudoprogram statement is in effect to call it a new statement in the programming language. Refinements to carry out this new statement are collected elsewhere in a *subprogram*. In Pascal, such subprograms are called PROCEDUREs and FUNC-TIONs, which differ somewhat in form and usage. They are defined in the declarations part of the program, between VAR declarations and the BEGIN of the main program. A procedure or function is executed only when its name is invoked in the main program or a subprogram itself gotten to in this way. We think of this name invocation as being the language extension mentioned previously.

EXAMPLE 2.3.1 A report-writing program is to produce its output in numbered pages. A variable LINESSOFAR keeps track of the number of lines already printed on the page and a constant PAGE-LEN is the number of lines per page. PAGENO is the number of the current page. At many places in the program, we wish to execute the pseudoinstruction

skip to new page

Rather than refining this statement each place it occurs, we add a new statement to the language, NEWPAGE say, and then declare a procedure of this name to accomplish "skip to new page." "Skip to new page" is refined as follows:

write enough blank lines to set to the top of the next page;
print page number and one blank line

(We count lines because on a terminal there may be no "new page" carriage control.) The procedure, together with the relevant declarations, is

```
CONST PAGELEN = 66;      (* LINES PER PAGE *)
        PAGEWIDTH = 80;   (* CHARS PER LINE *)
   .
   .
   .


VAR    PAGENO, LINESSOFAR: INTEGER;
   .
   .
   .

PROCEDURE NEWPAGE;
      (* GO TO TOP OF NEXT PAGE AND NUMBER IT *)
   BEGIN (* NEWPAGE *)
      FOR LINESSOFAR := LINESSOFAR + 1 TO PAGELEN DO
         WRITELN;
      PAGENO := PAGENO + 1; LINESSOFAR := 2;
         WRITE(' ': PAGEWIDTH-8):
         WRITELN('PAGE   ', PAGENO:1); WRITELN
```

```
    END;  (* NEWPAGE *)
    .
    .
    .
BEGIN (* MAIN PROGRAM *)
    PAGENO := 1; LINESSOFAR := 0; (* DON'T NUMBER FIRST PAGE *)
        etc.
```

Now wherever the statement "skip to new page" appears in the main program, it is replaced by the command

```
    NEWPAGE;
```

(no keyword CALL, as in FORTRAN or PL/I.) The NEWPAGE statement causes the procedure NEWPAGE to be executed from its BEGIN till its END, after which control returns to the statement following the NEWPAGE statement. (There is no RETURN statement in Pascal.) NEWPAGE can access variables, constants, and the like, defined in the main program. These are called *global* items. The body of the procedure is just like a main program, except that it has no PROGRAM statement and its last END is followed by a semicolon (;) instead of a period. The procedure may have its own LABEL, CONST, TYPE, VAR, PROCEDURE, and FUNCTION declarations. These are *local* items. They are visible only within the procedure itself. In the Example 2.3.2, I is a local variable. It is possible for local and global items to have the same name, but this can be confusing and is not advised at this point. A detailed discussion of local and global data items is found in Section 6.3.

One of the most powerful capabilities of procedures is that they can have *parameters*. As an example, look at the part of NEWPAGE in Example 2.3.1 which prints PAGEWIDTH-8 blanks. It seems possible that there are many occasions when we might like to print N copies of a character C. N and C are called parameters here.

EXAMPLE 2.3.2 Write a procedure to execute the pseudo-statement

```
    print N copies of character C
```

We will call our procedure PRINCOPY, and the new programming language statement to accomplish this will be PRINCOPY(C, N). In the declaration of PRINCOPY, parameters are listed in parentheses after the procedure name, together with their type, just as in VAR declarations. In this case, we would have

```
PROCEDURE PRINCOPY(C: CHAR; N: INTEGER);
     (* PRINT N COPIES OF C *)
   VAR I: INTEGER; (* COUNTER *)
   BEGIN (* PRINCOPY *)
     IF (C = ' ') THEN WRITE(' ':N)
     ELSE FOR I := 1 TO N DO WRITE (C)
   END;   (* PRINCOPY *)
```

Note the ; between parameter declarations. Possible calls of PRINCOPY include

```
PRINCOPY('*', 20);
PRINCOPY(CH, K-18);
```

PRINCOPY can of course be used to print the PAGEWIDTH–8 blanks in NEWPAGE, but if output is to an ASCII terminal it can also be used to skip to the top of the next page:

```
PRINCOPY(CHR(10), PAGELEN - LINESSOFAR)
```

instead of the FOR loop. (10 is the ASCII code for line-feed.)

A procedure must always be declared before it is used in Pascal. If we wish to use PRINCOPY in NEWPAGE, there are two possibilities:

1. PRINCOPY is a *global* procedure; that is, it may be used anywhere in the main program or any of its subprograms:

```
     .
     .
     .
PROCEDURE PRINCOPY( . . . );
   VAR I: INTEGER;
   BEGIN
     . . .
   END;
PROCEDURE NEWPAGE;
   BEGIN
     FOR LINESSOFAR . . .
     PAGENO := . . .
     PRINCOPY(' ', PAGEWIDTH–8);
       . . .
   END;
```

2. PRINCOPY is a *local* procedure, available to NEWPAGE only:

```
PROCEDURE NEWPAGE;
   PROCEDURE PRINCOPY( . . . );
     VAR
     BEGIN
       . . .
     END;
```

```
BEGIN (* NEWPAGE *)
    same body as in 1.
END:   (* NEWPAGE *)
```

If PRINCOPY is used only by NEWPAGE, it is probably a good idea to make it local (method 2) to express that fact.

It is also possible to write FUNCTION subprograms and then use them just like built-in functions such as SQR and CHR. They are similar to procedures: they have just one specific value and, when used as part of an expression, are replaced by that value. Their declaration is of the form

```
FUNCTION name(parameters, if any): type of value;
    body
```

FUNCTION values must be of type REAL, INTEGER, BOOLEAN, CHAR, enumerated, subrange, or pointer.

"Body" is like a procedure body except that at some place it must execute a statement

name := expression

The last such statement executed before the function drops through its END determines the function's value.

When assigning a value to FUNCTION name using "name := expression," the parameters to the function do not follow "name."

EXAMPLE 2.3.3 In certain applications it is desired to print numbers right-justified with other than blank fill (for example, protection of check amounts, ***23.45, or floating $ sign, $23.45). Unfortunately, we may not get quite the effect we want because some Pascals always print a blank before a positive real number, but the idea is worthwhile anyway. We develop a function NUMLEN(X) with real parameter X whose value is the number of character positions required to print the whole part of X [e.g., NUMLEN(X) = 2 if $10 \leqslant X < 100$]. NUMLEN(X) is just 1 more than the integer part of $\log_{10}(X)$, and $\log_{10}(X) = LN(X)/LN(10)$, LN being Pascal's built-in natural logarithm function. (This is because $10 ** (LN(X)/LN(10)) = (e ** LN(10)) ** (LN(X)/LN(10)) = e ** (LN(10) * LN(X) / LN(10)) = e ** LN(X) = X$). The function is

```
FUNCTION NUMLEN(X: REAL): INTEGER;
    (* RETURN NUMBER OF DIGITS IN X LEFT OF DEC PT *)
```

```
BEGIN (* NUMLEN *)
   IF (X < 10) THEN NUMLEN := 1 (* MOSTLY FOR X < 1 *)
   ELSE
      NUMLEN := 1 + TRUNC(LN(X) / LN(10))
END;  (* NUMLEN *)
```

We can get a sort of floating dollar sign using

```
PROCEDURE FLOATDOL(AMT: REAL; COLS: INTEGER);
   BEGIN (* FLOATDOL *)
      PRINCOPY('  ', COLS - 3 - NUMLEN(AMT));
      WRITE('$', AMT:1:2)
   END;  (* FLOATDOL *)
```

Main program statements of

```
FLOATDOL(3.21, 9);
WRITELN;
FLOATDOL(12345.67, 9)
```

will produce the output

```
    $3.21
$12345.67
```

on a Pascal that does not force leading blanks on real output.

Pascal only allows functions to have a single value; to get a sub-program to return multiple values, use a procedure and return values through some of the procedure parameters. This is done by resetting their values within the procedure. However, to protect the outside world, Pascal normally does not allow procedures (or functions) to change values of parameters in the outside world. For this to be possible, such parameters must be explicitly declared as VARiable parameters in the procedure or function declaration. For example,

```
PROCEDURE SOMETHING(VAR X: REAL; Y: REAL);
   BEGIN
      X := 8;  (* CHANGES EXTERNAL VALUE OF PARAMETER X *)
      Y := 5   (* CHANGES ONLY INTERNAL VALUE OF Y *)
   END;
```

When SOMETHING is executed in the main program, its first parameter (corresponding to X) must be a variable, while the parameter corresponding to Y can be a variable, constant, or expression. The value for Y is used to initialize Y, but any further changes to Y change only the local variable Y within SOMETHING, not anything outside.

Pascal Pointer 20

Parameters whose outside values are to be changed by a subprogram must be VAR parameters.

We should also note that

| Pascal Pointer 21 ⟩ | *Types of parameters and function values must be simple type names.* |

Thus we could not declare

    PROCEDURE P(X: ARRAY [1 .. 10] OF REAL);

but would have to declare

    TYPE AR = ARRAY [1 .. 10] OF REAL;
    . . .
    PROCEDURE P(X: AR);

The parameter names used in a subprogram declaration are called *formal* parameters. When the subprogram is actually executed, these are replaced by *actual* parameters:

    PROCEDURE XXX(A: REAL; B: INTEGER);
       (* A and B are formal parameters *)
       . . .
       XXX(R/2, 14); (* R/2 and 14 are actual parameters *)

There must be essentially exact agreement between data types of formal and actual parameters, although some minor latitude is allowed. Just how much is or should be allowed is one of the problems with the language (see for instance the paper of Welsh, Sneeringer, and Hoare in the Bibliography). Newer compilers, and the proposed Pascal standard, tend to be *more* rigid. To be safe, formal and actual parameters should be declared with the same type *name*.

It should be possible to have a real non-VAR formal parameter and corresponding integer actual parameter; the automatic conversion integer → real takes place. As we would expect, a real VAR formal cannot take an integer actual as this would also imply an automatic conversion real → integer, which as we have seen Pascal will never do.

It should be emphasized that the dimensions of a Pascal array are very much a part of its data type, and in most Pascals the dimensions of formal and actual array parameters must be *identical*. Thus, if your Pascal does not have the whole-line character reading feature and you wish to write a PROCEDURE to do this (using Model Program 4, for instance), you must write a different version for each different length of line variable that you wish to read. (The new standard has dynamic sizing of ARRAY parameters, which alleviates this problem; see Section B.7 of the Appendix.)

There is much more to be said about procedures and functions; we will discuss various features as the need for them arises.

Exercises 2.3

1. Suppose that for each of the following PROCEDURE definitions we execute the same main program, which is

```
X := 5; Y := 18;
PROC(X, Y);
WRITELN(X, Y)
```

What is printed, given the following definitions of PROC:

```
PROCEDURE PROC(A, B: INTEGER);
   BEGIN
      A := A + 1; B := B - 2; WRITELN(A, B)
   END;


PROCEDURE PROC(A: INTEGER; VAR B: INTEGER);
   BEGIN
      A := A + 1; B := B - 2; WRITELN(A, B)
   END;


PROCEDURE PROC(VAR A: INTEGER; B: INTEGER);
   BEGIN
      A := A + 1; B := B - 2; WRITELN(A, B)
   END;


PROCEDURE PROC(VAR A, B: INTEGER);
   BEGIN
      A := A + 1; B := B - 2; WRITELN(A, B)
   END;
```

2. Suppose we have declared

```
TYPE CHAR80 = PACKED ARRAY [1 .. 80] OF CHAR;
```

(a) Write a function LASTNB with one parameter, a CHAR80, which returns as its value the integer index of the last nonblank character in the parameter (0 if all blank).

(b) Using LASTNB, PRINCOPY, and character array READ, write a program segment which reads a line and prints the part up to the last nonblank centered in 80 columns surrounded by asterisks; for example,

```
*****AN EXAMPLE*****
```

is printed centered in 20 columns.

(c) Write a procedure READTOCOMMA which reads into a single CHAR80 parameter LINE up to but not including the first comma on the input line and fills the rest of LINE with blanks. If EOLN occurs before ",", HALT (Section 1.14) with an appropriate error message.

(d) Assuming an input line of the form

chapter-name, page-number

write a program segment using READTOCOMMA, LASTNB, and PRINCOPY to produce a table-of-contents line in 80 columns of the form

chapter-name . . . . page-number

Note that READTOCOMMA will automatically eat up the comma.

   3. Write a program which reads and prints lines of text until it encounters the word STOP *anywhere* on an otherwise blank line. (*Hint:* write a Boolean function ENDOFINPUT which is TRUE when such a line has occurred. This avoids repeating a sizable piece of code or using a GOTO.)

Programming Problems

   2.1 Write a program which takes an input line sss . . . s/pp . . p/rr . . r/, where sss . . . s is a *subject* string, pp . . p is a *pattern* string, and rr . . r is a *replacement* string. The program searches for the first occurrence of pp . . p in sss . . . s and replaces that occurrence with rr . . r and prints the result. The / can be replaced by any other character not in sss . . . s, pp . . p, and rr . . r except $. Processing is repeated until a line whose first character is $ is encountered. Write a procedure to read the three strings, declared by

```
TYPE STRTYPE = PACKED ARRAY [1 . . 100] OF CHAR;
    . . .
PROCEDURE READTODELIM(VAR S: STRTYPE; VAR LEN: INTEGER);
```

where LEN is to be the length of string actually read. A sample run might be

```
?  /ABCFGH/C/CDE/
ABCDEFGH
?  /I WILL NOT RETURN/NOT//
I WILL  RETURN
?  $
```

   2.2. Write a procedure CONJUGATE which does present-tense first conjugations of Spanish verbs. The declarations include

```
TYPE WORD = PACKED ARRAY [1 . . 20] OF CHAR;
     PERSON = 1 . . 3;
     NUMBER = (SING, PLURAL);
         . . .
PROCEDURE CONJUGATE(INF: WORD; P: PERSON; N: NUMBER;
     VAR CONJ: WORD);
```

Conjugation consists of finding the "AR" at the end of the infinitive and removing it and replacing it with the appropriate ending:

	sing	plural
1	O	AMOS
2	AS	AIS
3	A	AN

Test your procedure by printing the complete conjugations of REFLEJAR (to reflect) and DESEAR (to want). For example, the conjugation of DESEAR should appear

DESEO   DESEAMOS
DESEAS   DESEAIS
DESEA   DESEAN

chapter 3

files: searching and sorting

3.1 FILES AND FILE TERMINOLOGY

A file is a collection of related information. It might consist of a program (source or object), a collection of programs, or, our principal concern here, a collection of data. A data file generally contains the same types of data about each of a number of objects. The data about any one individual object are called a *record*. Usually, different records have the same general organization and differ only in particular values. Each datum within a record is called a *field*.

EXAMPLE 3.1.1 A personnel file consists of one record for each employee in the firm. Each record contains, for its particular employee, such data as name, social security number, age, and job classification. These data items would be called fields, and if one record had a particular field, such as salary, then all would.

To allow us to make the structure of the data fit the structure of the problem, Pascal allows us to group several types of data in a single conglomerate. By analogy with file terminology, this conglomerate is called a RECORD. Note that a Pascal RECORD need not be a record in a file (and *vice versa*).

EXAMPLE 3.1.2 We wish to represent a part-file, each record of which has the following information:

> part-name, a PACKED ARRAY OF 20 CHARs
> part-number, an INTEGER
> quantity-on-hand, an INTEGER
> price, a REAL

We can declare PART to be a variable whose "value" is the collection of the four items above as follows:

```
VAR PART: RECORD
              NAME: PACKED ARRAY [1 . . 20] OF CHAR;
              NUMBER, ONHAND: INTEGER;
              PRICE: REAL
          END;
```

The words RECORD and END are keywords which must always be used in this way. NAME, NUMBER, ONHAND, and PRICE are the names of fields in the RECORD and are identifiers chosen by the programmer according to the usual rules. They are declared as though they were variables, but they really are not. They are called *selectors* and act more like subscripts of an array, with PART corresponding to the array name. To manipulate part-name, write PART.NAME, where the "." represents the field selection operation. For example, PART. NAME[3] is the third character of the part-name.

When we wish to process files in Pascal, we will distinguish two cases:

Case 1: All the file is to be contained in main memory at once. In this case the file will be represented as an array of RECORDs.

EXAMPLE 3.1.2, continued Assume that the part-file is to contain (at most) 100 records. It can be declared by the statement

```
VAR PARTFILE: ARRAY [1 . . 100] OF
                  RECORD
                      NAME: . . .
                        . . .
                  END;
```

PARTFILE[8] is the record corresponding to the eighth part in the file. PARTFILE[8].PRICE is the price of the eighth part in the file, and PARTFILE[I].NAME[5] is the fifth character in the name of the Ith part in the file. (You may wonder why the subscript I itself was not used for the part-number. This is because, in the real world, new parts appear, old parts are modified or become obsolete, and it would be very confining to attempt to maintain all these numbers in the range 1 . . 100.)

We could redo this example as

```
TYPE PNM = PACKED ARRAY [1 . . 20] OF CHAR;
     PARTREC = RECORD
                   NAME: PNM;
                   NUMBER, ONHAND: INTEGER;
                   PRICE: REAL
               END;


     VAR PARTFILE: ARRAY [1 . . 100] OF PARTREC;
```

Case 2:   In the second possible file type, only one record at a time is to be held in main memory. In Pascal such a file is referred to by a variable of type "FILE OF recordtype."

EXAMPLE 3.1.2, concluded   If only one record at a time of the part-file is to be in memory, and we have the TYPE declarations given previously, we can declare

```
     VAR PARTFILE: FILE OF PARTREC;
         PART: PARTREC;
```

Such files can be accessed only from the beginning in sequential order. The next record can be read from the file into the variable PART or written from PART into the file. A commonly used special case will be discussed in Section 3.6, but we defer a general discussion of such files until Section 9.1. For now we will assume that all our files are contained entirely in main memory, as in Case 1.

Usually there are one or more fields in each record of a file that serve to identify the record. Such a field is called the *key*. For example, in the part-file, the likely key would be NUMBER, although NAME might also be used. One very frequently used operation on files is to find a record in the file with a given key. This operation is called *searching*.

3.2   THE LINEAR SEARCH

We have already considered the simplest form of searching, the *linear search*. Here we consider an example placed in the context of the last section, which we will also then rework to demonstrate other methods in this chapter.

EXAMPLE 3.2.1 Create an internal file with 10 records, one for each number from 1 to 10. Each record has two fields, the number in English and the number in German. The program is to read German numbers from the input (terminal) and print their English translations, stopping when the word 'HALT' is read.

The fundamental loop is

```
read first WORD;
WHILE (WORD <> 'HALT            ') DO
    BEGIN
        look up WORD;
        print translation;
        read next WORD
    END
```

In our program we use the extended form of READ to read an array of characters, in this case the ALFA variable WORD. See Model Program 4, Section 1.13, concerning what to do if such a READ is not available. The fundamental loop is in the standard form for processing lines of input assuming lazy input (Section 1.13.5, Method B):

```
READLN(WORD);
WHILE (WORD <> 'HALT            ') DO
    BEGIN
        look up WORD and translate;
        READLN(WORD)
    END
```

(READLN must be used instead of READ as the character array READ will not read beyond an end of line.) The fundamental loop of "look up word" is a linear search. The program is

```
            (* EXAMPLE 3.2.1: LINEAR            *)
            (* TRANSLATE GERMAN NUMBERS TO *)
            (* ENGLISH USING LINEAR SEARCH    *)

            PROGRAM LINEAR(INPUT, OUTPUT);

            CONST MAXNUM = 10;    (* NUMBER OF GER-ENG PAIRS *)

            TYPE   WORDPAIR = RECORD GER, ENG: ALFA END;

            VAR    NUM: ARRAY[0 . . MAXNUM] OF WORDPAIR; (* GER-ENG PAIRS *)
                       I: INTEGER;          (* SEARCH INDEX *)
                       WORD: ALFA;       (* INPUT GERMAN WORD *)
            BEGIN (* LINEAR *)
```

```
NUM[  1] .GER := 'EINS           '; NUM[  1] .ENG := 'ONE           ';
NUM[  2] .GER := 'ZWEI           '; NUM[  2] .ENG := 'TWO           ';
NUM[  3] .GER := 'DREI           '; NUM[  3] .ENG := 'THREE         ';
NUM[  4] .GER := 'VIER           '; NUM[  4] .ENG := 'FOUR          ';
NUM[  5] .GER := 'FUNF           :; NUM[  5] .ENG := 'FIVE          ';
NUM[  6] .GER := 'SECHS          '; NUM[  6] .ENG := 'SIX           ';
NUM[  7] .GER := 'SIEBEN         '; NUM[  7] .ENG := 'SEVEN         ';
NUM[  8] .GER := 'ACHT           '; NUM[  8] .ENG := 'EIGHT         ';
NUM[  9] .GER := 'NEUN           '; NUM[  9] .ENG := 'NINE          ';
NUM[10] .GER := 'ZEHN           '; NUM[10] .ENG := 'TEN           ';

WRITELN('TYPE IN GERMAN NUMBERS TERMINATING WITH "HALT"');
READLN(WORD);  (* READ FIRST WORD *)
WHILE (WORD <> 'HALT            ') DO
    BEGIN
        I:= MAXNUM; NUM[0] .GER := WORD; (* SENTINEL *)
        WHILE (WORD <> NUM[I] .GER) DO I := I - 1;
        IF (I = 0) THEN WRITELN('ILLEGAL NUMBER')
        ELSE WRITELN('THE ENGLISH IS  ', NUM[I] .ENG);
        READLN(WORD) (* READ NEXT WORD *)
    END
END.  (* LINEAR *)
```

A sample terminal session might run

```
TYPE IN GERMAN NUMBERS, TERMINATING WITH 'HALT'
? EINS
THE ENGLISH IS ONE
? AVERYLONGTESTNUMBER
ILLEGAL NUMBER
? ACHT
THE ENGLISH IS EIGHT
? HALT
```

3.3   THE BINARY SEARCH

The linear search is satisfactory for small files, but unduly time-consuming for large ones. For a better method, let us look at a typical searching procedure for inspiration: looking up a word in a dictionary. In this case one never uses a linear search, that is, starting from the beginning and reading until the desired word is found. The usual procedure is to open the dictionary at the approximate location of the word; if the word desired comes before the words on that page, proceed backward with another (presumably better) guess; otherwise proceed forward. Continue this procedure until the word is found. This method is abstracted into the *binary search*. We look at the middle record of the file. If its key is greater than the search key, we search the first half of the file, looking first at its middle record, and so on. For this method to work, two conditions on the file are required:

1. The keys of the file must be in increasing or decreasing order.
2. Records of the file must be accessible in random order. This usually means that the whole file must be in main memory.

We will give two versions of the binary search. The first is somewhat crude but easy to program; the second is more sophisticated but also more subtle.

EXAMPLE 3.3.1 (Binary Search) We will redo our German-to-English example (3.2.1). We use the fact that PACKED ARRAYs of characters of equal length can be compared and that the result is lexicographic ordering; that is, string A $<$ string B if they are the same up to a given position and the character in that position in string A is less than the one in string B. (See Section 1.11.) At each stage we have to keep track of which part of the file we are still searching, and for that purpose we use the indices LO and HI. The fundamental loop is the same as in Example 3.2.1. The difference lies in the interior loop "look up WORD." We will use a Boolean variable FOUND to help terminate the search. This is rather awkward and unesthetic, but it makes the program easier to write. Recall also that DIV is integer division, with no remainder. The complete program is

```
(* EXAMPLE 3.3.1: BINARY            *)
(* GERMAN-ENGLISH NUMBER TRANS-  *)
(* LATION VIA BINARY SEARCH        *)

PROGRAM BINARY(INPUT, OUTPUT);

CONST MAXNUM = 10;       (* NUMBER OF GER-ENG PAIRS *)

TYPE   WORDPAIR = RECORD GER, ENG: ALFA END;

VAR    NUM: ARRAY [1 .. MAXNUM] OF WORDPAIR; (* GER-ENG PAIRS *)
       HI, LO,              (* SUBFILE BOUNDS *)
       MID: INTEGER;        (* SUBFILE MIDPOINT *)
       WORD: ALFA;          (* INPUT GERMAN NUMBER *)
       FOUND: BOOLEAN;      (* LOOP TERMINATOR *)

BEGIN (* BINARY *)
     NUM[ 1].GER := 'ACHT        '; NUM[ 1].ENG := 'EIGHT       ';
     NUM[ 2].GER := 'DREI        '; NUM[ 2].ENG := 'THREE       ';
     NUM[ 3].GER := 'EINS        '; NUM[ 3].ENG := 'ONE         ';
     NUM[ 4].GER := 'FUNF        '; NUM[ 4].ENG := 'FIVE        ';
```

```
          NUM[ 5].GER := 'NEUN          '; NUM[ 5].ENG := 'NINE          ';
          NUM[ 6].GER := 'SECHS         '; NUM[ 6].ENG := 'SIX           ';
          NUM[ 7].GER := 'SIEBEN        '; NUM[ 7].ENG := 'SEVEN         ';
          NUM[ 8].GER := 'VIER          '; NUM[ 8].ENG := 'FOUR          ';
          NUM[ 9].GER := 'ZEHN          '; NUM[ 9].ENG := 'TEN           ';
          NUM[10].GER := 'ZWEI          '; NUM[10].ENG := 'TWO           ';
                  (* NOTE—GERMAN IS IN ALPHABETICAL ORDER! *)


          WRITELN('TYPE IN GERMAN NUMBERS, TERMINATING WITH ''HALT''');
          READLN(WORD);  (* READ FIRST WORD *)
          WHILE (WORD <> 'HALT          ') DO
              BEGIN
                  LO := 1; HI := MAXNUM; FOUND := FALSE;
                  WHILE (LO <= HI) AND NOT FOUND DO
                      BEGIN
                          MID := (LO + HI) DIV 2;
                          IF (NUM[MID].GER = WORD) THEN FOUND := TRUE
                          ELSE IF (WORD <  NUM[MID].GER) THEN
                              HI := MID - 1
                          ELSE
                              LO := MID + 1
                      END;
                  IF FOUND THEN WRITELN('THE ENGLISH IS  ', NUM[MID].ENG)
                  ELSE WRITELN('ILLEGAL NUMBER');
                  READLN(WORD)  (* READ NEXT WORD *)
              END
      END   (* BINARY *)
```

The method may become clearer if we trace two examples, one in which the item sought is found and the other in which it is not.

Example 1: The search key is 'FUNF   '. Each column represents the state of LO, MID, and HI just after MID is computed inside the loop.

LO →	ACHT	LO →	ACHT		ACHT		ACHT
	DREI	MID →	DREI		DREI		DREI
	EINS		EINS	LO,MID →	EINS		EINS
	FUNF	HI →	FUNF	HI →	FUNF	LO,MID,HI →	FUNF
MID →	NEUN		NEUN		NEUN		NEUN
	SECHS		SECHS		SECHS		SECHS
	SIEBEN		SIEBEN		SIEBEN		SIEBEN
	VIER		VIER		VIER		VIER
	ZEHN		ZEHN		ZEHN		ZEHN
HI →	ZWEI		ZWEI		ZWEI		ZWEI

Note that when we reset LO and HI, we must set HI := MID – 1, not HI := MID, or LO := MID + 1, not LO := MID, as otherwise an infinite loop may result. In this example if we used HI := MID and LO := MID and the search key was ZWEI, the successive values of LO, MID, and HI would be

$$1,5,10; \quad 5,7,10; \quad 7,8,10; \quad 8,9,10; \quad 9,9,10; \quad 9,9,10; \ldots$$

forever. The important thing is that each time through the loop the subfile being searched is at least one item smaller than on the last execution. This means that eventually we will find our key or the file under consideration will become empty, that is, LO > HI, as in our next example.

Example 2: The search key is 'HUIT   '. As in Example 1, we show LO, MID, and HI just after MID has been set.

LO →	ACHT	LO →	ACHT		ACHT	ACHT
	DREI	MID →	DREI		DREI	DREI
	EINS		EINS	LO,MID →	EINS	EINS
	FUNF	HI →	FUNF	HI →	FUNF LO,MID,HI →	FUNF
MID →	NEUN		NEUN		NEUN	NEUN
	SECHS		SECHS		SECHS	SECHS
	SIEBEN		SIEBEN		SIEBEN	SIEBEN
	VIER		VIER		VIER	VIER
	ZEHN		ZEHN		ZEHN	ZEHN
HI →	ZWEI		ZWEI		ZWEI	ZWEI

Then when the loop is exited we have

```
              ACHT
              DREI
              EINS
HI,MID  →     FUNF
   LO   →     NEUN
              SECHS
              etc.
```

and the search terminates unsuccessfully.

While hand tracing a program can be useful in understanding and debugging it, another somewhat more abstract approach can be even more convincing. The idea is to study a loop by looking for an *invariant relation*, or *loop invariant*, some condition on the program variables which is true before the loop begins (usually trivially), and if true each time before the loop body is executed, remains true after it is executed. The loop invariant is then true when the loop is done. If properly chosen, this should tell us that the loop has accomplished its purpose.

There are always many invariant relations, most of which are not useful. Often great cleverness is required in finding the proper loop invariant. Let us look at the binary search, but this time at the second more sophisticated version promised earlier. The most obvious difference is the omission of FOUND. We will be searching for X in an array A[1 .. N]. The program segment is

```
LO := 1; HI := N;
WHILE (LO <= HI) DO
    BEGIN
        MID := (LO + HI) DIV 2;
        IF (X < A[MID]) THEN HI := MID - 1
        ELSE LO := MID + 1
    END
```

At any time in the course of this program, we intuitively expect X to be between A[LO] and A[HI], which unfortunately will not be the case if X is originally out of range of the A's (or after X = A[MID] happens). To avoid this special case, assume that there is an A[0] smaller than every possible X and an A[N+1] larger than every possible X. We will try

$$A[LO - 1] \leqslant X \leqslant A[HI + 1]$$

as our invariant relation. It is clearly true (by choice of A[0] and A[N+1]) before the loop is executed, and remains true after each execution of the loop body, as the only change in LO or HI is to make LO - 1 or HI + 1 equal to MID. Therefore, when the loop ends, we can assert that the invariant relation is *still true*, and that the WHILE condition is false. The latter means that HI < LO, and as, until the end, LO ≤ MID ≤ HI, it must be the case that HI = LO - 1. Therefore, the invariant relation becomes

$$A[HI] \leqslant X \leqslant A[HI + 1]$$

We could check each of the two possibilities to see if X has been found, but if we go back and choose our invariant relation a bit more carefully, we will see that that is not necessary. The proper relation is the slightly stronger one:

$$A[LO - 1] \leqslant X < A[HI + 1]$$

(Note that the second inequality is <, not ≤! In fact the first ≤ is initially < also, but this < is not preserved by the loop body.) This invariant gives us the final condition

$$A[HI] \leqslant X < A[HI + 1]$$

which means that X must be A[HI] if it is in the array. Note, finally, that as 1 ≤ LO ≤ MID ≤ HI ≤ N whenever the loop is executed, A[0] and A[N+1] are never referenced, so they do not need to be set, or even exist! The only problem is that at the end it is possible that HI = 0, and if we check X = A[HI], we could get bounced for a subscript error. To avoid this, we simply insert a special test for HI = 0 at the end. Recall from Section 2.1, solution 2, that we cannot say IF (HI > 0) AND (A[HI] = X) THEN . . ., so we still use a BOOLEAN, FOUND:

```
FOUND := FALSE;
IF (HI > 0) THEN
    IF (A[HI] = X) THEN FOUND := TRUE
```

This version of the binary search algorithm has the disadvantage of going all the way to the end of the search even if by chance the item sought is found early on. However, that should be balanced against the following facts:

1. About 50% of the file cannot be seen until the last time through the loop anyway.

2. The second version requires two tests each time through the loop and the first version (Example 3.3.1) requires four.

3. Version 2 generalizes easily to searches for X in a range between two items in the table.

Model Program 6:   Binary search $A[1 .. N]$, in increasing order, getting $A[HI] \leqslant X < A[HI+1]$ ($X < A[1]$ if $HI = 0$, $A[N] \leqslant X$ if $HI = N$).

```
LO := 1; HI := N;
WHILE (LO <= HI) DO
    BEGIN
        MID := (LO + HI) DIV 2;
        IF (X < A[MID]) THEN HI := MID – 1
        ELSE LO := MID + 1
    END
```

Exercise 3.3

Income tax tables are set up as follows: there is a range table RANGE[0 .. N+1], a base amount table BASE[0 .. N], and a percent table PCT[0 .. N]. $0 = RANGE[0] < RANGE[1] < ... < RANGE[N+1]$, which is larger than any possible income. If net income NET satisfies

$$RANGE[I] \leqslant NET < RANGE[I+1]$$

then income tax TAX is given by

```
TAX := BASE[I] + PCT[I] * (NET – RANGE[I])
```

Write a Pascal program segment to READ NET and find and print the income tax using a binary search of the RANGE table. Use Model Program 6.

A sample tax table might begin

| Not over $3,200 | | Tax is | -0- |

| | But not | | of the amount |
Over —	over —		over —
$3,200	$4,200	14%	$3,200
$4,200	$5,200	$140+15%	$4,200
$5,200	$6,200	$290+16%	$5,200

etc.

In this case we would have RANGE[0] = 0, RANGE[1] = 3200, RANGE[2] = 4200, . . ., BASE[0] = BASE[1] = 0, BASE[2] = 140, . . ., PCT[0] = 0, PCT[1] = 0.14, PCT[2] = 0.15, ...

3.4 RELATIVE EFFICIENCY OF ALGORITHMS

An *algorithm* is a completely described procedure for accomplishing something. In the last two sections, we have discussed two searching algorithms. At this point, one should ask: is the binary search really better than the linear search and, if so, by how much? This is actually an amazingly difficult sort of question to answer, even in this simple case, and the final answer will in fact be "it all depends." However, if we are to call ourselves computer *scientists*, it is important that we try to answer such questions.

Let $T(n)$ be the time required to process n objects according to some algorithm. We say that $T(n)$ is *big oh* of "something," and write

$$T(n) = O(\text{something})$$

if, for some constant K independent of n, we have

$$T(n) \leqslant K * \text{something}, \quad \text{for } n \text{ beyond some point}$$

The O stands for "order of magnitude." For our purposes here, $T(n)$ will be the average time to search a file of n records; to be exact, let $Tl(n)$ be the time to linear search a file of n elements and $Tb(n)$ the time to binary search such a file. We hope to be able to compare these two times by getting "big oh" estimates for them and comparing the estimates, the idea being that the K's absorb differences due to computer, language, and the like, and the "something" should express the time taken by the algorithm in some essential way.

First, consider $Tl(n)$. We want to show that $Tl(n) = O(n)$, that is, that the linear search is a $O(n)$ method. The nonmathematically inclined can skip to (*** end $Tl(n) = O(n)$ ***).

If $K1$ is the time it takes to go through the loop once, and $K2$ includes any one-time overhead, we have

$$Tl(n) \leqslant n * K1 + K2 \leqslant n * K1 + n * K2$$
$$= n(K1 + K2) = K3 * n, \quad \text{where } K3 = K1 + K2$$

Thus $Tl(n) = O(n)$ as claimed. This may seem crude, but in fact it is the best we can do. If each item in the file is sought about equally often, so that the loop will be executed $n/2$ times on the average, $Tl(n) \geqslant (n/2) * K1 = (K1/2) * n$, so in some sense $O(n)$ is the best we can do.

$$(*** \text{ end of } Tl(n) = O(n) ***)$$

Turning to the binary search, we wish to show that $Tb(n) = O(\log_2(n))$, the logarithm to the base 2 of n. We need the following simple mathematical fact, which recurs again and again in computer science:

The HALVING Principle

If $n > 1$, we must replace n by n DIV 2 a total of TRUNC($\log_2(n)$) times to get 1.

This is because if we set $p = \log_2(n)$, then by definition of logarithms $n = 2 ** p$. Then n DIV $2 \leqslant 2 ** (p - 1)$, $(n$ DIV 2) DIV $2 \leqslant 2 ** (p - 2)$, ..., and so on, and if we DIV by 2 TRUNC(p) times, we get

$$n \leqslant 2 ** (p - \text{TRUNC}(p))$$

Since $p - \text{TRUNC}(p) < 1$, we have $n < 2 ** 1 = 2$, so n is at most 1.

Now on the binary search, each pass through the loop the size of the file under consideration, HI − LO + 1, is at most half the size of the file the last time through. Thus the number of times through the loop is roughly the number of times we must divide n by 2 until we get 1. But, by the halving principle, that is at most $\log_2(n)$ and an argument similar to the one for linear search now gives us that $Tb(n) = O(\log_2(n))$.

But what does all this mean? $Tl(n) \leqslant Kn$ and $Tb(n) \leqslant K'\log_2(n)$, and $\log_2(n)$ is much smaller than n when n is large ($\log_2(1024) = 10$, $\log_2(1,000,000)$ is approximately 20); but this does not tell us much if $K < K'$. And this is most certainly the case here, as the loop for the binary search is more complicated than the loop for the linear search. What this does tell us is that $Tl(n)$ is larger than $Tb(n)$ *if n is large enough!* For example, suppose that $K = 0.001$ and $K' = 0.05$. Then the times for the searches are

n	$\log_2(n)$	linear	binary
8	3	0.008	0.150
64	6	0.064	0.300
512	9	0.512	0.450
4096	12	4.096	0.600

In this particular example, we can see that the time to perform the linear search catches up with and passes the time to perform the binary search at about $n = 400$, and the relative performance of the binary search continues to improve dramatically. In general, determining the crossover n usually requires running a few simple test cases, but a reasonable rule of thumb is to use the binary search for files of more than 20 to 30 records.

A third method of searching called *hashing* can be even faster than the binary search; in fact, it is $O(1)$! We must postpone consideration of this method until Chapter 8 when we have studied other concepts.

Exercises 3.4

1. If it requires 10 seconds to search a file with 64 items, estimate the time required to search a file of 4096 items (= 64 ** 2) using (a) the linear search, and (b) the binary search.

2. For the mathematically inclined:
   (a) Show that, if $T(n) = O(\log_2(n))$, then $T(n) = O(n)$ [*Hint:* $\log_2(n) \leqslant n$ if $n \geqslant 1$.]
   (b) Show that, if $T(n) = O(2n)$, then $T(n) = O(n)$.
   (c) Show that, if $T1(n) = O(n)$ and $T2(n) = O(\log_2(n))$, then $T1(n) + T2(n) = O(n)$.

3.5   SORTING

The binary search has one weakness compared to the linear search, which we have glossed over: the file to be searched must have its keys in increasing or decreasing order; that is, the file must be *sorted*. Often the file must be sorted anyway, so this is no additional penalty, but in cases where sorting is not necessary, it is an additional overhead on the binary search and may lead one to choose the linear search instead. In this section we will consider how sorting can be carried out if desired. Even more so than in searching, there are a bewildering variety of sorting methods. We will consider only one here, the *insertion sort*. This method is one of the simplest and is the method of choice for (1) relatively small files (perhaps fewer than 20 records) with relatively small records, or (2) files which are already nearly sorted (see the paper by Cook and Kim in the Bibliography). We will discuss a more exotic method in Section 6.4.

The idea of the insertion sort is quite simple: assume that the first K records R[1] , . . ., R[K] , are already sorted. It is desired to insert R[K+1] in its rightful position. This can be done by finding where R[K+1] should go in the sequence:

$$R[1] , \ldots , R[J], R[J+1], \ldots , R[K]$$

$$\uparrow$$
$$R[K+1]$$

sliding the records to the right of it in the list one farther to the right,

$$R[1], \ldots , R[J], \ //////// , R[J+1], \ldots , R[K]$$

$$\uparrow$$
$$R[K+1]$$

and inserting R[K+1] in the position vacated. The process can now be repeated with R[K+2] and the (now) ordered records R[1 . . K+1]. When this process is repeated for K = 1, 2, . . ., N − 1, the file will be sorted.

The fundamental loop for the insertion sort is

```
FOR K := 1 TO N − 1 DO
    BEGIN
        find J so that R[K+1] goes between R[J] and R[J+1] ;
        X := R[K+1] ;
        FOR I := K DOWNTO J+1 DO R[I+1] := R[I] ;
        R[J+1] := X
    END
```

The loop invariant is "R[1 . . K] is a rearrangement of the original R[1 . . K] in sorted order." This is trivially true when K = 1, and the business of the loop keeps it true as K increases. Therefore, when the loop is finished, we have K = N and R[1 . . K] is sorted, so the whole R array is sorted.

The "find J . . ." part of the loop is a search, and since the file being searched is sorted, either the binary or the linear search may be used. The simplest method is to use the linear search, starting from the K down, and combine the search with the move in a single inner loop.

EXAMPLE 3.5.1 Sort the NUM file of Example 3.2.1 into alphabetical order by GER field.

```
(* EXAMPLE 3.5.1: INSORT     *)
(* INSERTION SORT GER-ENG*)
(* WORD PAIRS.               *)
```

```
PROGRAM INSORT(INPUT, OUTPUT);

CONST MAXNUM = 10; (* NUMBER OF GER-ENG PAIRS *)

TYPE   WORDPAIR = RECORD GER, ENG: ALFA END;

VAR    NUM: ARRAY [0 .. MAXNUM] OF WORDPAIR; (* GER-ENG PAIRS *)
                          (* 0 ENTRY IS FOR SENTINEL *)
       K, J: INTEGER; (* INDICES FOR SORTING *)

BEGIN (* INSORT *)
   (* INITIALIZE NUM[1 .. 10] .GER, NUM[1 .. 10] .ENG  *)
   (* EXACTLY AS IN EXAMPLE 3.2.1                       *)
   FOR K := 1 TO MAXNUM – 1 DO
      BEGIN
         NUM[0] := NUM[K+1] ; (* SAVE NUM[K+1] AND SET SENTINEL *)
         J := K;
         WHILE (NUM[J] .GER > NUM[0] .GER) DO
            BEGIN
               NUM[J+1] := NUM[J] ; (* SLIDE UP ONE *)
               J := J – 1
            END;
         NUM[J+1] := NUM[0]
      END;

   FOR K := 1 TO MAXNUM DO
      WRITELN(NUM[K] .GER, NUM[K] .ENG)
END.  (* INSORT *)
```

The program will produce the output

```
ACHT      EIGHT
DREI      THREE
EINS      ONE
etc.
```

Let's trace through the insertion of a couple of records. When K is set to 2, the situation is

```
      GER            ENG

      ////           /////
      ———            ————
      EINS           ONE
K→    ZWEI           TWO
      DREI           THREE
```

where the dashes separate the sentinel entry from the true file. On successive executions of the test in the WHILE loop, the GER part is

```
        DREI              DREI           J→ DREI
        ───               ───               ───
        EINS          J→ EINS              EINS
J,K→ ZWEI             K→ ZWEI          K→  EINS
        DREI              ZWEI             ZWEI
```

And at the end of the main FOR loop, GER becomes

```
J→   DREI
     ───
     DREI
K→   EINS
     ZWEI
```

Looking at GER on successive WHILE loop tests when K = 5, we have

```
        SECHS            SECHS            SECHS
        ────             ────             ────
        DREI             DREI             DREI
        EINS             EINS             EINS
        FUNF             FUNF         J→ FUNF
        VIER         J→ VIER              VIER
J,K→ ZWEI            K→ ZWEI          K→ VIER
        SECHS            ZWEI             ZWEI
```

and at the end of the FOR loop, GER is

```
        SECHS
        ────
        DREI
        EINS
J→     FUNF
        SECHS
K→     VIER
        ZWEI
```

The insertion sort is called an *internal* sorting method because the file is contained entirely in memory while it is being sorted. The method is *stable*, meaning that if two records have identical keys their original order is preserved.

To obtain a big oh estimate for the insertion sort, we need another simple and often used mathematical fact:

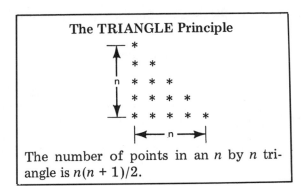

The number of points in an n by n triangle is $n(n + 1)/2$.

This is easily seen if we fit two copies of the triangle into an n by $(n + 1)$ rectangle:

```
* + + + + +
* * + + + +
* * * + + +
* * * * + +
* * * * * +
```

Returning to the insertion sort, we see that when the outer loop index is K, we go through the inner loop at most K times. As K runs from 1 to $n - 1$, the inner loop is executed at most $1 + 2 + \ldots + (n - 1)$, which is the number of dots in an $(n - 1)$ by $(n - 1)$ triangle, which, by the triangle principle, is $(n - 1) * (n - 1 + 1)/2 = (n - 1) * n/2 < n ** 2/2$. As before, adding in the extra overhead for loop setup does not outweigh this, so we see that the insertion sort is a $O(n ** 2)$ method. [It can be shown that the bubble sort, discussed in Exercise 2.2.1, is also a $O(n ** 2)$ method, but that its K is much larger than the K for the insertion sort.]

Exercises 3.5

1. For what sort of file would the method of insertion sorting with binary searching be efficient? (*Hint:* Binary searching works best for larger files.)

2. The *selection sort* is another $O(n ** 2)$ method. The fundamental loop for sorting records R[1 .. N] is

```
FOR I := 1 TO N-1 DO
    BEGIN
        get R[J], the record with smallest key in R[I .. N];
        interchange R[I] and R[J]
    END
```

The invariant relation for this loop is "R[1 . . I-1] consists of the I-1 smallest-keyed records in the file, in order."

Advantages of the Selection Sort: There tends to be much less record moving than in the insertion sort, an advantage if records are large.

Disadvantages of the Selection Sort: The search phase must look at all the remaining file rather than half of it on the average, and the search must be linear. The selection sort does not take advantage of any inherent ordering already in the file.

The exercise: write a selection sort program to sort the NUM file of Example 3.2.1.

3.6 PASCAL TEXT FILES

In various examples in this chapter, the NUM file has had to be written out in full in various programs. This is tedious and error prone, and would have been totally impractical if the file had been much larger. Also, the program of Example 3.5.1 produced sorted output for use by the binary search program, but in a form in which it would have to be hand transcribed. Better solutions might be to have NUM on a separate file which would be read in at the start of programs and for the sorting program to write its output onto a file in a form in which it could be used directly by other programs. It is the purpose of this section to give you the background necessary to do this.

As discussed in Section 3.1, a file in Pascal is a variable of type FILE OF record type. A special case of interest here is the FILE OF CHAR, a file which behaves much like the standard INPUT and OUTPUT files. The built-in type TEXT is short for FILE OF CHAR. Pascal maintains pointers to the current position in all TEXT files, and objects of various types can be read or written as in Sections 1.6 and 1.13.

To initialize a TEXT file properly, execute

> RESET(file variable) — before first READ
> REWRITE(file variable) — before first WRITE

REWRITE has the effect of emptying the file and preparing it to receive fresh contents. RESET is called "rewind" in some languages, and both of these statements have some of the functions of the "open" statement in other languages.

Once the file has been initialized, it is operated on by

> READ(file variable, variable list) — if RESET

or

> WRITE(file variable, variable list) — if REWRITE

In READing, the Boolean function EOF(file variable) becomes true just *before* trying to read off the end of the file (as opposed to just after as in most other languages). It is a fatal error to try to READ a file F when EOF(F) is TRUE. The end-of-line function EOLN(F) is also applicable to all TEXT file variables F, as are READLN and WRITELN.

The two standard files INPUT and OUTPUT (the card reader and line printer on batch systems, the two aspects of the user's terminal in time-sharing systems) are predefined and must *not* be declared in the VAR area, RESET, or REWRITEn. When INPUT is READ or OUTPUT is WRITEn, the file name can be omitted from the READ or WRITE statement. EOF (and EOLN) without parameter always refers to INPUT.

There are two problems in relating file variables to actual physical files: (1) physical file names are often long and complicated and contain characters which are illegal in Pascal variables, and (2) it is useful to be able to write a single program to process several different files. There are roughly two methods of associating files with file variables (see also Appendix B).

Method 1:   In standard Pascal, the PROGRAM name statement must include in parentheses the names of all the file variables which will be associated with permanent outside files. In addition, it must always contain INPUT and OUTPUT if they are used. For example,

```
PROGRAM XXX(X, INPUT, Y, OUTPUT, Z);
     .
     .
     .

VAR X, Y: FILE OF RECORD . . . END;
    Z: TEXT;
     .
     .
     .
```

X, Y, and Z are short temporary names for files which are assigned to physical files before the program is executed. For instance, in the CDC NOS system, we could assign X to a file via

```
GET, X=long permanent file name
```

It is also possible to change the short names used at run time. As an example, suppose that COPY is a Pascal program which copies the text file INPUT to the text file OUTPUT. COPY has PROGRAM statement

```
PROGRAM COPY(INPUT, OUTPUT);
```

Assume this program has been compiled and resides on a file called COPY. Then

1.   COPY copies INPUT to OUTPUT.
2.   COPY(A) copies file A to OUTPUT, that is, lists A.
3.   COPY(,B) copies INPUT into B.
4.   COPY(A, B) copies file A into file B.

The serious disadvantage of the standard solution to the file problem is that all file names must be known before the program starts executing. This makes it *impossible* to write certain useful programs, (for example, the text insertion program of Example 4.2.3). Recognizing this problem, many implementations have taken a different tack (and we shall do so, also, when necessary):

Method 2: A nonstandard approach is used in several systems with minor variations. The listing of FILEs in the PROGRAM statement becomes optional. A file variable is associated with a physical file name via RESET or REWRITE; for example,

    RESET(file variable, 'physical file name')

or

    RESET(file variable, array of CHAR)

where "array of CHAR" contains the physical file name.

EXAMPLE 3.6.1   Write the output from the insertion sort example (3.5.1) onto a file in a form in which it can be used directly as text in a Pascal program. Alterations to the program of Example 3.5.1 are chiefly to the final FOR loop, and are

```
PROGRAM INSORT(ORDOUT, INPUT,OUTPUT);
    .
    .
    .

VAR ORDOUT: TEXT;
    .
    .

    REWRITE(ORDOUT);
    FOR I := 1 TO MAXNUM DO
        WRITELN(ORDOUT, '      NUM[', I:2, '].GER  :=  ''', NUM[I].GER,
        '''; NUM[', I:2, '].ENG  :=  ''', NUM[I].ENG, ''';');
END.
```

This produces the output

```
NUM[  1] .GER := 'ACHT       ';NUM[  1] .ENG := 'EIGHT        ';
NUM[  2] .GER := 'DREI       ';NUM[  2] .ENG := 'THREE        ';
NUM[  3] .GER := 'EINS       ';NUM[  3] .ENG := 'ONE          ';
   etc.
```

in the file ORDOUT, which can then be punched on cards or inserted in a program text via the editing process.

EXAMPLE 3.6.2 Read a text file A and for each line, print (1) the first N characters of each line (presumable identification), (2) four blanks, then (3) the integer starting in column N of file A. N and M are to be read from INPUT. The fundamental loop is

```
WHILE NOT EOF(A) DO
    BEGIN
        read and write a line
    END
```

Character array read cannot be used, as a different number of characters is to be read on different executions of the program. "read and write a line" consists of

```
read and write N characters;
write 4 blanks;
read and skip M – N – 1 characters;
read and print integer;
READLN(A)
```

The program is

```
(* EXAMPLE 3.6.2: PRNT           *)
(* READ AND PRINT THE TEXT FILE *)
(* A IN A SPECIFIED FORMAT       *)

PROGRAM PRNT(A, INPUT, OUTPUT);

CONST BL = 4;        (* SPACES TO SKIP BETWEEN TWO OUTPUTS *)

VAR   C: CHAR;        (* FILE CHARACTER READ *)
      N,              (* PRINT THIS MANY CHARS AT START OF LINE *)
      M,              (* THEN SKIP TO THIS COLUMN ON INPUT *)
      INT: INTEGER;   (* THEN READ AN INTEGER INTO HERE *)
      A: TEXT;        (* THE FILE TO BE READ *)

BEGIN (* PRNT *)
    READ(N, M); RESET(A);
    WHILE NOT EOF(A) DO
```

```
BEGIN
   FOR I := 1 TO N DO
      BEGIN
         READ(A, C);
         WRITE(C)
      END;
   WRITE(' ':BL); (* SKIP BL SPACES *)
   FOR I := 1 TO M - N - 1 DO
      READ(A, C); (* SKIP TO COL M IN A *)
   READ(A, INT);
   WRITELN(INT);
   READLN(A)
END
END.  (* PRNT *)
```

If we wished to execute the program with the STATES file (see Appendix A) in which the state name is in the first 15 places on each line and the admission year begins in column 32, in the CDC NOS system we would code the lines

```
GET,A=STATES
PRNT
? 15 32
output
```

or

```
GET,STATES
PRNT(STATES)
? 15 32
output
```

assuming the translated version of the program PRNT is a file called PRNT. In systems with the more general RESET, the following changes are made:

```
      .
      .
      .
VAR C: ...
    A: TEXT;
    FNAME: PACKED ARRAY [1 .. 30] OF CHAR;

BEGIN (* PRNT *)
   READ(FNAME); READ(N, M);
   RESET(A, FNAME)
      .
      .
```

where the input for the program would now be

```
? STATES
? 15 32
output
```

Programming Problems

3.1 Write a program which READs a sequence of words from INPUT, storing them in an internal file of at most 100 records, each containing a WORD part, which is ALFA, and a COUNT part, which is an INTEGER. Each word should be stored in the table only once, and COUNT should contain the number of times the word has occurred. Stop when the word **** is typed in and print out all words and counts. A (too brief) sample run might be

```
? THE
? CAT
? ATE
? THE
? KANGAROO
? ****
WORD COUNTS:
    THE         2
    CAT         1
    ATE         1
    KANGAROO    1
```

3.2 Write a program which reads a date in the form JULY 4, 1976 and prints it in the form 7/4/76. The program should check that the day of the month is legal (for non-leap years). Use the binary search to find the month number and maximum number of days in the month. Use a file like

```
VAR MO: ARRAY [1 . . 12] OF
            RECORD
                NAME: PACKED ARRAY [1 . . 3] OF CHAR;
                NUM: 1 . . 12;
                MAXDAY: 28 . . 31
            END;
```

Read the date as follows: three characters of month name, then read and discard characters until a blank is read. Read the day number, then read and discard a character to get rid of the ",", and finally read the year. (A few Pascals won't work correctly for an input number terminated by a comma; if yours is such, omit the comma.) (Note: this file probably is not large enough for binary searching to be optimal. I specified it for the exercise.)

3.3 Write a program which reads a real number R and prints it in "scientific notation" of the form

$$sN.NNNNN \times 10 ** E$$

where s is the sign if negative and N the first non-zero digit of R unless R = 0. The method is as follows: so that the program will work on all computers, assume that

$$10 ** (-30) \leqslant ABS(R) < 10 ** 30$$

(unless R = 0). Use an array TENTOTHE[I] of reals initialized so that TENTTO-THE[I] = 10 ** I, - 30 ≤ I ≤ 30. By binary searching, find E such that

$$TENTOTHE[E] \leqslant ABS(R) < TENTOTHE[E+1]$$

and then you can write R/TENTOTHE[E]:p:q and E. Do not use LN!

3.4 The file STATES described in Appendix A contains information on the 50 states of the union, the first 15 columns of each line being the state name. Write a program to READ in the 50 state names and print them out in alphabetical order. *Hint:* The following program simply reads and prints state names:

```
PROGRAM PRSTATE(SF, INPUT, OUTPUT);

TYPE SNAME = PACKED ARRAY [1 . . 15] OF CHAR;

VAR  ST: ARRAY [1 . . 50] OF SNAME;
     I, J: INTEGER; SF: TEXT;

BEGIN (* PRSTATE *)
   RESET(SF);
   FOR I := 1 TO 50 DO
      READLN(SF, ST[I] );
   FOR I := 1 TO 50 DO WRITELN(ST[I] )
END.   (* PRSTATE *)
```

3.5 Write a program to determine the largest ten states in population and print state names in descending order of population. The STATES file (Appendix A) has state name in columns 1-15 (see the previous problem) followed by population (which must be read as a real number as it is too large to be an integer on most machines). Suggested method: read and sort the first ten states by population. Then read the remaining states, comparing each with the smallest of the ten. If the new state is larger, discard the old smallest and insert the new state in its proper position.

chapter 4

dynamic data structures: linear representation

In many types of programming problems, the size of the data being processed and perhaps even their structure will vary during execution of a program. In a program simulating waiting lines at a bank, for example, the individual lines may grow and shrink fairly independently of each other, and lines may be opened or closed as need arises. In this chapter and the next we will discuss some of the most important dynamically varying data structures.

4.1 LISTS

A *list* is a sequence of objects

$$X1, X2, \ldots, Xn$$

The X's can be numbers, records, character strings, even other lists. There would of course be no problem in representing lists in a computer if the list stayed put; we would just represent it as an array. Unfortunately, if the list changes with time, this may be a very poor way to represent it. The fundamental principle of dynamic data structures is

> ### The MIKADO Principle
>
> Make the data structure fit the application.

This rule may seem obvious in the abstract, but when real problems arise, there is a tendency to think that there must be one data structure, usually the most complicated one, which is best in all applications. In fact there are tradeoffs: storage versus time, time versus complexity, one application versus another. It is often not even possible to find a "best" structure for one particular program, and the programmer may have to choose between the best structure for the most common application and the "least worst" one for the least common.

Some possible operations which might be desirable on lists are the following:

1. Examining or changing individual items at random places in the list.

2. Examining or changing items in the list in order, or in reverse order, or both.

3. Adding or deleting items at one or both ends of the list.

4. Inserting or deleting items at arbitrary points in the list.

We have already seen that operation 1 is required for the binary search and operation 4 is required for sorting. Whereas the array representation is very efficient for operation 1, it is not for operation 4, as large amounts of data may have to be moved.

Lists with certain types of operations occur so often that they have been given special names: stacks, queues, and deques.

4.1.1 Stacks

A *stack* is a list in which items are added to, deleted from, or examined at one end only. This end is called the *top* of the stack. A useful mental picture is of the typical cafeteria tray stacker: only the top of the stack is readily visible. When a new tray is added to the stack, the stack "goes down one" and appears the same externally except for the different tray on top. When a tray is removed, the stack "goes up one," a new tray is visible, but the general appearance of the stack is the same. By analogy, the operation of adding an item to the stack is called *pushing* it onto the stack. The operation of removing an item is called *popping* the stack. An example of a *stack discipline* is the seniority system used by many employers to determine layoffs—the "last hired, first fired" system.

Stacks are by far the most important dynamic data structure. They are also sometimes called push-down lists or LIFO lists (for last in, first out, the order in which items put into the list are removed).

4.1.2   Queues

A *queue* is a list in which items are added at one end and removed from the other. Think in terms of a waiting line with customers being added to one end and removed from the other as they are served. Most computer applications are related to this example. Queues are used extensively in operating systems to keep track of users waiting for specific resources (e.g., the line printer). They also occur in programs simulating the "waiting in line" process.

4.1.3   Deques

Knuth has coined the term *deque* (double-ended queue, pronounced "deck") for lists in which additions and deletions can take place at both ends of the list. Deques usually occur in applications which are slight generalizations of queue applications. Example 4.4.1 discusses a terminal input deque in which characters are added to one end of the deque, deleted from that end by the "rubout" key, and removed from the other end by the program's READ statement.

We will spend the rest of this chapter showing how stacks, queues, and deques can be represented linearly, that is, as items in an array in array order. More exotic representations will be discussed in Chapter 5.

4.2   LINEAR REPRESENTATION OF STACKS

In programs in which only one or two stacks are used, the linear representation is often the best, as well as the easiest. To represent a stack of items of type "itemtype," we use an array S of itemtype and an integer TOP called the *top of stack pointer*. When the stack contains 37 members, they will be stored as S[1], S[2], . . ., S[37], with S[37] the top of the stack, and TOP = 37. At any time, if the stack is nonempty, S[TOP] will be the contents of the top of the stack.

To *push* X onto the stack, we code

```
TOP := TOP + 1; S[TOP] := X
```

To *pop* the top of the stack into X, we code

```
X := S[TOP] ; TOP := TOP - 1
```

(Of course, the old S[TOP] is still lying around in storage and will be destroyed only when some new number is pushed over it. This representation of a stack actually has more information than we are using.)

In the real world it is possible that the stack will be full when we want to push (will *overflow*) or empty when we want to pop (will *underflow*). Overflow is usually a fatal problem, meaning either that there is an error in the program or that the program must be rerun with a larger stack. Underflow, on the other hand, is often a good sign, meaning perhaps that processing is complete.

A complete description of how to operate on linear stacks is as follows:

1. Declarations:

```
CONST SMAX = 100; (* MAXIMUM STACK SIZE *)
     .
     .
     .
VAR   S: ARRAY [1 .. SMAX] OF itemtype;
      TOP: INTEGER; X: itemtype;
     .
     .
     .
BEGIN (* MAIN PROGRAM *)
   TOP := 0; (* SET STACK EMPTY *)
```

2. Push X:

```
IF (TOP >= SMAX) THEN overflow
ELSE BEGIN TOP := TOP + 1; S[TOP] := X END
```

The sometimes built-in procedure HALT (see Section 1.14) is very useful in this situation. "Overflow" would be replaced by the statement HALT('STACK OVERFLOW').

3. Pop to X:

```
IF (TOP = 0) THEN underflow
ELSE BEGIN X := S[TOP] ; TOP := TOP - 1 END
```

EXAMPLE 4.2.1   Read a list of student names and grade averages, stopping on the average -1. Find the highest grade average and print it and all names of students having that average.

If we could go through the list of students twice, once to find the highest average and the second time to collect all the students with that average, the program would be easy, although this would be an inefficient way to do the problem. Virtually all the time spent here is I/O time, so if we go through the students twice, the program is going to take twice as long. Instead we will make one pass through the students and use a stack (in a rather rudimentary way) to save the list of students with the current highest grade average.

We will assume that the input for each student is in the form "grade space name." The somewhat unnatural order is so that we can use the character array READ to read the name. The fundamental loop is

```
READ(GRADE);
WHILE (GRADE <>-1) DO
    BEGIN
        read NEWNAME;
        IF (GRADE > HIGHGRADE) THEN
            flush (empty) stack and push NEWNAME
        ELSE
            IF (GRADE = HIGHGRADE) THEN
                push NEWNAME;
        READ(GRADE)
    END
```

The *only* reliable way to start a maximum or minimum calculation is to treat the first item as a special case, in this problem, using it to initialize HIGHGRADE and the stack. Also, before reading NEWNAME we will have to skip over the blank that terminates reading GRADE. READLN is unnecessary as READ(GRADE) will take us to the next line. The program is

```
(* EXAMPLE 4.2.1: LARGEST    *)
(* FIND LARGEST GRADE AND *)
(* PRINT ALL NAMES WITH IT   *)

PROGRAM LARGEST(INPUT, OUTPUT);

CONST SMAX = 100;        (* MAXIMUM STACK SIZE *)
      EOI = -1;          (* END OF INFORMATION *)

VAR   S: ARRAY [1 .. SMAX] OF ALFA; (* STACK OF NAMES *)
      TOP,               (* TOP OF STACK POINTER *)
      I: INTEGER;        (* INDEX FOR PRINTING STACK *)
      NEWNAME: ALFA;     (* NAME FROM INPUT *)
      GRADE,             (* GRADE FROM INPUT *)
      HIGHGRADE: REAL;   (* HIGHEST GRADE ENCOUNTERED *)
      C: CHAR;           (* BLANK SKIPPER *)
```

```
BEGIN (* LARGEST *)
   WRITELN('TYPE IN "GRADE NAME", TERMINATED BY ',EOI:1);
   READ(HIGHGRADE,C);
   TOP := 1; READ(S[TOP] ,GRADE);
   WHILE(GRADE< >EOI)DO
      BEGIN
         READ(C); READ(NEWNAME);
         IF (GRADE > HIGHGRADE) THEN
            BEGIN (* NEW HIGHGRADE *)
               HIGHGRADE := GRADE;
               TOP := 1; (* FLUSH STACK *)
               S[TOP] := NEWNAME
            END
         ELSE
            IF (GRADE = HIGHGRADE) THEN
               IF (TOP >= SMAX) THEN
                  HALT('STACK OVERFLOW')
               ELSE
                  BEGIN (* PUSH NEWNAME *)
                     TOP := TOP + 1;
                     S[TOP] := NEWNAME
                  END;
         READ(GRADE)
      END;

   WRITELN('THE HIGHEST GRADE OF ', HIGHGRADE:1:2,
      ' IS HELD BY . . .'); WRITELN;
   FOR I := 1 TO TOP DO WRITELN('          ', S[ I ] )
END.    (* LARGEST *)
```

Assume the following lines of input: 3.5 ANN; 3.5 BOB; 3.5 CAL; 3.8 DAN; 3.6 EVE; 3.8 FAY. The stack will appear successively as in Figure 4.1, and the final printout is

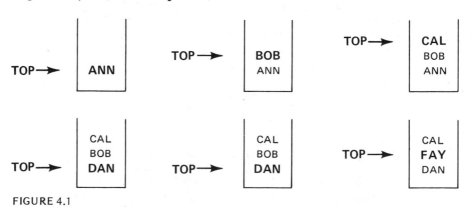

FIGURE 4.1

THE HIGHEST GRADE OF 3.80 IS HELD BY . . .

DAN
FAY

EXAMPLE 4.2.2   READ a number N and print out the different
ways in which it can be written as the sum of positive integers. For
example,

4 = 4 = 3 + 1 = 2 + 2 = 2 + 1 + 1 = 1 + 1 + 1 + 1.

The tricky part of this program is to generate the sums in an
orderly fashion so that we get all the sums and get them only once
(i.e., 2 + 1 and 1 + 2 should *not* both be given). We will keep the terms
of the sum on a stack in decreasing order. To get from one sum to the
next, pop all the 1's off the top of the stack, reduce the new stack top
by 1, and push the largest numbers possible back onto the stack until
the sum is back up to N. The fundamental loop is

```
initialize stack to one item, N;
WHILE stack non-empty DO
    BEGIN
        write out sum on stack;
        pop 1's off the stack;
        IF stack non-empty THEN
            BEGIN
                subtract 1 from top of stack;
                refill stack to sum to N
            END
    END
```

To avoid having to keep summing the stack, we keep a variable STAK-
SUM which always contains an up-to-date value for this sum. The
program is

```
(* EXAMPLE 4.2.2: SUMS      *)
(* PRINT OUT ALL WAYS OF  *)
(* SUMMING INTEGERS TO N  *)

PROGRAM SUMS(INPUT, OUTPUT);

CONST NMAX = 20;      (* LARGEST VALUE FOR N *)

VAR    S: ARRAY [0 .. NMAX] OF INTEGER;
                      (* STACK OF NUMBERS ADDING UP TO N *)
       N,             (* THE INPUT NUMBER *)
       STAKSUM,       (* SUM OF NUMBERS CURRENTLY ON STACK *)
```

```
      I,                      (* INDEX TO PRINT STACK *)
         TOP: INTEGER;   (* STACK TOP POINTER *)

  BEGIN (* SUMS *)
    WRITELN('TYPE IN NUMBER BETWEEN 2 AND   ', NMAX:1);
    READ(N);
    WHILE (N <= 1) OR (N > NMAX) DO
       BEGIN WRITELN('TRY AGAIN'); READ(N) END;
    TOP := 1; (* INITIALIZE STACK TO 1 ITEM, N *)
    S[TOP] := N;
    S[0] := 2; (* SENTINEL TO STOP POPPING 1'S *)
    STAKSUM := N; (* SUM OF STACK *)
    WRITE(N:3, '  =  '); (* START PRINTOUT *)
    WHILE (TOP > 0) DO
       BEGIN
             (* WRITE OUT SUM ON STACK *)
          FOR I := 1 TO TOP-1 DO WRITE(S[I] :1, '  +  ');
          WRITELN(S[TOP] :1);
             (* POP 1'S OFF STACK *)
          WHILE (S[TOP] = 1) DO
             BEGIN
                TOP := TOP - 1;
                STAKSUM := STAKSUM - 1
             END;
          IF (TOP > 0) THEN
             BEGIN (* STACK NOT EMPTY *)
                S[TOP]  := S[TOP] - 1;
                STAKSUM := STAKSUM - 1;
                WHILE (STAKSUM < N) DO (* REFILL STACK *)
                   BEGIN
                      TOP := TOP + 1; (* OVERFLOW IMPOSSIBLE *)
                      IF (N - STAKSUM <= S[TOP-1]) THEN
                         BEGIN
                            S[TOP]  := N - STAKSUM;
                            STAKSUM := N
                         END
                      ELSE (* CAN'T ADD FULL AMOUNT NEEDED *)
                         BEGIN
                            S[TOP]  := S[TOP-1];
                            STAKSUM := STAKSUM + S[TOP]
                         END
                   END; (* OF REFILL *)
                WRITE('      =  '); (* PREPARE FOR NEXT SUM *)
             END
       END
  END.  (* SUMS *)
```

Execution results for N = 6 are

```
? 6
  6 = 6
    = 5 + 1
    = 4 + 2
    = 4 + 1 + 1
    = 3 + 3
    = 3 + 2 + 1
    = 3 + 1 + 1 + 1
    = 2 + 2 + 2
    = 2 + 2 + 1 + 1
    = 2 + 1 + 1 + 1 + 1
    = 1 + 1 + 1 + 1 + 1 + 1
```

EXAMPLE 4.2.3   (This example may be skipped on first reading; See also Programming Problem 6.1.) Process a text file by transferring its contents to another file, inserting the contents of other text files where requested to do so. The user specifies the main input file and the output file. When any line of the current input file starts with the characters

$INSERT

the remainder of the line is interpreted as the name of a text file to be inserted at this point. Inserted files can also have the $INSERT feature. This program could be quite useful in maintaining a source program library, for instance. Since files to be inserted are not known until after execution begins, the nonstandard form of the RESET statement described in Section 3.6 is required.

As an example of the insertion process, suppose our main input file is

```
X
$INSERT ATXT
Y
$INSERT BTXT
Z
```

and ATXT is

```
MMM
NNN
```

and BTXT is

```
PP
$INSERT ATXT
QQ
```

then the output file will be

```
X
MMM
NNN
Y
PP
MMM
NNN
QQ
Z
```

Since inserts can contain inserts, we have to keep a variable list of the files currently active. We do so in a stack, in this case a stack of files represented as an ARRAY OF TEXT.

The insertion program is quite complicated in a language like Pascal, which has very primitive string-handling facilities, but the top-down approach can be used to handle the complexity well. As one concession to the complexity though, we will not check for things like lines too long or stack overflow, allowing Pascal to do that for us even though Pascal's error messages will not be very useful to the unsophisticated user.

The fundamental loop is

```
set stack equal to 1 item, the main input file;
WHILE stack not empty DO
    BEGIN
        process top-of-stack file;
        pop top-of-stack
    END
```

"Process top-of-stack file" is

```
WHILE NOT EOF(top-of-stack file) DO
    read and process line from top-of-stack file
```

"Read and process . . ." is

```
read top-of-stack file line into LINE;
IF start of LINE = '$INSERT' THEN
    push new file onto stack
ELSE
    write out line
```

"Write out line" is relatively straightforward once we have "read top . . .." The whole-line character reading capability does not help us here if we do not want to write out extra trailing blanks, so we go back to Model Program 4:

```
I := 0;
WHILE NOT EOLN(top-of-stack file) DO
```

```
BEGIN
    I := I + 1;
    READ(top-of-stack file, LINE[I] )
END;
READLN(top-of-stack file)
```

I now contains the number of characters in the current line. To check for the character string '$INSERT' at the beginning of the line requires expansion of the condition in the preceding IF statement into several statements. First, we assume an array INSERT has been initialized with the character string '$INSERT'. To avoid blowing up on an illegal subscript, the INSERT array must have an extra character (equal to anything) at its end.

For "IF start of line = '$INSERT' THEN . . . " we code

```
J := 1;
IF (I >= 7) THEN
    WHILE (J <= 7) AND (LINE[J] = INSERT[J] ) DO
        J := J + 1
```

"start of line = '$INSERT'" is now the condition $J > 7$! Finally, we have to refine "push new file onto stack":

```
skip J over blanks in LINE;
transfer rest of line to array FNAME;
RESET(new top-of-stack, FNAME)
```

At this point the final refinements are straightforward, so we proceed to the program. We will use the multicharacter read for FNAME.

```
(* EXAMPLE 4.2.3: INSRT              *)
(*TEXT-FILE INSERTION PROGRAM   *)

PROGRAM INSRT(INPUT, OUTPUT);

CONST FNLEN = 30;      (* MAXIMUM LENGTH OF FILE NAME *)
      LINELEN = 150;  (* MAXIMUM INPUT FILE LINE LENGTH *)
      FMAX = 10;      (* MAXIMUM DEGREE OF NESTING OF INSERTS *)
      INSLEN = 8;     (* LENGTH OF $INSERT COMMAND *)
      INSCMD = '$INSERT   '; (* INSERT COMMAND *)


VAR   INP: ARRAY [1 .. FMAX] OF TEXT; (* STACK OF FILES *)
      OUT: TEXT;       (* OUTPUT FILE *)
      FNAME : PACKED ARRAY[1 .. FNLEN] OF CHAR;
      LINE : PACKED ARRAY[1 .. LINELEN] OF CHAR;
                       (* FILE NAME FROM INPUT *)
      I,               (* LINE READ INDEX *)
      J,               (* INDEX FOR '$INSERT', OUTPUT *)
      K,               (* INDEX FOR FILE NAME TRANSFER *)
```

```
          TOP: INTEGER;  (* TOP OF STACK POINTER *)
          INSERT: ARRAY [1 .. INSLEN] OF CHAR: (* THE STRING '$INSERT' *)

BEGIN (* INSRT *)
    INSERT := INSCMD; (* INITIALIZE INSERT ARRAY *)
    WRITELN('INPUT FILE NAME'); (* GET MAIN INPUT FILE *)
    READLN(FNAME);
    RESET(INP[1] , FNAME); TOP := 1; (* SET UP FILE STACK *)
    WRITELN('OUTPUT FILE NAME'); (*GET OUTPUT FILE *)
    READLN(FNAME); REWRITE(OUT, FNAME);

    WHILE (TOP > 0) DO (* FUNDAMENTAL LOOP *)
        BEGIN
            (* PROCESS TOP-OF-STACK FILE *)
            WHILE NOT EOF(INP[TOP]) DO
                BEGIN
                    (* READ AND PROCESS LINE FROM TOP-OF-STACK FILE *)
                    I := 0;
                    WHILE NOT EOLN(INP[TOP]) DO
                        BEGIN
                            I := I + 1;
                            READ(INP[TOP] , LINE[I])
                        END;
                    READLN(INP[TOP] );
                    J := 1; (* DOES LINE START '$INSERT'? *)
                    IF (I >= INSLEN–1) THEN
                        WHILE (J < INSLEN) AND (LINE[J] = INSERT[J] ) DO
                            J := J + 1;
                    IF (J >= INSLEN) THEN
                        (* $INSERT HAS OCCURRED *)
                        BEGIN
                            (* PUSH NEW FILE ONTO STACK *)
                            WHILE (J <= I) AND (LINE[J] = ' ') DO
                                J := J + 1; (* SKIP OVER BLANKS *)
                            FOR K := J TO I DO (* TRANSFER FILE NAME *)
                                FNAME[K–J+1] := LINE[K] ;
                            FNAME[I–J+2] := ' ';
                            TOP := TOP + 1;
                            RESET(INP[TOP] , FNAME)
                        END

                    ELSE (* $INSERT HASN'T OCCURRED *)
                        BEGIN (* WRITE OUT LINE *)
                            FOR J := 1 TO I DO WRITE(OUT, LINE[J] );
                            WRITELN(OUT)
                        END

                END; (* OF WHILE NOT EOF *)
            (* POP TOP-OF-STACK *)
```

```
                TOP := TOP - 1
            END
    END.  (* INSRT *)
```

Exercises 4.2

1. An airline wishes to assign seats in a 200 seat plane in such a way that (1) smokers and non-smokers are segregated and (2) there are no wasted seats if, say, on one flight there are 10 smokers and 190 non-smokers while on the next these figures are reversed. Suggest a scheme for seat allocation.

2. In the BASIC programming language, the program segment

```
FOR I = 1 to N
S1
. . .
SK
NEXT I
```

is equivalent to the Pascal segment

```
FOR I := 1 TO N DO BEGIN S1 . . . SK END
```

Such "FOR-NEXT" loops can be nested arbitrarily, as in

```
FOR I = 1 TO 10
S1
FOR J = 1 TO 100
FOR K = 1 TO N
S2.
NEXT K
S3
NEXT J
NEXT I
```

(a) Suggest a method of keeping track of what to do when a NEXT statement occurs.

(b) Is the I in "NEXT I" required (for anything but error checking)?

4.3   POLISH NOTATION

Stacks are intimately related to machine evaluation of arithmetic expressions. The intermediary is Polish notation, which we study here. The usual notation for algebraic expression, in which the operators are written *between* the operands (e.g., $a + b$) is called *infix* notation. In the early 1950s, the Polish mathematician Lukasiewicz discovered that if the operator were written *before* the operands (*prefix*, or *Polish*, notation; e.g., $+ a b$) or *after* the operands (*suffix*, *postfix*, or *reverse Polish* (RPN) notation; e.g., $a b +$), then parentheses could be omitted.

In reverse Polish notation,

$$a + b * c \qquad \text{becomes} \qquad a\ b\ c * +$$

and

$$(a + b) * c \qquad \text{becomes} \qquad a\ b + c *$$

(To standardize the translation, the variables in the Polish expression should appear in the same order as the variables in the infix expression. $b\ c * a +$ is also a representation of $a + b * c$, but not the standard one.)

The following method can be used to evaluate RPN expressions by hand. Starting from the left, move across the expression until an operator ($+$, $-$, $*$, etc.) is encountered. Assuming it takes two operands, these should be the two numbers immediately to the left of it. (There can be nothing but numbers since this is the first operator, and if there are not at least two, the RPN expression is malformed.) Draw a circle around these three and write the value of the operation on the two operands above the circle. Henceforth, consider that all that is inside the circle has been replaced by the single number outside. Now continue to the right looking for operators. After the last operator has been processed, the expression should consist of a single number, its value. For example, let's evaluate $a\ b\ c + d\ e * / -$, where $a = 6$, $b = 3$, $c = 2$, $d = 4$, and $e = 5$ (see Figure 4.2).

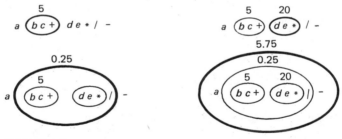

FIGURE 4.2

Shortly after Lukasiewicz's discovery, it was realized that RPN had important applications in computer science. In fact, many compilers now translate arithmetic expressions first into some form of RPN and then translate the RPN into machine code. Some brands of hand calculators also use RPN. This is because it is much easier to evaluate a RPN expression mechanically than the usual parenthesized infix form. As the reader might expect from its location in the text, stacks will play a crucial role, both in conversion and evaluation. We will give the RPN *evaluation* informally to avoid mechanics of I/O. Its fundamental loop is

    initialize stack empty;

```
WHILE more input DO
    IF input is a constant THEN push it
    ELSE
        IF input is a variable THEN push its value
        ELSE
            it's an operator; let n be the number of operands it takes (2 for + and –,
            1 for square root, etc); pop the top n numbers from the stack (error if
            too few), apply the operator to them, and push the result
```

If at loop termination the stack contains precisely one number, that is the value of the expression. Otherwise an error has occurred.

Let's apply this procedure to the RPN expression $a\ 3 + 4\ b - /$, where $a = 5$, $b = 2$ (see Figure 4.3).

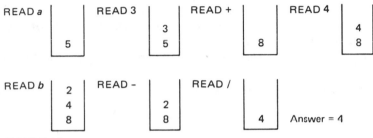

FIGURE 4.3

The fact that RPN expressions are easy to evaluate would not help much if it were not for the fact that it is fairly easy to translate infix to RPN expressions. First let's see how to do it by hand. Number the operators of the expression in the order they are evaluated, left to right if of equal precedence:

$$\overset{1}{a} * \overset{3}{b} + \overset{2}{c} * d$$

Reading from left to right, copy variables until all those required for the first operation are copied; then write the first operation. Here,

$$a\ b *$$

Continue copying variables, if necessary, until all those required for the second operation are copied; then copy it too:

$$a\ b * c\ d *$$

Repeat the process for all remaining operators. In this case we finally obtain

$$a\ b * c\ d * +$$

If we try the same procedure on

$$2 \quad 1 \quad 3$$
$$a * (b + c) * d$$

we obtain, successively, $a\ b\ c\ +$, $a\ b\ c\ +\ *$, and $a\ b\ c\ +\ *\ d\ *$.

The computer algorithm for doing the translation is a reasonable imitation of this process. When variables or numbers are READ, they are output immediately. Operators and parentheses are saved on a stack and only sent along to the output when an operator of lower or equal precedence comes along and pops them to the output. This allows us to determine the order of operations "on the fly."

EXAMPLE 4.3.1 Translate an input string consisting of single-letter variables and binary (having two operands) operators +, -, *, /, and ^ (to the power) into RPN. (+ or - in expressions like +a and -14.2 are called *unary* operators. To simplify the example, we do not allow them.)

A *precedence* is assigned to each operator:

OP	prec(OP)
'^'	largest
'*','/'	.
'+','-'	.
'('	smallest

We assume one formula per line, and a terminating line starting with ".". The fundamental loop of our program is

```
READLN(LINE);
WHILE (LINE[1] <> '.') DO
    BEGIN
        translate LINE;
        READLN(LINE)
    END
```

"translate LINE" is

```
initialize stack;
FOR I := 1 TO line length DO
    CASE LINE[I] OF
        alphabetic: output it;
             '(': push it;
             ')': pop and output stack until '(' is
                  reached; and pop it too;
        operator: WHILE (prec(stack top) >= prec (LINE[I] ) DO
                                pop and output stack items;
```

```
                    push LINE[I] ;
          other: ignore
    END;
flush remainder of stack to output
```

(You may wish to review the CASE statement in Section 1.12.)

The simplest method of assigning precedence is to use a character class array as we did in Example 1.11.2. At the same time we can also use this array to detect alphabetic characters. To enhance program readability, we define an enumerated type for character class values, with values for operators in increasing order of precedence:

```
TYPE CCTYPE = (SKIPIT, ALPHABETIC, LPAREN, RPAREN, ADDOP,
   MULOP, EXPOP);
```

As pushing and popping are done at several places, we will make them procedures. The program is

```
(* EXAMPLE 4.3.1: INTORPN     *)
(* INFIX TO RPN TRANSLATOR *)


PROGRAM INTORPN(INPUT, OUTPUT);


CONST SMAX = 100;      (* STACK LIMIT *)
        STOPCHAR = '.'; (* INPUT TERMINATOR IN COL 1 *)
        LINELEN = 80;   (* LONGEST INPUT LINE *)
        LOWORD = 0;     (* LOWEST ORD OF A CHAR *)
        HIGHORD = 127; (* HIGHEST ORD OF A CHAR—ASCII *)


TYPE   CCTYPE = (SKIPIT, ALPHABETIC, LPAREN, RPAREN,
                      ADDOP, MULOP, EXPOP);


VAR    S: ARRAY [1 .. SMAX] OF CHAR;   (* OPERATOR STACK *)
        TOP: INTEGER;                       (* TOP OF STACK POINTER *)
        LINE: PACKED ARRAY [1 .. LINELEN] OF CHAR; (* INPUT LINE *)
        CC: ARRAY [CHAR] OF CCTYPE;   (* CHARACTER CLASSES *)
        C: CHAR;                        (* LOOP INDEX FOR CC *)
        I: INTEGER;                     (* INDEX FOR LINE *)
PROCEDURE PUSH(OP: CHAR); (* PUSH OP ONTO STACK *)
    BEGIN (* PUSH *)
        IF (TOP >= SMAX) THEN HALT('EXPRESSION TOO COMPLEX');
        TOP := TOP + 1; S[TOP] := OP
    END;  (* PUSH *)


PROCEDURE POPOUT; (* POP AND WRITE OUT TOP OF STACK *)
    BEGIN (* POPOUT *)
        WRITE(S[TOP]); (* UNDERFLOW NOT POSSIBLE *)
        TOP := TOP - 1
    END; (* POPOUT *)
```

```
BEGIN (* INTORPN *)
     (* INITIALIZE CC *)
   FOR C : = CHR(LOWORD) TO CHR(HIGHORD) DO CC[C] := SKIPIT;
   FOR C := 'A' TO 'Z' DO CC[C] := ALPHABETIC;
   CC['('] := LPAREN; CC[')'] := RPAREN;
   CC['+'] := ADDOP; CC['-'] := ADDOP;
   CC['*'] := MULOP; CC['/'] := MULOP; CC['^'] := EXPOP;

   READLN(LINE);
   WHILE (LINE[1] <> STOPCHAR) DO
      BEGIN
         TOP := 0; PUSH('('); (* SENTINEL *)
         FOR I := 1 TO LINELEN DO
            CASE CC[LINE[I]] OF
         ALPHABETIC: WRITE(LINE[I]);
             LPAREN: PUSH('(');
             RPAREN: (* FLUSH TO '('; SENTINEL MAY STOP *)
               BEGIN
                  WHILE (S[TOP] <> '(') DO POPOUT;
                  IF (TOP = 1) THEN
                     HALT('')'' WITHOUT ''('');
                  TOP: = TOP - 1 (* DISCARD '(' *)
               END;
   ADDOP,MULOP,EXPOP: (* POP ANY OP WITH BIGGER PREC ON STACK *)
               BEGIN
                  WHILE (CC[S[TOP]] >= CC[LINE[I]]) DO
                     POPOUT; (* SENTINEL MAY STOP *)
                  PUSH(LINE[I])
               END;
             SKIPIT: (* DO NOTHING *)
            END; (* OF CASE *)
         WHILE (S[TOP] <> '(') DO POPOUT (* FLUSH STACK *)
         WRITELN;
         IF (TOP > 1) THEN WRITELN('UNMATCHED ''(''');
         READLN(LINE)
      END
END.  (* INTORPN *)
```

To clarify the program, we will trace it for two sample infix expressions. To simplify the diagrams, we will use "prec(X)" as a shorthand for ORD(CC[X]), the ORD being used so that the ordering becomes obvious.

1. Input = A+B*C-D. The position at the start of the FOR I loop is as in Figure 4.4.

2. Input = (A+B)*C-D. Tracing as before results in Figure 4.5.

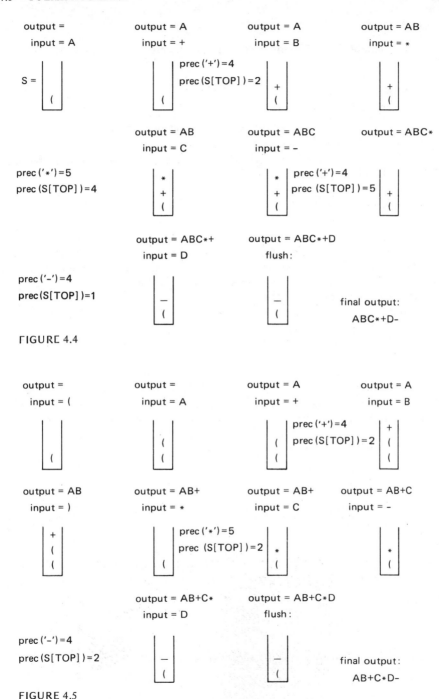

FIGURE 4.4

FIGURE 4.5

Exercises 4.3

1. Evaluate the following RPN expressions, assuming that $a = 3$, $b = 4$, $c = -2$, and $d = 1$:
   (a) $abc + d *-$
   (b) $abc -/ d +$
   (c) $ab * cd *+$

2. Note that in RPN, $abc++$ is the same as $ab + c +$. Does $abc - - = ab - c -$ for all values of a, b, and c?

3. Convert the following infix expressions to RPN. Be sure that the order of the variables is unchanged.
   (a) $a - b/c + d$
   (b) $(a - b)/c + d$
   (c) $a - b/(c + d)$
   (d) $(a - b)/(c + d)$

4. There is a technique for checking the validity of RPN expressions much like the usual parenthesis counting trick: start the count at 0 and, counting from the left, add 1 whenever a number or variable is encountered, and subtract 1 whenever an operator is encountered.
   (a) Give conditions based on this count under which the RPN expression is valid.
   (b) How is the count related to the stack method of evaluation of RPN expressions?

5. In infix expressions it is possible to use the same symbol for binary and unary + and - (see Example 4.3.1 for definitions of binary and unary operators), but this is not so in RPN. For instance, does $ab - - = a - (-b)$ or $- (a - b)$? Unary + can simply be omitted, but a separate symbol is necessary for unary -, say, $\sim$. Then $a - (-b)$ would be written $ab \sim -$ and $-(a - b)$ would be written $ab -\sim$. Translate the following infix expressions to RPN:
   (a) $-a + b - c$
   (b) $a * (-b)$

4.4 LINEAR REPRESENTATION OF QUEUES AND DEQUES

There is a fairly obvious way to implement a queue as a linear array: simply keep two pointers, one for each end of the queue. If we have declared

```
VAR Q: ARRAY [1 .. 100] OF itemtype;
     FRONT, REAR: INTEGER;
```

then we can add X to the rear of the queue by

```
REAR := REAR + 1; Q[REAR] := X
```

and remove X from the front of the queue by

```
FRONT := FRONT + 1; X := Q[FRONT]
```

Some refinements are necessary for, as in stacks, we must worry about underflow and overflow. But even before we get to that, it is very important to define the meaning of FRONT and REAR precisely. Unless this is done, the meaning has a tendency to change, with disastrous results. Examining the preceding program segments, we see that

FRONT points one before the current first item

and

REAR points directly at the last item.

Underflow then occurs when FRONT = REAR. We can set FRONT and REAR initially to 0.

Testing for overflow is also easy, but it brings up a serious problem: even though the queue may never contain more than a few items, the array may eventually overflow. This is because the part of the array containing the queue "marches across" the array as items are added or deleted. If the queue became completely empty often enough, then we could reset FRONT and REAR to 0 when that occurs, but we would still be in trouble in cases when the queue never contained more than two items, but was never empty. If A represents an addition to the queue and R a removal, the sequence $AARARARAR$ . . . will eventually exhaust the array no matter how large it is.

One possible solution is to slide everything to the left when the queue overflows to the right. But if the occupied part of the queue gets fairly long or the queue items are large, this is time consuming.

A better solution in general is to think of the Q array as being *circular*, with Q[1] immediately following Q[100]. A typical situation might be as in Figure 4.6 where the X's represent active items in the queue and the .'s represent empty spots in the Q array which can house further entries. Now, however, we must be very careful about overflow, because if the queue becomes full we set REAR = FRONT, which makes the queue appear empty! (If we have FRONT point to the first item instead of one before the first, we have the same problem:

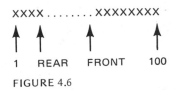

FIGURE 4.6

FRONT = REAR + 1 can indicate either a full or an empty queue.) One solution, which is discussed in Exercise 4.4.1, is always to require the array to contain at least one empty slot. A more straightforward way is to keep an auxiliary variable QCOUNT containing the number of items currently in the queue.

The basic queue declarations are

```
VAR Q: ARRAY [1 .. QLEN] OF itemtype;
    FRONT, REAR, QCOUNT: INTEGER;
       .
       .
       .
BEGIN
    FRONT := 0; REAR := 0; QCOUNT := 0; (* INITIALIZE QUEUE *)
```

To add X to the queue,

```
IF (QCOUNT = QLEN) THEN overflow;
REAR := REAR + 1;
IF (REAR > QLEN) THEN REAR := 1;
Q[REAR] := X; QCOUNT := QCOUNT + 1
```

To remove X from the queue,

```
IF (QCOUNT = 0) THEN underflow;
FRONT := FRONT + 1;
IF (FRONT > QLEN) THEN FRONT := 1;
X := Q[FRONT] ; QCOUNT := QCOUNT – 1
```

A typical application of the techniques of this section is to what is called *circular buffers*. When a file is being read or written in sequential order and the operating system knows this, it can take advantage of the fact and read ahead or write behind the program. Storage is allocated for several records, a record-sized piece of storage being called a *buffer*. The buffers are kept in the form of a circular queue. When reading, for instance, the front of the queue will be the record from which the user's program is currently taking data, while the operating system is actually reading into the buffer at the rear of the queue (see Figure 4.7). As long as a buffer is available, the operating system's reading program will continue to read ahead. If the user's

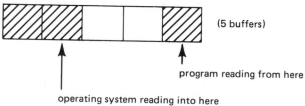

(5 buffers)

program reading from here

operating system reading into here

FIGURE 4.7

program needs a record before the operating system has had a chance to read it, the program is halted until the operating system has done the reading. A queue discipline is used so that the records are shipped to the user in the same order that they appear in the file. Similarly, circular buffering on output allows the user's program to start filling new output buffers before old buffers are completely written out. Most commonly, only two buffers are used; but if I/O takes place at irregular intervals, buffering with more than two buffers can help to smooth out the lumps.

Deques can be implemented using the same scheme as for queues. An extremely important example is a generalization of the buffering idea discussed previously for computer terminal input. In this example, characters may be added to the rear of the queue (by keying them in at the terminal) and removed either from the front of the queue (by a READ in the computer) or the rear (by striking the delete, rubout, or whatever, key). This is called an *input restricted deque*, as input is allowed at only one end.

EXAMPLE 4.4.1 Simulate a terminal input deque. The deque will contain at most 256 characters. Any character typed in will be added to the rear of the deque except for '\', which will act as the delete key, and '$', which will cause a simulated READ from the deque in which all characters from the front up to and including the first "." will be printed and deleted from the deque. The program will process one line of input only.

The fundamental loop is

```
WHILE NOT EOLN DO
    BEGIN
        READ(C);
        IF (C = '\') THEN delete char
        ELSE IF (C = '$') THEN fake read line
            ELSE queue up C
    END
```

We will make "delete char," "fake read line," and "queue up C" all separate procedures. We refine "fake read line" further to

```
REPEAT
    get a char and print it
UNTIL (char = '.') OR deque empty
```

The program is a little subtle because of the necessity for testing for empty deques and lines in the proper places. It is as follows:

```
(* EXAMPLE 4.4.1: INDEQUE            *)
(* SIMULATE TERMINAL INPUT DEQUE *)
```

```
PROGRAM INDEQUE(INPUT, OUTPUT);

CONST DELCHAR = '\';       (* DELETE CHAR *)
      READCHAR = '$';      (* SIMULATE LINE READ *)
      EOLNCHAR = '.';      (* END OF LINE CHAR *)
      DLEN = 256;          (* LENGTH OF DEQUE *)

VAR   D: ARRAY [1 .. DLEN] OF CHAR; (* INPUT DEQUE *)
      FRONT, REAR,         (* DEQUE POINTERS *)
      DCOUNT: INTEGER; (* NUMBER OF ITEMS IN DEQUE *)
      C: CHAR;             (* INPUT CHARACTER *)

PROCEDURE DELETECHAR; (* DELETE A CHAR FROM REAR OF QUEUE *)
   BEGIN (* DELETECHAR *)
      IF (DCOUNT > 0) THEN
         IF (D[REAR] <> '.') THEN
            BEGIN
               REAR := REAR - 1;
               IF (REAR = 0) THEN REAR := DLEN;
               DCOUNT := DCOUNT - 1
            END
   END;    (* DELETECHAR *)

PROCEDURE FAKEREAD; (* FAKE READ ONE LINE AND DELETE IT *)
                    (* DEQUE ASSUMED TO BE NON-EMPTY    *)
   BEGIN (* FAKEREAD *)
      REPEAT
         FRONT := FRONT + 1;
         IF (FRONT > DLEN) THEN FRONT := 1;
         DCOUNT := DCOUNT - 1;
         WRITE(D[FRONT])
      UNTIL (D[FRONT] = EOLNCHAR) OR (DCOUNT = 0);
      WRITELN
   END;  (* FAKEREAD *)

PROCEDURE QUEUEUPC;
      (* ADD C TO QUEUE *)
   BEGIN (* QUEUEUPC *)
      IF   (DCOUNT = DLEN) THEN
         HALT('QUEUE OVERFLOW');
      REAR := REAR + 1;
      IF (REAR > DLEN) THEN REAR := 1
      DCOUNT := DCOUNT + 1; D[REAR] := C (* C IS GLOBAL *)
   END;   (* QUEUEUPC *)

BEGIN (* INDEQUE *)
   FRONT := 1; REAR := 1; DCOUNT := 0;
   WHILE NOT EOLN DO
```

```
BEGIN
    READ(C);
    IF (C = DELCHAR) THEN DELETECHAR
    ELSE
        IF (C = READCHAR) THEN
            BEGIN
                IF (DCOUNT > 0) THEN FAKEREAD (****)
            END
            ELSE QUEUEUPC
    END;
    WRITELN('LINES LEFT OVER:');
    WHILE (DCOUNT > 0) DO FAKEREAD
END.  (* INDEQUE *)
```

Consider the following sample execution, shown with DLEN = 8:

Input	Deque	Output
T	T———	
H	TH——	
U	THU—	
\	TH——	
I	THI—	
S	THIS—	
.	THIS.—	
I	THIS.I—	
S	THIS.IS—	
$	———IS—	THIS.
N	———ISN	
T	T——ISN	
.	T:——ISN	
\	T.——ISN	
H	T.H ISN	
$	—H———	ISNT.
A	—HA——	
R	—HAR—	
D	—HARD-	
eoln		LINES LEFT OVER:
		HARD

Comments

1. Note that we have started FRONT and REAR at 1 and not 0.
    I felt more comfortable having FRONT and REAR always
    be legal subscripts.

2. The BEGIN-END brackets around the main program statement marked (****) are necessary to make the ELSE following apply to IF (C = READCHAR) . . .

3. There must be a test of DCOUNT outside of FAKEREAD in the final WHILE loop (to terminate it), so the test is also outside at (****).

Exercises 4.4

1. Another common way to solve the overflow-underflow problem in queues is not to allow the last slot to be filled; that is, when adding an item, if FRONT = REAR after REAR has been updated, overflow has occurred.

(a) Write the declarations and initializations for such a queue and program segments to add X to the rear and delete it from the front.

(b) Compare the two methods in terms of program length and storage used (e.g., the method here "wastes" one queue slot but does not require the use of QCOUNT. What difference does size of queue item make?).

Programming Problems

4.1 In the STATES file (Appendix A), the state name is in columns 1-15 and its admission year in columns 32-35. Read the current year CY and anniversary year number AN and produce a list of the states which will next celebrate their ANth anniversary. For instance, if CY = 1982 and AN = 200, the output should be

IN 1987, THE FOLLOWING STATES WILL CELEBRATE ANNIVERSARY 200:

PENNSYLVANIA
DELAWARE
NEW JERSEY

You should read the STATES file only once and keep a stack of potential next states to celebrate their ANth anniversary. The reading can be done using READLN (NAME, SKIP, YEAR) where NAME is a PACKED ARRAY [1 . . 15] OF CHAR, SKIP, which is ignored, is a PACKED ARRAY [1 . . 16] OF CHAR, and YEAR is an integer.

4.2 Write a program to simulate a RPN calculator. Each line of input is either (1) an operator +, -, *, or /, (2) a # character followed by a number, indicating an operand, or (3) =, which causes a check to be made that the stack has only one item, prints it if so, and stops. The following is a possible sample run:

```
?  #2
?  #3
?  #4
?  +
?  *
?  =
RESULT =    1.4000000000000E+001
```

4.3 Write a program which reads expressions involving parentheses ( ), brackets [ ], and, if available, braces {   }. Your program should check to see that they are properly nested and that) matches (,] matches [, and }matches {. If your computer doesn't have {   }, use < > instead. You may assume that each line of input contains exactly one expression. You should keep a single stack corresponding to unmatched left parentheses, brackets, and braces. *Ignore all other characters!* The program should be terminated by a '$' at the first of an input line. Using character-array read, the overall structure can be

```
READLN(LINE);
WHILE (LINE[1] <> '$') DO
    BEGIN
        process LINE;
        READLN(LINE)
    END
```

A sample run is as follows:

```
?  A[F + X {Y - 2}]
LEGAL
?  B+[3 - {X/2})*19 + 2/(X - 7)
ERROR--] EXPECTED
?  $
```

chapter 5

dynamic data structures: linked representations

5.1 LINKED LISTS

In many applications it is desirable to reorder a list without physically moving its items, for instance, when sorting a file with large records. To do this, we distinguish two orders for a list, the *logical order* and the *physical order*. The physical order is the actual order of the items in the list in the physical places in which they are stored. The logical order of a list may be entirely different from the physical order, and a file may have more than one logical order. Since in logical order the order of items is not determined by their physical position, there must be some explicit way of giving the order, usually a *pointer* field in each item which points to the next item in logical order. The pointer to an item is often simply the memory address of the beginning of the item.

For example, let I1, I2, . . . , I8 be a list of information with the physical order I1, . . . , I8, that is, stored in that order. We wish to give it the logical order I3, I5, I7, I8, I4, I1, I2, I6. We do this by associating with each information field In a *link* field LINK pointing to, that is, giving the address of, the next information item. We also need a pointer FIRST to the first item on the list. The end of the list is indicated by the *nil pointer*, 0. If 0 were actually a legal pointer value, then some other value would be chosen to represent the nil pointer. Supposing that the In's are stored as follows, the value of the LINKs are

	address	Info	LINK
	1200	I1	1210
	1210	I2	1250
FIRST =	1220	I3	1240
	1230	I4	1200
	1240	I5	1260
	1250	I6	0
	1260	I7	1270
	1270	I8	1230

FIRST = 1220, so the address of the first item in the list is 1220. The LINK part of the first item (I3) is 1240, so the address of the second item is 1240 and the second item is I5. The address of the third item is therefore 1260, and the third item is I7, and so on.

The Info-LINK list item is called a *node*, which can be represented pictorially as in Figure 5.1(a). The value of LINK is often represented as an arrow, as in Figure 5.1(b), with the last item on the list having a nil pointer represented as in Figure 5.1(c).

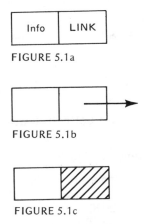

FIGURE 5.1a

FIGURE 5.1b

FIGURE 5.1c

One representation of the preceding I3, I5, . . . , list is shown in Figure 5.2. We will usually simply picture such a list as in Figure 5.3.

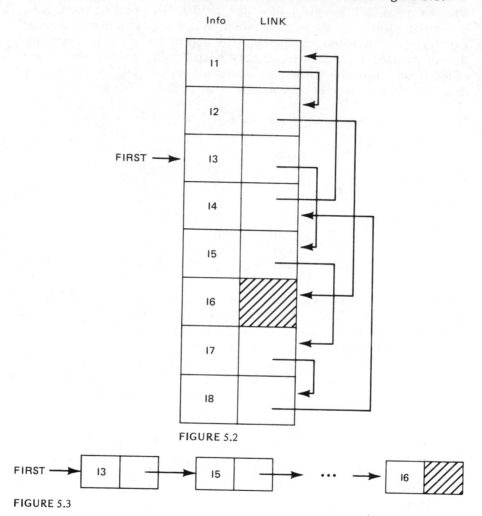

FIGURE 5.2

FIGURE 5.3

Exercises 5.1

(The following addresses below will not have gaps if interpreted as octal, base 8, numbers.)

1. Consider the following LINKed list:

address	Info	LINK
2020	27	2040
2030	47	2060
2040	23	2110

FIRST =	2050	74	2100
	2060	35	2040
	2070	14	0
	2100	32	2020
	2110	17	2070

(a) Give the Info parts of the list starting at FIRST in logical order.

(b) Redraw the list with LINKs shown geometrically.

2. Fill in the LINKs so that the following list is logically in alphabetical order. Draw the appropriate LINK arrows between nodes.

FIRST = _ _ _ _ _

address	Info	LINK
10244	HAL	
10246		
10250	BOB	
10252	IVY	
10254	EVE	
10256	ANN	
10260		
10262	GIL	
10264	JAY	
10266	DAN	
10270	CAL	
10272		
10274	FAY	

3. Give the Info part of the following list in logical order:

FIRST = 322

address	Info	LINK
310	OR	332
312	OFF	340
314	BE	326
316	AND	312
320	TO	314
322	TO	334
324	QUESTION	0
326	THAT	342
330	THE	324
332	NOT	320
334	BE	310
336	ON	340
340	AGAIN	320
342	IS	330

5.2 POINTERS IN PASCAL

In many old-fashioned languages, pointers are simply integers. This, however, can encourage the programmer to fall into the error of doing arithmetic on them, using them as FOR loop indices, or otherwise using them like ordinary integers, to the programmer's ultimate sorrow. Thus modern languages like Pascal have a pointer data type on which only operations appropriate to pointers can be performed. As a further safeguard, the programmer must specify the type of data to which a pointer may point when it is declared. This is done in a statement like

```
VAR P, Q: ^sometype;
```

(*Read:* pointer to sometype; on some terminals, ^ is an upward-pointing arrow ↑.) "sometype" must the name of a type, not a complicated type definition. A pointer variable generally occupies a single memory cell and is the same size no matter what type it points to, but the data pointed to may comprise many memory cells. Pascal distinguishes between the pointer P and what it points to, denoted by P^ (see Figure 5.4). The operation of applying ^ to a pointer is sometimes called *dereferencing*, as a pointer is sometimes called a *reference variable*.

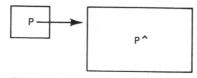

FIGURE 5.4

Suppose that we have declared

```
TYPE ALFREC = RECORD A, B, C: ALFA END;
VAR  P, Q: ^ALFREC;
```

and we have the example shown in Figure 5.5. Then if we executed Q := P, we would have Figure 5.6. If no other pointer is pointing to the former Q^ (EEE . . . , etc.), then access to it is lost forever. If instead we had executed Q^ := P^, then the result would have been as shown in Figure 5.7. And if, instead of that, we had executed Q^.B := P^.B,

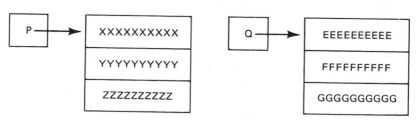

FIGURE 5.5

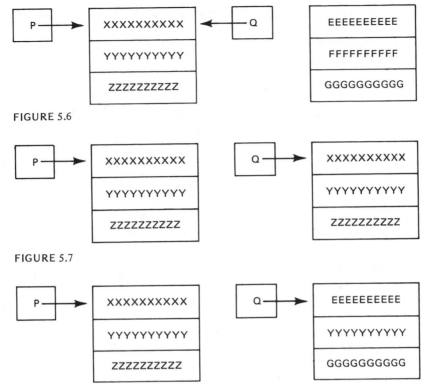

FIGURE 5.6

FIGURE 5.7

FIGURE 5.8

then we would have Figure 5.8.

Note that if P = Q (as in Figure 5.6), then changes to P^ also change Q^ (P still = Q), but changing P does *not* change Q (P may no longer = Q). Also, if P^ = Q^ but P ≠ Q (as in Figure 5.7), changes to P^ do *not* affect Q^.

When assigning a value to a pointer variable, the value assigned must be a pointer to the same data type. The one exception to this is the one pointer *literal*, NIL, a keyword representing the nil pointer. NIL is considered to be of type "pointer to anything," although in fact it points to nothing. NIL, not 0, must always be used as the nil pointer.

Pascal Pointer 22 ⟩   *If P = NIL, evaluation of P^ is a fatal error.*

The only operation on pointer variables other than ^ , assignment, and comparison for equality is the built-in procedure NEW. With P declared as in the preceding, NEW(P) allocates enough unused memory to hold three ALFAs and sets P pointing to it. P itself is *not* new; its value is. Once NEW(P) has been executed, values are given to the various parts of P ^ in separate statements.

Unfortunately in many Pascals, including the proposed standard, if we declare

VAR A: ^XXX; B: ^XXX;

then A and B are considered to be *different types*!! Statements like A := B would not then be allowed! Since it is often necessary to declare pointer variables in different places with the same type (in particular, for formal and actual procedure parameters and situations like Examples 5.3.1–3) I recommend that you follow

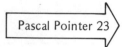

The type ^SOMETYPE should always be given a name like PTRTOSOMETYPE before its first use and that name only used in declarations.

The recommended form for the ALFREC declarations above would be

```
TYPE   PTRTOALFREC = ^ALFREC;
       ALFREC = RECORD A, B, C: ALFA END;
VAR    P, Q: PTRTOALFREC;
```

Finally, we handle the most important application of pointers, which is to linked lists. Since the LINK of a node must point to an item of the node's type, a TYPE declaration is always required in this case. It will be of the form

```
TYPE PTRTONODE = ^NODE;
     NODE = RECORD INFO: sometype;
            LINK: PTRTONODE END;
```

Note that we are not saying that a NODE contains another NODE. That would be impossible as that would in effect say that a NODE contains a NODE and something else, that is, that a NODE is larger than a NODE. A ^NODE is the same (small) size no matter what size a NODE is.

Notice also that in the declaration above, either PTRTONODE or NODE must be used before it is declared, something which Pascal does not in general allow. In this one special case though, one is allowed to use ^SOMETYPE before SOMETYPE is defined. (The reverse order for the definitions above is usually *not* allowed.)

Some diagrams may be helpful in understanding how the concepts of this section apply to linked lists. Assume that P is of type ^NODE, NODE as before, and we have Figure 5.9. P^.LINK is the variable (box) of Figure 5.10 whose *value* is the pointer (arrow) of Figure 5.11, so that P^.LINK^.LINK is as shown in Figure 5.12.

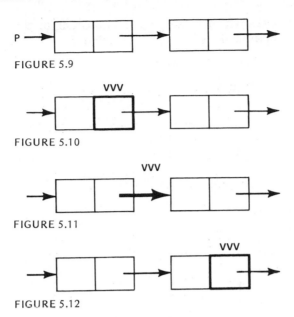

FIGURE 5.9

FIGURE 5.10

FIGURE 5.11

FIGURE 5.12

5.3   BASIC OPERATIONS WITH LINKED LISTS

There are three basic operations with linked lists: item insertion, item deletion, and sequential traversal. In all these examples, we will assume that the type NODE is declared as in the end of the last section and that P and Q are declared as type PTRTONODE = ^NODE.

5.3.1   Item Insertion

Assume that a new element with INFO part X is to be inserted after the node pointed to by P and before P's successor (see Figure 5.13). The necessary code is

```
NEW(Q); Q^.INFO := X;
Q^.LINK := P^.LINK; P^.LINK := Q
```

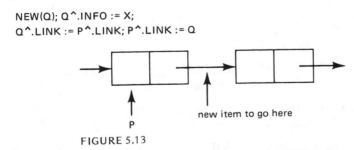

FIGURE 5.13

and the result is shown in Figure 5.14. The order of the statements is crucial. If we executed the second line in the order

```
P^.LINK := Q; Q^.LINK := P^.LINK (*????*)
```

then we would get Figure 5.15.

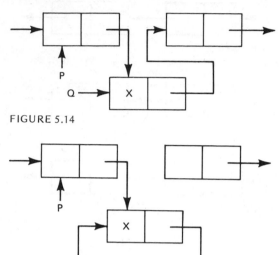

FIGURE 5.14

FIGURE 5.15

5.3.2 Item Deletion

We need a pointer to the node *before* the node to be deleted, not

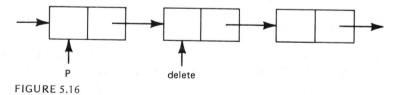

FIGURE 5.16

just to the to-be-deleted node itself (see Figure 5.16). The code is

```
P^.LINK := P^.LINK^.LINK
```

which produces Figure 5.17. The preceding statement may be easier to grasp if it is broken up into two pieces:

```
Q := P^.LINK; (* Q POINTS TO NODE TO BE DELETED *)
P^.LINK :=Q^.LINK
```

Another sort of order is crucial here. If we wrote Q^.LINK := P^.LINK instead, we would get Figure 5.18.

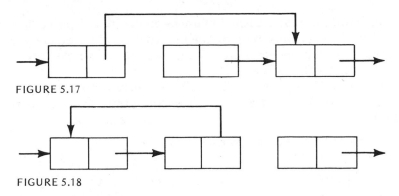

FIGURE 5.17

FIGURE 5.18

5.3.3 Sequential Traversal

This involves going through a linked list in order. This operation sometimes gives people fits. They have managed to learn FOR loops for going through arrays sequentially and often find that technique difficult to unlearn. But unlearn it you must, as it is *worthless* for linked lists. Pascal is some help here because it will not even let us try a FOR loop on linked lists.

To keep track of our position on the list we need a pointer, say P, called a *running pointer*, which is analogous to the index of a FOR loop. This should be a separate variable from the variable, say FIRST, which points to the beginning of the list, because P changes, and we do not want to lose our pointer to the start of the list.

> **Model Program 7:** Sequentially process a linked list pointed to by FIRST.
>
> ```
>     P := FIRST;
>     WHILE (P <> NIL) DO
>         BEGIN
>             Process P^;
>  →          P := P^.LINK (* P TO NEXT NODE *)
>         END
> ```

As a simple example, the following program segment prints out all the INFO values in logical order. Notice that it works even if the list is empty (FIRST = NIL)!

```
P := FIRST;
WHILE (P <> NIL) DO
    BEGIN
        WRITELN(P^.INFO);
        P := P^.LINK
    END
```

Some minor modifications must be made in this procedure if we wish to go through only part of the list, that is, when we are searching for a node which meets some condition. For example, say FIRST points to a list with integer INFOs and we are to print the value of the first INFO that is negative, NOT FOUND if there is none. Once we have found a negative INFO, it would be a waste of time to continue traversing the list. Just as in Section 2.1, Solution 2, we cannot use

```
WHILE (P <> NIL) AND (P^.INFO >= 0) DO
    P := P^.LINK
```

as if no P^.INFO is less than 0; the last time the test is performed P will be NIL, and when we try to evaluate P^, a fatal error results. One solution is

> **Model Program 8:** Set P pointing to the first node in the list starting at FIRST such that "P^ satisfies condition."
>
> ```
>     P := FIRST; FOUND := FALSE;
>     WHILE (P <> NIL) AND NOT FOUND DO
>         IF P^ satisfies condition THEN
>             FOUND := TRUE
>         ELSE P := P^.LINK
> ```

Most obvious variants of this code are wrong! See Exercise 5.3.3.

As we discovered in Section 2.1, it is often useful to end a list with a sentinel, a special node with a fixed pointer to it which we will usually call SENTINEL (see Figure 5.19). The sentinel is not considered to be a real element of the list but is merely there to see that a search condition will always be met.

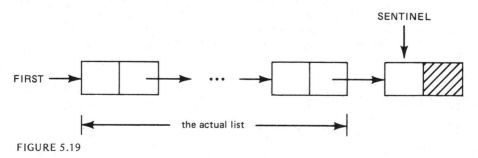

FIGURE 5.19

Model Programs 7 and 8 can be easily rewritten for lists terminated with sentinels:

Model Program 7s: Sequentially process a list pointed to by FIRST and ended by SENTINEL.

```
P := FIRST;
WHILE (P <> SENTINEL) DO
   BEGIN
      Process P^;
      P := P^.LINK
   END
```

and

Model Program 8s: Set P pointing to the first node in the list starting at FIRST and ended by SENTINEL such that "P^ satisfies condition." If no such P is found, P will be left equal to SENTINEL.

```
P := FIRST;
Make SENTINEL^ satisfy condition;
WHILE (P^ doesn't satisfy condition) DO
   P := P^.LINK;
IF (P = SENTINEL) THEN not found
```

EXAMPLE 5.3.1 Read integers, ending on 0, and put them in a linked list. Print the list.

In this example the list will be treated like a stack, with each new item added at the beginning. Before is shown in Figure 5.20 and after the addition in Figure 5.21. The program is on the next page.

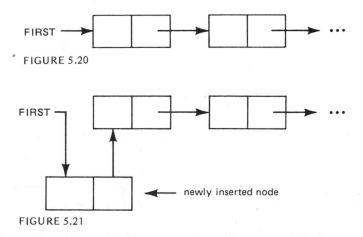

FIRST

FIGURE 5.20

FIRST

newly inserted node

FIGURE 5.21

```
(* EXAMPLE 5.3.1: LIST1        *)
(* READ INTEGERS AND PLACE *)
(* IN LINKED LIST              *)

PROGRAM LIST1(INPUT, OUTPUT);

CONST EOI = 0;                    (* END OF INPUT SENTINEL *)

TYPE   PTRTONODE = ^NODE;
       NODE = RECORD INFO: INTEGER; LINK: PTRTONODE END;

VAR    FIRST,                     (* POINTER TO START OF LIST *)
       P: PTRTONODE;             (* RUNNING POINTER TO LIST *)
       X: INTEGER;               (* INPUT ITEM *)

BEGIN (* LIST1 *)
   FIRST := NIL;
   READ(X);
   WHILE (X <> EOI) DO
      BEGIN
         NEW(P);
         P^.INFO := X;
         P^.LINK := FIRST;
         FIRST := P;
         READ(X)
      END;

   P := FIRST; (* NOW PRINT OUT THE LIST *)
   WHILE (P <> NIL) DO
      BEGIN
         WRITE(P^.INFO:1, ' ');
         P := P^.LINK
      END;
   WRITELN
END. (* LIST1 *)
```

Execution of the program produces:

```
?  1  3  5  7  9  11  0       (* input *)
11  9  7  5  3  1              (* output *)
```

EXAMPLE 5.3.2   As you can see, Example 5.3.1 gave us a list in reverse order of input. If we want it in the same order, the program is a little trickier. We maintain another pointer, LAST, to the current last item on the list, where the new item will be attached, so that we do not have to keep searching through the list for it (see Figure 5.22). The question marks indicate that at that point we do not care what the LINK is. After a new last item is added, we have Figure 5.23. As often

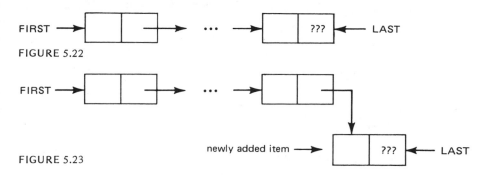

FIGURE 5.22

FIGURE 5.23

newly added item

happens, the first node is a special case, because at that point LAST does not have anything to point to. To keep from checking for this case each time through the main reading loop, it is treated as a special case at the beginning, which gives the program a somewhat awkward appearance. It is

```
(* EXAMPLE 5.3.2: LIST2          *)
(* READ IN ITEMS AND PLACE ON *)
(* LIST, PRESERVING ORDER        *)

PROGRAM LIST2(INPUT, OUTPUT);

CONST EOI = 0;               (* END OF INPUT SENTINEL *)

TYPE   PTRTONODE = ^NODE;
       NODE = RECORD INFO: INTEGER; LINK: PTRTONODE END;

VAR    FIRST,                (* FIRST OF LIST POINTER *)
       LAST,                 (* END OF LIST POINTER *)
       P: PTRTONODE;         (* RUNNING POINTER TO LIST *)
       X: INTEGER;           (* INPUT DATA ITEM *)

BEGIN (* LIST2 *)
   (* SET UP FIRST NODE, IF ANY *)
   READ(X);
   IF (X <> EOI) THEN
      BEGIN
         NEW(FIRST); LAST := FIRST;
         FIRST^.INFO := X;
         READ(X)
      END
   ELSE FIRST := NIL; (* AND X STILL = EOI *)

   (* GET REST OF LIST *)
```

```
    WHILE (X<> EOI) DO
        BEGIN
            NEW(P); P^.INFO := X;
            LAST^.LINK := P; LAST := P;
            READ(X)
        END;

    (* FINISH OFF LIST *)
    IF (FIRST <> NIL) THEN LAST^.LINK := NIL;

    (* PRINT OUT LIST AS IN EXAMPLE 5.3.1 *)
    END. (* LIST2 *)
```

A sample execution might be

```
? 1  3  5  7  9  11  13  0        (* input *)
  1  3  5  7  9  11  13           (* output *)
```

Now let's consider the problem of searching for and deleting a particular number X from the list. The problem is that if P points to the node being examined, we need a pointer to the previous node in order to delete $P^$. One method is to keep a *trailing pointer* TRAILP which follows one behind P through the list. TRAILP is then used for the deletion. This does not completely solve the problem as there is no value for TRAILP at the start of the list. Deletion of the first item in a list is always a special case anyway, as the pointer to its start, FIRST say, must be changed. Using a BOOLEAN FOUND as in Model Program 8, we can write

```
FOUND := FALSE; P := FIRST;
WHILE (P <> NIL) AND NOT FOUND DO
    IF (P^.INFO = X) THEN FOUND:= TRUE
    ELSE
        BEGIN
            TRAILP := P;
            P := P^.LINK
        END;
IF FOUND THEN
    IF (P = FIRST) THEN FIRST := FIRST^.LINK
    ELSE TRAILP^.LINK := P^.LINK
```

Remember the INSIDE-OUT Principle of Chapter 2!

One can try to avoid using a trailing pointer by having P point to the item *before* the item being examined; that is, we are interested in $P^.LINK^.INFO = X$. There are several complications to this method: (1) the first item on the list must be examined as a special case, and (2) we must stop on $P^.LINK = NIL$, but before we can safely compute this, we must know initially that $P <> NIL$. A solution by this method is

```
IF (FIRST <> NIL) THEN
   IF (FIRST^.INFO = X) THEN FIRST := FIRST^.LINK
   ELSE
      BEGIN
         FOUND := FALSE; P := FIRST; (* KNOWN <> NIL *)
         WHILE (P^.LINK <> NIL) AND (NOT FOUND) DO
            IF (P^.LINK^.INFO = X) THEN FOUND := TRUE
            ELSE P := P^.LINK;
         IF FOUND THEN P^.LINK := P^.LINK^.LINK
      END
```

It seems to me that the first method is shorter and less tricky and therefore preferable. It is even better if we add a sentinel as in Model Program 8s.

EXAMPLE 5.3.3   Read in integers and store in a list as in Example 5.3.1. Then read in integers to be deleted from the list. Finally, print out the resulting list.

```
(* EXAMPLE 5.3.3: LIST3            *)
(* READ INTEGERS AND MAKE LIST; *)
(* THEN DELETE SELECTED ITEMS    *)

PROGRAM LIST3(INPUT, OUTPUT);

CONST EOI = 0;                    (* END OF INPUT SENTINEL *)

TYPE   PTRTONODE = ^NODE;
       NODE = RECORD INFO: INTEGER; LINK: PTRTONODE END;

VAR    FIRST,                   (* START OF LIST POINTER *)
       P,                       (* LIST RUNNING POINTER *)
       TRAILP,                  (* ONE BEFORE P *)
       SENTINEL: PTRTONODE;     (* FIXED END OF LIST *)
       X: INTEGER;              (* INPUT DATA ITEM *)

BEGIN (* LIST3 *)
   NEW(SENTINEL); FIRST := SENTINEL;

   (* READ IN LIST EXACTLY AS IN EXAMPLE 5.3.1 *)

   WRITELN('TYPE IN INTEGERS TO DELETE, ENDING WITH   ',EOI:1);
   READ(X);
   WHILE (X <> EOI) DO
      BEGIN
         SENTINEL^.INFO := X; P := FIRST;
         WHILE (P^.INFO <> X) DO
```

```
BEGIN
    TRAILP := P;
    P := P^.LINK
END;
IF (P = SENTINEL) THEN
    WRITELN (X:1,'NOT FOUND')
ELSE IF (P = FIRST) THEN FIRST: = P^.LINK
    ELSE TRAILP^.LINK: = P^.LINK ;
    READ(X)
END;

P := FIRST; (* NOW PRINT OUT THE LIST *)
WHILE (P <> SENTINEL) DO
    BEGIN
        WRITE(P^.INFO:1,' ');
        P := P^.LINK
    END;
WRITELN
END. (* LIST3 *)
```

A test run might be

```
?  1  3  5  7  9  11  13  15  0                    (* initial input *)
TYPE IN INTEGERS TO DELETE, ENDING WITH 0
?  1  9  8  15  0
8 NOT FOUND
13  11  7  5  3
```

Note that both *boundary cases*, X the first and last item on the list, were tested. This is important as errors often creep in at the edges of problems. This leads us to

---

The MASON-DIXON Principle

Always test boundary cases.

A comparison of the performance of linear and linked methods of representing lists is useful.

	linear	linked
random access	$O(1)$	$O(n)$
item insert	$O(n)$	$O(1)$

[The $O(n)$ on random access comes from having to search half the list, on the average, and the $O(n)$ on item insert comes from having to move half the list, on the average. On item insertion, we assume that the place for the insertion has already been found.]

Exercises 5.3

1. You are given a linked list with first item pointer FIRST and each node in the usual INFO-LINK form, INFO an integer and no sentinel node. Write Pascal program segments to accomplish the following (P, Q, R, etc., are assumed to be declared as ^NODEs):

(a) Set CT equal to the number of nodes on the list.

(b) Check to see if consecutive INFOs are in increasing order throughout the list, and print an error message if not.

(c) Find the first INFO on the list which is a perfect square and print its value.

(d) Set P pointing to the last item on the list. If the list is empty, set P = NIL.

(e) Delete the first node on the list whose INFO is 0.

(f) Delete all nodes on the list whose INFOs are 0.

(g) Create a sentinel node and attach it to the end of the list.

(h) Find and delete the node on the list with the smallest INFO. (This can be done on one pass through the list, but be careful!)

2. Assume a list as in Exercise 1, only now with a sentinel node pointed to by SENTINEL. Write Pascal program segments to

(a) Set CT equal to the number of nodes on the list.

(b) Find the first INFO on the list which is a perfect square and print its value.

(c) Delete the first node on the list whose INFO is 0.

(d) Delete *all* nodes on the list whose INFOs are 0.

3. The following are supposed to be solutions to the problem of finding the first negative item on a list and printing it (which was discussed earlier in this section). What is wrong with each solution?

(a)

```
P := FIRST; FOUND := FALSE;
WHILE (P <> NIL) AND NOT FOUND DO
    BEGIN
        IF (P^.INFO < 0) THEN FOUND := TRUE;
        P := P^.LINK
    END;
IF FOUND THEN WRITELN(P^.INFO)
ELSE WRITELN('NOT FOUND')
```

(b)

```
P := FIRST; FOUND := FALSE;
WHILE (P <> NIL) AND NOT FOUND DO
    BEGIN
        IF (P^.INFO < 0) THEN
            BEGIN
                FOUND := TRUE;
                WRITELN(P^.INFO)
            END
```

```
      ELSE WRITELN('NOT FOUND');
         P := P^.LINK
   END
```

(c) Using a SENTINEL:

```
P := FIRST; SENTINEL^.INFO := –1;
WHILE (P^.INFO >= 0) DO P := P^.LINK;
IF (P^.INFO = –1) THEN WRITELN('NOT FOUND')
ELSE WRITELN(P^.INFO)
```

(d) Trying to write out all negative entries:

```
P := FIRST;
WHILE (P <> NIL) DO
   IF (P^.INFO < 0) THEN WRITELN (P^.INFO)
   ELSE P := P^.LINK
```

4. Given a list in INFO-LINK format with first pointer FIRST, what does the following code do (assume that P, Q, and R are ^NODEs)?

```
P := NIL; Q := FIRST;
WHILE (Q <> NIL) DO
   BEGIN
      R := Q^.LINK;
      Q^.LINK := P;
      P := Q;
      Q := R
   END;
FIRST := P
```

5. Assume we have declared

```
TYPE   PTRTOCNODE = ^CNODE;
          CNODE = RECORD COLOR: ALFA;
             PT, LINK: PTRTOCNODE END;

VAR    FIRST, P, FRED: PTRTOCNODE;
```

What does the following program segment do?

```
FRED := NIL; P := FIRST;
WHILE (P <> NIL) DO
   BEGIN
      IF (P^.COLOR = 'RED          ') THEN
         BEGIN
            P^.PT := FRED; FRED := P
         END;
      P := P^.LINK
   END
```

Trace the program using Figure 5.24.

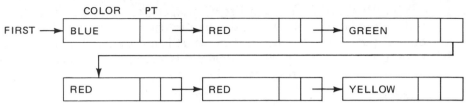

FIGURE 5.24

6. Many list algorithms are simplified by attaching a special node with no (or meaningless) INFO at the head of the list; this node is called a *listhead* (Figure 5.25). The basic loop for processing such a list is

```
P := FIRST ^.LINK;
WHILE (P <> NIL) DO
    BEGIN
        Process P^;
        P := P^.LINK
    END
```

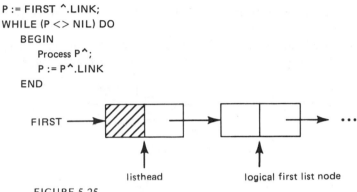

listhead   logical first list node

FIGURE 5.25

To initialize a list with listhead, we would code NEW(FIRST); FIRST^.LINK := NIL;

(a) Rewrite the list-reading part of Example 5.3.1 to use a list with listhead.

(b) Rewrite the search and delete part of Example 5.3.3, assuming the list has a listhead. (Note that there is now a convenient initial value for TRAILP, and the first item on the list does not need to be treated as a special case.)

5.4   POINTERS AND SORTING

When files have large records, the regular insertion sort is undesirable because of the amount of data movement necessary. Two alternatives, in which only pointers need be moved, are presented in this section.

The first method is the *list insertion sort*. In this method, a link field is added to each record and the links arranged so that the logical order of the file is the one desired. No actual physical movement of records takes place. The method is very similar to that of Section 3.5, except that we can only traverse the file from the start, so we must search forward instead of backward, and no record movement is necessary.

EXAMPLE 5.4.1 Read a list of integers, terminating on 0. Sort them into increasing order using the list insertion sort and print out the sorted list. (Of course the list insertion sort is not the method of choice here because the records are so small; this example is just to demonstrate the method.) The fundamental loop is

```
READ(X);
WHILE (X <> 0) DO
    BEGIN
        make a node for X and insert it;
        READ(X)
    END
```

The place to insert X is shown in Figure 5.26. The reason for requiring $\ldots \leqslant X < \ldots$ instead of $\ldots < X \leqslant \ldots$ is that the former gives a *stable* sorting method; that is, if two records have equal keys, they end up in the same order they started in. To simplify the searching proce-

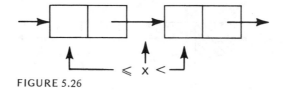

FIGURE 5.26

dure, we use a sentinel node as usual, and to make sure that the search for $X < INFO$ stops on the sentinel, we initialize the sentinel to $X+1$ (or any other value larger than X). The insert loop is

```
P := FIRST; SENTINEL^.INFO := X+1;
WHILE (X >= P^.INFO) DO
    BEGIN
        TRAILP := P; P := P^.LINK
    END;
Insert X after TRAILP
```

The program is

```
(* EXAMPLE 5.4.1: LISTSORT        *)
(* LIST INSERTION SORT NUMBERS *)

PROGRAM LISTSORT(INPUT, OUTPUT);

CONST EOI = 0;                      (* END OF INPUT SENTINEL *)

TYPE PTRTONODE = ^NODE;
    NODE = RECORD INFO: INTEGER; LINK: PTRTONODE END;
```

```
VAR FIRST,                    (* FIRST OF LIST POINTER *)
    P,                        (* RUNNING POINTER FOR ORDER SEARCH *)
    TRAILP,                   (* ONE BEHIND P FOR INSERTION *)
    Q,                        (* POINTER TO NEW NODE *)
    SENTINEL: PTRTONODE;      (* FIXED POINTER TO END OF LIST *)
    X: INTEGER;               (* INPUT DATA *)


BEGIN (* LISTSORT *)
    NEW(SENTINEL); FIRST := SENTINEL;
    WRITE('ENTER NUMBERS, TERMINATING WITH ',EOI:1);
    READ(X);
    WHILE (X <> EOI) DO
        BEGIN
            P := FIRST; SENTINEL^.INFO := X + 1;
            WHILE (X >= P^.INFO) DO
                BEGIN
                    TRAILP := P; P := P^.LINK
                END;
            NEW(Q); Q^.INFO := X; Q^.LINK := P;
            IF (P = FIRST) THEN FIRST := Q
            ELSE TRAILP^.LINK := Q;
            READ(X)
        END;
    P := FIRST;
    WHILE (P <> SENTINEL) DO
        BEGIN WRITE(P^.INFO,'  '); P := P^.LINK END;
    WRITELN  .
END. (* LISTSORT *)
```

A sample run might look like

```
ENTER NUMBERS, TERMINATING WITH 0
?  5  18  2  37  -4  12  9  3  0
-4  2  3  5  9  12  18  37
```

A problem with the list insertion sort is that the sorted file can be accessed only sequentially. This means, among other things, that the list method does not generalize to other methods of sorting which require random access to the file (for example, doing the searching using a binary search). A solution to this problem is our second method, the *address table sort*. In this method, an ARRAY [1 .. n] OF ^ file-record is kept, say called AD, and after the sorting is performed, AD[1] ^, AD[2] ^, . . . , are in order. Once again the records themselves are not moved. Note that this method requires the same amount of extra storage as the list insertion sort; it is just that in the list insertion sort the pointers are kept in the records, and in the address table sort they are kept all together in a separate table.

EXAMPLE 5.4.2 Same problem as Example 5.4.1, except now use the address table sort. The fundamental loop is

```
read AD[1] ^; K := 1;
WHILE NOT EOF DO
    BEGIN
        read and insert AD[K+1] ^;
        K := K + 1
    END
```

The "read and insert . . . " part is

```
NEW(AD[0] ); read (AD[0] ^); (* SENTINEL *)
J := K;
WHILE (AD[J] ^.INFO > X) DO
    BEGIN
        AD[J+1] := AD[J] ; (* ONLY POINTERS MOVE HERE! *)
        J := J – 1
    END;
AD[J+1] := AD[0]
```

The declarations might be

```
TYPE PTRTOREC = ^REC;
    REC = RECORD INFO: INTEGER (* other stuff *) END:

VAR AD: ARRAY [1 . . MAXREC] OF PTRTOREC;
```

(MAXREC, the maximum number of records, is a CONST, so there may be some waste storage. Note that REC does not (necessarily) include a PTRTOREC.) You can compare this with the ordinary insertion sort in which the declarations would be similar, except that AD could be an ARRAY [1 . . MAXREC] OF REC, not PTRTOREC, and the inner loop would appear to be the same as in the preceding, with no NEW statement and all the ^s deleted. The difference in execution would be that whole records would be moved rather than just pointers. We leave the actual program as an exercise for the reader.

We will close this section by summarizing the advantages and disadvantages of the two methods discussed here.

Advantages of Both Methods over Regular Insertion: Faster for files with large records; allows files to be sorted in more than one order at once.

Disadvantages of Both Methods: File is not physically reordered; extra storage required for pointers (insignificant for large records).

Advantages of List Insertion over Address Table: Pointers and records are kept together so that only one file access per record is required for sequential processing of the file (one each for address table and record may be required if the address table is too large to be kept in memory); for a file with several logical orders, switching order of traversal is easy; extra waste storage in address table not required.

Advantages of Address Table over List Insertion: File can be accessed in random order and the method generalizes to other sorting methods (such as the quicksort, to be introduced in Chapter 6).

5.5   STACKS AND QUEUES

In situations where there are many stacks and/or queues growing and shrinking more or less independently, or where the node size is relatively large so that the overhead of an extra field for a pointer is not too great, it may be preferable to represent stacks and queues by linked lists. Given the techniques we have developed so far, this is quite easy. For instance, a stack can be represented as in Figure 5.27. To push X

FIGURE 5.27

onto the stack, the code is

```
NEW(P); P^.LINK := TOP; P^.INFO := X; TOP := P
```

(No check for stack overflow is necessary; NEW does that.) To pop the top of the stack into X, the code is

```
IF (TOP = NIL) THEN underflow; X := TOP^.INFO; TOP := TOP^.LINK
```

The one problem here is that when a node is popped from the stack, it is lost forever. One solution to this problem is to keep a list of currently unused nodes called the *available storage list*. This too is treated as a stack, but only because that is the easiest way to manipulate it. Declarations might be

```
TYPE   PTRTONODE = ^NODE;
       NODE = RECORD (* . . . *) LINK:PTRTONODE END;

VAR    AVAIL:PTRTONODE; (* POINTS TO AVAILABLE STORAGE LIST *)
```

Simple subprograms to get and return nodes are

```
FUNCTION GETNODE: PTRTONODE;
   VAR P: PTRTONODE
```

```
      BEGIN (* GETNODE *)
        IF (AVAIL = NIL) THEN
           BEGIN
              NEW(P); GETNODE := P
           END
        ELSE
           BEGIN
              GETNODE := AVAIL; AVAIL := AVAIL^.LINK
           END
      END; (* GETNODE *)
```

and

```
   PROCEDURE PUTNODE(PT: PTRTONODE);
      BEGIN (* PUTNODE *)
         PT^.LINK := AVAIL;
         AVAIL := PT
      END;   (* PUTNODE *)
```

Note that even though PT is not a VAR parameter in PUTNODE and thus the value of PT itself cannot be changed, PT^ can be changed; in fact, when we execute, say, PUTNODE(P), P^ *will* be changed! [Can you figure out why we were not able to say NEW(GETNODE) in GETNODE?]

The code for pushing and popping X now is

```
   P := GETNODE; P^.INFO := X; P^.LINK := TOP; TOP := P
```

and

```
   IF (TOP = NIL) THEN underflow; X := TOP^.INFO;
   P := TOP; TOP := TOP^.LINK; PUTNODE(P)
```

Linked representation of queues is described in the exercises. The methods so far can be used to represent output-restricted deques (input at both ends, output from the front only). To represent deques in full generality, a *doubly linked list* is usually used. This is a list in which each node has two pointers, one to its predecessor as well as one to its successor in the list. We will not discuss these lists here; a treatment of them can be found in any book on data structures. (For example, see Knuth, volume 1, and Wirth listed in the Bibliography.)

Exercises 5.5

1. A queue can be represented as in Figure 5.28. The empty queue is represented by FRONT = NIL. Using GETNODE and PUTNODE, write code segments to (a) add a node to the rear of the queue with INFO = X (see Example 5.3.2) and (b) remove the front node of the queue and put its INFO into X (see the preceding stack example). Be careful of the empty list and the list with one node.

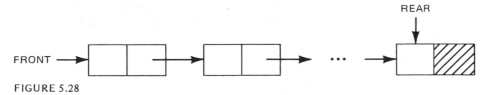

FIGURE 5.28

2. Do the same exercise as (1) for a queue with a listhead (see Exercise 5.3.4 and Figure 5.29.) What condition indicates an empty queue?

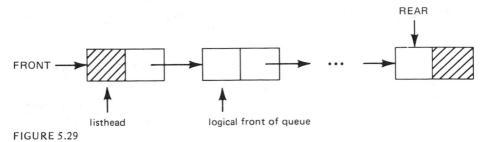

FIGURE 5.29

Programming Problems

5.1 The STATES file in Appendix A contains state names in columns 1-15 followed by population followed by area (both of which should be read as real numbers because of their size). Read the file (once) and make three linked lists—one of SMALL states with areas less than 10000, one of MEDIUM states whose areas are between 10000 and 100000, and one of LARGE states whose areas are greater than or equal to 100000. Then print each list of states with appropriate identification. (Given the small amount of data involved, this problem could easily be solved without resorting to linked lists; it is, however, characteristic of problems involving several lists of data of unpredictable and widely varying lengths.)

5.2 The STATES file in Appendix A contains state names in columns 1 to 15 of each line, and order of admission, a number from 1 to 50, in columns 37 to 38. Give the file two logical orders, according to these fields. Print the file in both orders with no sorting in between.

Suggested method: Use the declarations

```
TYPE PTRTOSREC = ^SREC;
        SREC = RECORD NAME: PACKED ARRAY [1 . . 15] OF CHAR;
                    ORD: INTEGER; LINK: PTRTOSREC END;

    VAR AD: ARRAY [1 . . 50] OF PTRTOSREC;
```

Ordering by admission is arranged by using AD as an address table, AD[N] ^.ORD = N. Use the list insertion sort to order the state names, using the LINK field in SREC. Note that each state name can be stored only *once*. Data can be read as in Programming Problem 4.1.

5.3 Write a program to create, manage, and retrieve information from a *self-reorganizing* list of names and telephone numbers. List nodes are of the form

```
TYPE PTRTONODE = ^NODE;
     NODE = RECORD NAME: ARRAY [1 . . 30] OF CHAR;
                   PHONE: ARRAY [1 . . 8] OF CHAR;
                   CT: INTEGER;
                   LINK: PTRTONODE END;
```

When a node is created its CT is set to 0 and it is placed at the first of the list. Every time a node is referenced, its CT is increased by 1 and when CT reaches 3 (a magic number?), the node should be deleted from its current place on the list, replaced at the head of the list, and its CT reset to 0. The program should recognize three commands, requested by the prompt CMD:

1. A   Add a phone number. The program prompts with NAME and PHONE.
2. L   Look up a number. The program prompts with NAME.
3. C   Change a phone number. The program prompts with NAME and NEW NUMBER, printing an error message if the name did not previously exist.

The program should initialize itself from a TEXT file of names and phone numbers (called, perhaps, MABELL and, perhaps, empty) and when given an S command, should REWRITE this file with the list in its updated form.

5.4   Write a program to sort the state names in the STATES file (Appendix A) using a method similar to the old-fashioned mechanical card sorter: Define nodes by

```
TYPE   PTRTONMNODE=^NMNODE;
       NMNODE=RECORD
                      NAME: PACKED ARRAY [1 . . 15] OF CHAR;
                      LINK: PTRTONMNODE
              END;
```

twenty seven lists with first and last pointers defined by

```
VAR    FIRST, LAST: ARRAY ['A' . . 'Z'] OF PTRTONMNODE;
       FIRSTB, LASTB: PTRTONMNODE;
```

and a list pointer SLIST for the whole file.

Start by reading state names and placing them on the end (pointed to by LAST) of the appropriate FIRST list according to their first character. Using FIRST and LAST, merge the resulting twenty six lists into one pointed to by SLIST. Now repeat the process on the second character, then the third, etc. After the first character, blanks can occur so FIRSTB and LASTB must be used. This list should be merged onto the output list ahead of the letter lists. State names must be added to the ends of their appropriate lists so that ordering already due to letters further to the left will be preserved.

chapter 6

recursion

A recursive program is one which either directly or indirectly calls itself as a subprogram; for example, A calls A or A calls B which calls C which calls A. A number of problems in computer programming which are quite difficult to solve nonrecursively are quite easy to solve using languages such as Pascal, which allow recursive programs to be expressed easily and naturally. (Languages like FORTRAN and COBOL do not allow them at all.) In this chapter we will learn how to write and trace recursive programs and how to apply recursive techniques to problems in searching, sorting, and infix to RPN translation.

One of the most common uses of recursive programming is with data structures which are defined recursively, that is, in terms of themselves. One of the simplest and most commonly used such structures is the tree, which we discuss next.

6.1 TREES

A *tree* is a structure like the one shown in Figure 6.1. It can represent many things, for instance, a family tree giving either the ancestors or descendants of a person, or a decision tree in which each circle represents a particular situation and the lines leading down from it represent possible actions in that situation. The circles are called the *nodes* of the tree and, just like nodes of a list, may contain a substantial information part.

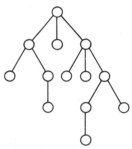

FIGURE 6.1

We will consider only binary trees here; they are the easiest to represent in a computer and suffice for most applications (and any tree can be represented as a binary tree). A binary tree is a finite set of nodes which is either empty or consists of a special node called the *root* and two sets of nodes, which are themselves binary trees, called the *left* and *right subtrees.* The two subtrees can have no common nodes. (The root is normally drawn at the top.)

You may think it odd that a binary tree can be empty. This is a matter of convenience; if we did not allow empty trees we would either have to say that a subtree can be empty and hence is not necessarily a tree, or we could say that a tree has left and right "things" which are either empty or subtrees, either of which is much more awkward.

From now on, whenever we say "tree" we will mean "binary tree." The definition of binary tree is recursive because it defines tree in terms of subtrees, which are other trees. This is all right though, because subtrees are necessarily smaller than the whole tree (they do not contain the root), so when we look at their subtrees, they are smaller still, and eventually we will get down to trees with no nodes. To see how this works, let's first reverse the process and see what sort of trees we can manufacture from a given small number of nodes.

First, the empty set (zero nodes) is a tree, and the set of one node is a tree with that node being the root and empty left and right subtrees [see Figure 6.2]. There are two binary trees with two nodes [see Figure 6.3]. Now let's get all binary trees with three nodes. The

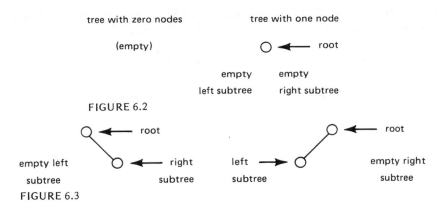

FIGURE 6.2

FIGURE 6.3

root takes care of one, so we must partition the remaining two nodes into left and right subtrees. There are three ways: (1) two left, none right; (2) one left, one right; and (3) none left, two right. There are two different two-node trees, so cases 1 and 3 give us two trees each, while there is only one tree with one node, so case 2 gives us one. Thus there are a total of five trees with three nodes, as shown in Figure 6.4. Continuing this way, you can see that there are fourteen binary trees with four nodes (see Exercise 6.1.1).

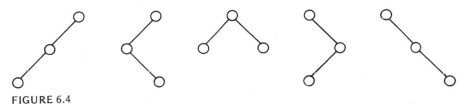

FIGURE 6.4

Going the other direction, suppose we wanted to use the definition to show that Figure 6.5 is a tree. Picking the top node as root,

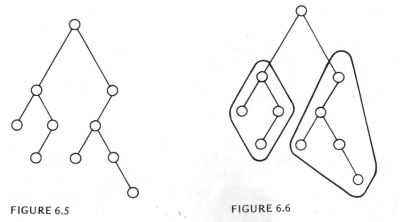

FIGURE 6.5   FIGURE 6.6

it is a tree only if the (putative) left and right subtrees outlined in Figure 6.6 are trees. The left "subtree" [Figure 6.7] is a tree if its subtrees [Figure 6.8] are. But from our original discussion, we know these to be trees, so the left subtree is a tree. Similarly, Figure 6.9 is a tree if its left subtree is, since its right subtree is empty. Continuing in this way, we get that the right "subtree" of the original structure is in fact a tree, so the original structure is, too.

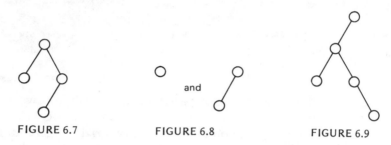

FIGURE 6.7   FIGURE 6.8   FIGURE 6.9

If we try to show that Figure 6.10 is a tree, we fail. We must show that the "subtrees" of Figure 6.11 are binary trees. The latter is, of course, but the former has left and right "subtrees" which have a node in common (see Figure 6.12).

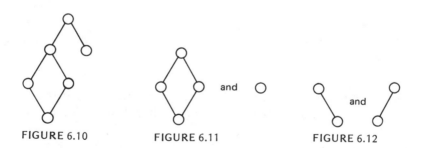

FIGURE 6.10   FIGURE 6.11   FIGURE 6.12

It should be fairly clear that, by proceeding down a tree in this way, eventually every node will be the root of some subtree. If its left subtree is nonempty, the root of the left subtree is called the *left child* of the original node. Similarly, the root of the right subtree is called the *right child*. A node with no children is called a *leaf* (Figure 6.13).

One application of binary trees is to the evaluation of infix expressions. The expression (A + B)∗C/(11 + A + B) might be represented as in figure 6.14. An expression in tree form is evaluated as follows: at each node evaluate the left and right children. Then evaluate the node itself by applying the operator at it to the values of the left and

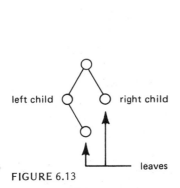

FIGURE 6.13

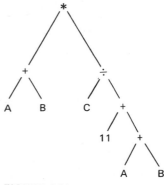

FIGURE 6.14

right children. A node which is not an operator is a constant or variable (which must be a leaf), and its evaluation is obvious. Note that this process is recursive, the value of a tree being defined in terms of the values of its subtrees. One advantage of the tree representation over RPN is that it can make the computation easier to optimize. For instance, it is possible to detect that the subtree shown in Figure 6.15 occurs twice above, so this subtree need only be evaluated once.

FIGURE 6.15

A simpler application is to the binary search. One of the flaws of the usual binary search is that the file must be sorted, which may represent an unacceptable overhead if the file is volatile, that is, if new entries are being added or old ones removed. One solution is the *binary search tree*. Each node contains a record, including the *key* field, and the fundamental property of a binary search tree is that

key of all nodes of left subtree
    < key of root
        < key of all nodes of right subtree

and that this property holds for all subtrees as well. A binary search tree for the German numbers might be as shown in Figure 6.16. Nodes in a binary search tree are declared as records with *two* pointer fields to left and right children. In this example, we could declare

```
TYPE PTRTONODE = ^NODE;
        NODE = RECORD GER, ENG: ALFA;
                    LCHILD, RCHILD: PTRTONODE END;
    VAR ROOT: PTRTONODE;
```

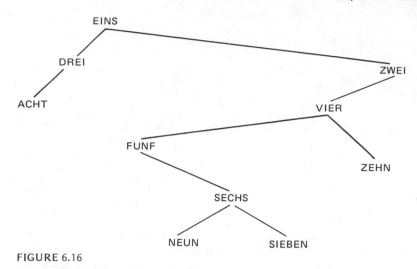

FIGURE 6.16

Such a node can be represented pictorially as in Figure 6.17, and the tree of Figure 6.16 as in Figure 6.18.

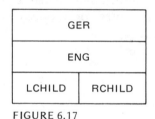

FIGURE 6.17

To search the tree for WORD and print its translation, we code

```
FOUND := FALSE; P := ROOT; (* RUNNING POINTER *)
WHILE (P <> NIL) AND NOT FOUND DO
    IF (WORD = P^.GER) THEN
        FOUND := TRUE
    ELSE
        IF (WORD < P^.GER) THEN
            P := P^.LCHILD (* GO LEFT *)
        ELSE
            P := P^.RCHILD; (* GO RIGHT *)
IF FOUND THEN WRITELN('THE ENGLISH IS  ',P^.ENG)
ELSE WRITELN(WORD, '  NOT FOUND')
```

Thus, in searching for SECHS, P would point successively to EINS, ZWEI, VIER, FUNF, and SECHS. As before, the search can be speeded up and simplified by terminating the search with a sentinal node. Now, however, there are many possible path terminations, and they must all lead to the sentinel. Thus all the nil pointers in the tree are replaced

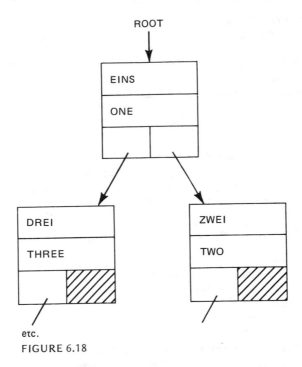

ROOT

etc.

FIGURE 6.18

by pointers to SENTINEL, and the tree really is not properly a tree any more unless we agree to ignore the sentinel node and treat pointers to it as terminations of branches of the tree. The search with sentinel is

```
SENTINEL^.GER := WORD; P := ROOT;
WHILE (P^.GER <> WORD) DO
    IF (WORD < P^.GER) THEN
        P := P^.LCHILD
    ELSE
        P := P^.RCHILD;
IF (P = SENTINEL) THEN WRITELN(WORD, '  NOT FOUND')
ELSE WRITELN('THE ENGLISH IS  ', P^.ENG)
```

The most straightforward method of constructing such a binary tree uses a trailing pointer. Assume for simplicity's sake that German and corresponding English words are typed in on separate lines:

```
EINS
ONE
ZWEI
 . . .
```

The following program segment constructs the binary tree in Figure 6.16 for the German numbers when the numbers come in in increasing numeric order. Its fundamental loop is

```
initialize ROOT and SENTINEL;
WHILE NOT EOF DO
    BEGIN
        read German WORD;
        find where it belongs;
        create new node for WORD and insert it
    END
```

The program is

```
NEW(SENTINEL); NEW(ROOT);
READLN(ROOT^.GER); READLN(ROOT^.ENG); READLN(WORD);
ROOT^.LCHILD := SENTINEL; ROOT ^.RCHILD := SENTINEL;
WHILE (WORD <> end-of-input signal) DO
    BEGIN
        P := ROOT;
        REPEAT
            TRAILP := P;
            IF (WORD < P^.GER) THEN
                P := P^.LCHILD (* GO LEFT *)
            ELSE
                P := P^.RCHILD (* GO RIGHT *)
        UNTIL (P = SENTINEL);
        NEW(Q); Q^.GER := WORD; READLN(Q^.ENG);
        Q^.LCHILD := SENTINEL; Q^.RCHILD := SENTINEL;
        IF (WORD < TRAILP^.GER) THEN TRAILP^.LCHILD := Q
        ELSE TRAILP^.RCHILD := Q;
        READLN(WORD)
    END
```

A more sophisticated method will be discussed in the next section.

One disadvantage of binary trees is that their efficiency is strongly dependent on the order in which keys occur when the tree is being constructed. If for instance keys came in in alphabetical order, the resulting tree would be as shown in Figure 6.19, and the search would

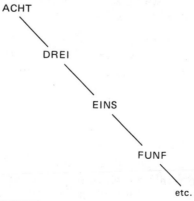

FIGURE 6.19

be a linear search. On the other hand, if we had an ideal key order, we would get an optimal binary search tree (Figure 6.20). [Optimal

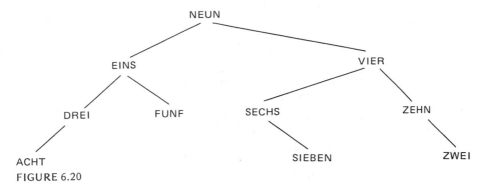

FIGURE 6.20

is defined as a tree requiring the fewest comparisons, maximum, to find any given item, that is, a tree with smallest height for a given number of nodes. By the halving principle, this optimal number of comparisons is about $\log_2(n)$, where n is the number of nodes; so in the best of circumstances, the binary search tree is a $O(\log_2(n))$ method.]

Exercises 6.1

1. Draw all possible binary trees with four nodes.
2. (a) Give a *different* optimal binary search tree for the German numbers.
   (b) Give two different orders for input of keys which will result in the optimal binary search tree given in Figure 6.20.

6.2   TREES AND RECURSION

Because trees are defined recursively, many algorithms involving trees are most easily expressed recursively.

EXAMPLE 6.2.1   Write a program which reads a list of words, stopping on ∗∗∗∗, and then prints out the words in alphabetical order together with a count of the number of times each word has occurred. The basic form of the program is

count words
print table

To count words, we will use a binary search tree whose nodes are declared

```
TYPE PTRTONODE = ^NODE;
      NODE = RECORD WD: ALFA;
                CT: INTEGER;
                LCHILD, RCHILD: PTRTONODE END;
```

The very definition of a binary tree suggests the following scheme for counting a word:

```
IF end of path (and word not found) THEN
    insert new WD with CT = 1
ELSE
    IF word = WD THEN CT := CT + 1
    ELSE
        IF word < WD THEN search left subtree
        ELSE search right subtree
```

We have defined searching in terms of searching, that is, recursively. Thus let us postulate a procedure SEARCH(P) where P points to the root of the tree to be searched. The definition of SEARCH is

```
PROCEDURE SEARCH(P: PTRTONODE);
    BEGIN (* SEARCH *)
→       IF (P = NIL) THEN
            insert new WD with CT = 1
        ELSE
            IF word = WD then CT := CT + 1
            ELSE
→               IF word < WD THEN SEARCH(P^.LCHILD)
→               ELSE SEARCH (P^.RCHILD)
    END;  (* SEARCH *)
```

(For now, take it on faith that it works; we will explain how later.)

The tricky part here is the "insert new WD . . ." statement. It seems we should need a trailing pointer of some sort; however, we can avoid this through a very subtle method. When P = NIL, the situation might be as in Figure 6.21, which we want to turn into Figure 6.22.

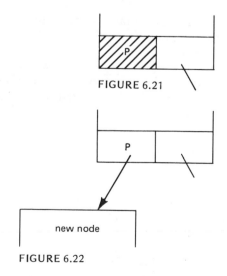

FIGURE 6.21

FIGURE 6.22

Normally, we would need a pointer to the node containing P (and some way of determining if P was the left or right child of that node), but in fact we can change the value of P without any of this information if P is a VAR parameter! Pascal itself, in effect, passes pointers to VAR parameters for us.

Turning to the "print table" statement, it is even easier. We simply notice that by the fundamental property of binary trees, we want to

> print left subtree
> print root
> print right subtree

If we postulate a procedure PRINT(Q: PTRTONODE) which prints a binary tree in alphabetical order, its definition is

```
PRINT(P^.LCHILD);
write out contents of P^;
PRINT(P^.RCHILD)
```

The only trouble with this is that it never stops (until P = NIL, so evaluating P^.LCHILD causes a fatal error). We need to treat P = NIL as a special case. This leads to the fundamental rule of recursive programs:

The RECURSION Principle

Always start a recursive procedure by testing for trivial cases, and handle these nonrecursively.

Note that SEARCH satisfies this rule, its trivial cases being "P = NIL" and "word = WD." It should also be the case that the recursive calls have the effect of getting the problem nearer to the trivial case; in both PRINT and SEARCH, the recursion is applied to a smaller tree.

The complete program is

```
(* EXAMPLE 6.2.1: BTREE        *)
(* MAKE BINARY SEARCH TREE *)
(* FOR WORDS AND COUNTS;    *)
(* PRINT IT OUT IN ORDER.      *)

PROGRAM BTREE(INPUT, OUTPUT);

CONST EOI = '****        '; (* END OF INPUT SENTINEL *)

TYPE   PTRTONODE = ^NODE;
       NODE = RECORD WD: ALFA; CT: INTEGER;
                     LCHILD, RCHILD: PTRTONODE END;
```

```
VAR    ROOT: PTRTONODE; (* ROOT OF BINARY SEARCH TREE *)
       WORD: ALFA;         (* GERMAN WORD TO SEARCH FOR *)

PROCEDURE PRINT(Q: PTRTONODE);
       (* PRINT TREE ROOTED AT Q IN ORDER *)
    BEGIN (* PRINT *)
       IF (Q <> NIL) THEN
          BEGIN
             PRINT(Q^.LCHILD);
             WRITELN(Q^.WD, '  ', Q^.CT);
             PRINT(Q^.RCHILD)
          END
    END;  (* PRINT *)


PROCEDURE SEARCH(VAR P: PTRTONODE);
       (* SEARCH TREE WITH  ROOT AT P FOR WORD *)
       (* IF NOT FOUND, ATTACH WORD IN PLACE *)
    BEGIN (* SEARCH *)
       IF (P = NIL) THEN
          BEGIN
             NEW(P); P^.WD := WORD; P^.CT := 1;
             P^.LCHILD := NIL; P^.RCHILD := NIL
          END
       ELSE
          IF (WORD = P^.WD) THEN
             P^.CT := P^.CT + 1
          ELSE
             IF (WORD < P^.WD) THEN SEARCH(P^.LCHILD)
             ELSE SEARCH (P^.RCHILD)
    END;  (* SEARCH *)

BEGIN (* BTREE *)
   ROOT := NIL; (* NOT A SPECIAL CASE! *)
   WRITELN('TYPE IN WORDS, TERMINATED BY   ', EOI);
   READLN(WORD);
   WHILE (WORD <> EOI) DO
      BEGIN
         SEARCH(ROOT);
         READLN(WORD)
      END;

   WRITELN('WORD TABLE:'); WRITELN;
   PRINT(ROOT)
END.  (* BTREE *)
```

The reader could probably construct a nonrecursive version of SEARCH without too much trouble, but would likely be completely stumped trying a nonrecursive version of PRINT. The ordering is extremely tricky, and variable amounts of information have to be remembered to keep track of where you are in the tree. For instance, in Figure 6.23, node 2 follows node 1 in printing order.

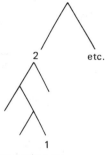

FIGURE 6.23

The PRINT procedure is a special case of a general process called *tree traversal*. Intuitively, tree traversal means that each node of the tree is visited (i.e., some action is performed on it) exactly once. There is a priori no order of traversal that's better than others; we generally use one of three orders:

1. *Preorder:* (first) visit the root
   (then) visit the left subtree
   (last) visit the right subtree

2. *Postorder:* (first) visit the left subtree
   (then) visit the right subtree
   (last) visit the root

3. *Inorder:* (first) visit the left subtree
   (then) visit the root
   (last) visit the right subtree

Notice that PRINT visits the nodes of the tree in inorder. Also, if an arithmetic expression is represented as a tree, as we did in Section 6.1, and the tree is printed out in *postorder*, the result is the RPN version of the expression.

As an example, let's visit the nodes of the tree in Figure 6.24 in inorder. First, we visit the left subtree (see Figure 6.25). The first thing we do there is visit its left subtree (see Figure 6.26), which means in turn that we first visit subtree H. H's left subtree is empty, so no visiting is required. We then visit the root of the subtree consisting of H, that is, H itself, and then visit its right subtree, again empty. Thus we have finished visiting the left subtree of the tree whose root is D, and can now visit its root, D itself, and then its right subtree, which, as with H, means visiting I. At this point we have visited the left subtree of the tree whose root is B, so we can visit B. The nodes visited

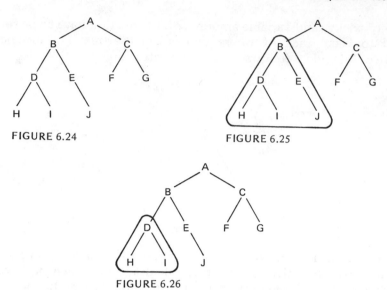

FIGURE 6.24   FIGURE 6.25

FIGURE 6.26

so far, in order, are H D I B, and we are ready to visit the right subtree of B (see Figure 6.27). We visit its left subtree (empty), root (E), and right subtree (J), and we have finished A's left subtree. After visiting A itself, we are then ready to visit A's right subtree (see Figure 6.28).

Continuing this way we see that the whole inorder traversal visits the nodes in the order HDIBEJAFCG. Traversing the same tree in preorder (root first) gives ABDHIEJCFG and in postorder (root last) gives HIDJEBFGCA.

We end this section with some applications of tree traversal.

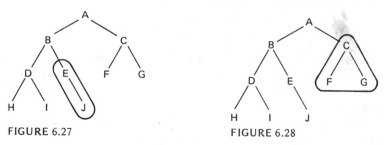

FIGURE 6.27   FIGURE 6.28

EXAMPLE 6.2.2 Write a function NODECOUNT(P) whose value is the number of nodes in the tree whose root is P. In this case, we count the root, the left subtree, and the right subtree, but the particular order does not matter.

```
FUNCTION NODECOUNT(P: PTRTONODE): INTEGER;
    (* RETURN NUMBER OF NODES IN TREE POINTED TO BY P *)
```

```
BEGIN (* NODECOUNT *)
  IF (P = NIL) THEN
     NODECOUNT := 0 (* TRIVIAL CASE *)
  ELSE
     NODECOUNT := 1 (* FOR ROOT *)
                     + NODECOUNT(P^.LCHILD)  (* RECURSIONS *)
                     + NODECOUNT(P^.RCHILD)
END;  (* NODECOUNT *)
```

EXAMPLE 6.2.3   Write a Boolean function EQUAL(P, Q) which has the value TRUE if the trees pointed to by P and Q have the same form with the same data at corresponding nodes. Assume that nodes are defined by

```
TYPE PTRTONODE = ^NODE;
     NODE = RECORD INFO: INTEGER; LCHILD, RCHILD: PTRTONODE END;
```

We do a preorder traverse of both trees simultaneously:

```
IF roots are the same THEN
    check left subtrees
    check right subtrees
```

The code is a bit complicated by the fact that one or the other root may not have children, but the code is still fairly straightforward:

```
FUNCTION EQUAL(P, Q: NODEPTR); BOOLEAN;
     (* RETURN TRUE IF TREES POINTED TO BY P AND Q *)
     (* HAVE SAME STRUCTURE AND SAME INFORMATION *)
     (* AT CORRESPONDING NODES *)
  BEGIN (* EQUAL *)
    IF (P = NIL) THEN (* FIRST OF 3 TRIVIAL CASES *)
        EQUAL := (Q = NIL)
    ELSE
       IF (Q = NIL) THEN
          EQUAL := FALSE (* AS P <> NIL *)
       ELSE
          IF (P^.INFO <> Q^.INFO) THEN
             EQUAL := FALSE
          ELSE (* RECURSION *)
             EQUAL := EQUAL(P^.LCHILD, Q^.LCHILD) AND
                        EQUAL(P^.RCHILD, Q^.RCHILD)
  END;  (* EQUAL *)
```

Exercises 6.2

1. Give the nodes of Figure 6.29 in pre-, post-, and inorder.

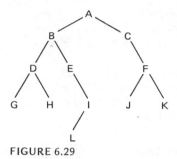

FIGURE 6.29

2. (a) The following is a list of the nodes in a tree in two orders:

preorder: ABCDEFGHIJK
inorder: DCEFBGAJIHK

Draw the tree.

(b) Is it always possible to reconstruct a tree from its preorder and postorder?

3. In Example 6.2.3, (a) why couldn't we have written

IF (Q = NIL) OR (P^.INFO <> Q^.INFO) THEN EQUAL = FALSE

(b) If the left subtree of P does not equal that of Q, then there is no reason to check right subtrees, but the given program does so anyway. Rewrite the recursion part so that if left subtrees are unequal the call of EQUAL for right subtrees is not made.

4. Suppose tree nodes are defined by

TYPE PTRTONODE = ^NODE;
      NODE = RECORD INFO: INTEGER; LCHILD, RCHILD: PTRTONODE END;

(a) Write a recursive function LEAFCOUNT(P) which returns the number of leaves in the tree pointed to by P.

(b) Write a recursive function HEIGHT(P) which returns the height of a tree pointed to by P. The height of a tree is the maximum number of nodes one can go through to get from the root to a leaf. Equivalently, it is 0 for an empty tree and 1 plus the larger of the heights of the left and right subtrees for a nonempty tree.

(c) Write a function COPY(P) which returns a PTRTONODE to a new tree which is a copy of P; that is, EQUAL (P, COPY(P)) is true by construction. (Note that INFO parts will be the same, but pointers must not be.)

5. Write a recursive function COMBO(N, M) which is the number of different ways of choosing M things from N things. Use the fact that COMBO(N, 0) = 1, COMBO(N, M) = 0 if M > N, and COMBO(N, M) = COMBO(N-1, M-1) + COMBO(N-1, M).

6. Write a recursive procedure DELETE(P, N) which searches for the number N in the linked list pointed to by P and deletes the node containing it. (This is a different version of part of Example 5.3.3. It makes no difference whether

you use a sentinel.) (*Hint:* see the discussion of program SEARCH in Example 6.2.1.)

6.3 TRACING RECURSIVE PROGRAMS

To understand recursive programs we must understand how Pascal treats variables (the rules are similar to those for ALGOL and PL/I). We will use the method of *contour diagrams* developed by Johnston (see the Bibliography). At the start, our description will be fairly intuitive, and gradually we will pin down the details.

Each program or subprogram in process of execution has associated with it one or more *environments*. An environment stores all the local variables and parameters and, in addition, for procedures and functions, stores information about where to return when execution is complete. Whenever a program or subprogram is entered, an environment is created for it (even if one already exists), and when the program's execution is complete, the environment is destroyed. (This is unlike languages such as FORTRAN and COBOL in which each program has only one environment, and it has life throughout the entire execution of the whole program.)

Consider the example program of Figure 6.30. The outlines (contours) are there to emphasize the nesting of the various programs. Similar outlines will be used to represent environments, which are also nested in the same way as their associated programs. (When we draw diagrams of environments, the size of various boxes is immaterial. It is the containment relationships of environments that matters. We will make them smaller to conserve space or larger when more detail must be shown.)

Now suppose that the main program AAA is executing. In this case, only an environment for AAA exists, which we represent as in Figure 6.31. The wavy arrow ⌇ indicates the environment of the currently executing program. If AAA calls CCC, a new environment for CCC is created (see Figure 6.32).

The nesting of environments can be used to picture the visibility of variables from one subprogram to another. You can think of the walls of an environment as being made of one-way mirrors, which allow you to see out of an environment but not into it. Thus in CCC we can see AAA's variables, but not vice versa.

Next, suppose that CCC calls DDD (see Figure 6.33), and that DDD calls itself recursively (see Figure 6.34). The second call to DDD creates a new environment for DDD, new copies of DDDs local variables and parameters. Its position shows that the variables of CCC and AAA are visible to it, but those of the other DDD environment are not.

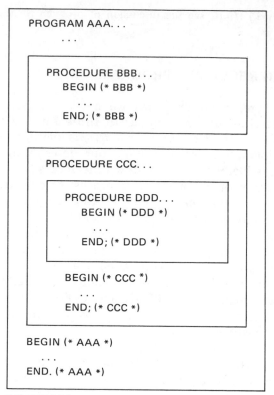

FIGURE 6.30

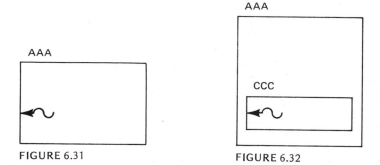

FIGURE 6.31   FIGURE 6.32

If at this point DDD were to call BBB, we would have the diagram of
Figure 6.35, which tells us several important things: (1) BBB can
access its own variables and AAA's, but not those of CCC and DDD;
however, the variables of CCC and DDD still exist and can be accessed
when we return to those procedures. (2) we see the necessity of the
wavy arrow. We cannot simply say that we are executing the innermost environment (order does not matter either; we will see later that
in certain cases we can call forward as well as backward). (3) Since BBB

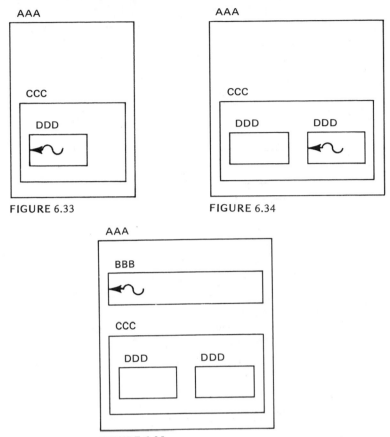

FIGURE 6.33

FIGURE 6.34

FIGURE 6.35

returns to DDD when it is done and there are two environments for DDD, we have a problem. In addition to knowing where in the program to return to, we have to know which environment to return to as well. Therefore, each environment except that for the main program will have a return indication in two parts (see Figure 6.36). Our last diagram would then become Figure 6.37.

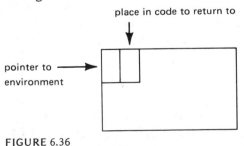

FIGURE 6.36

Each local variable is represented as a named box; for instance,

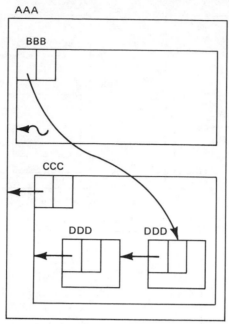

FIGURE 6.37

the variable X is represented as in Figure 6.38. Non VAR parameters

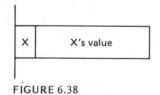

FIGURE 6.38

are represented the same way. The only difference in treatment is that they are given values immediately on entry to the subprogram. Local variables, on the other hand, contain garbage to start with (even if the subprogram has been executed previously, as values of local variables are not preserved between calls). Finally, VAR parameters are represented as having only the name part of their box and an arrow pointing to the variable they represent. Thus in the procedure

```
PROCEDURE WWW(X: REAL; VAR Y: REAL);
    VAR Z: REAL;
```

we would have the environment of Figure 6.39. If, say, we had made the call WWW(R, S), where R = 5.2 and S = –14.1, then initially the environment for WWW would look like Figure 6.40. In WWW, the

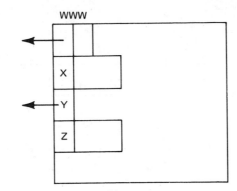

FIGURE 6.39

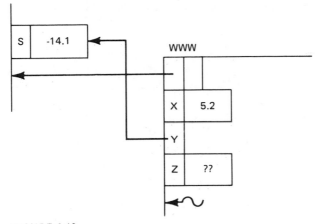

FIGURE 6.40

statement X := X + 1 produces Figure 6.41, and the statement Y :=
Y + 1 produces Figure 6.42.

Functions work the same way as procedures except that, in addition, they have something like a local variable which holds the func-

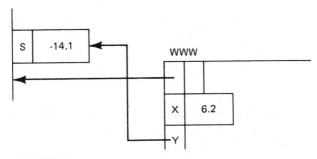

FIGURE 6.41

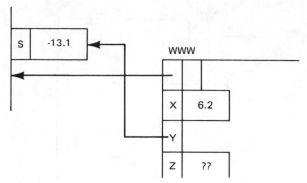

FIGURE 6.42

tion's current value. For example, if we declared

FUNCTION PPP(R, S, T . . .

an environment for PPP would look like Figure 6.43.

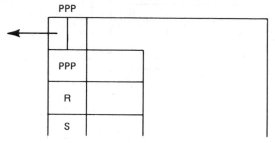

FIGURE 6.43

Now let's use what we have learned to trace a recursive program. We will do an inorder traverse of a binary tree.

```
    . . .
TYPE PTRTONODE = ^NODE;
      NODE = RECORD NAME: ALFA; LCHILD, RCHILD: PTRTONODE; END;
    . . .

PROCEDURE PRINT(P: PTRTONODE);
    BEGIN (* PRINT *)
      IF (P <> NIL) THEN
          BEGIN
(* 1 *)        PRINT(P^.LCHILD);
(* 2 *)        WRITELN(P^.NAME);
(* 3 *)        PRINT(P^.RCHILD)
(* 4 *)     END
      END;  (* PRINT *)
    . . .
```

```
(* 18 *) PRINT(ROOT);
(* 19 *) . . .
```

The numbers in the comments will be used as statement numbers to tell us where in the code various environments are to return.

Now we trace the program with Figure 6.44. Successive environ-

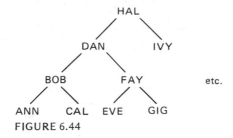

FIGURE 6.44

ments are shown in Figure 6.45. In Figure 6.45(f), since P is NIL, we

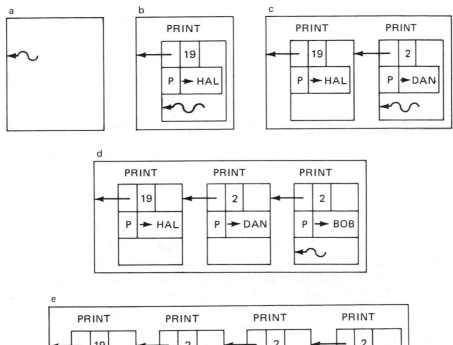

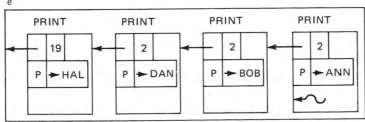

FIGURE 6.45 a–e

f

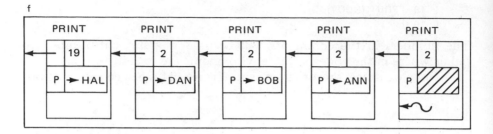

g

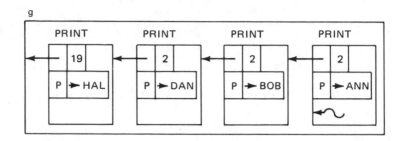

h

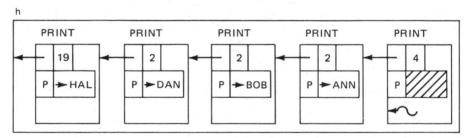

FIGURE 6.45 f–h

exit PRINT immediately and find ourselves ready to execute statement
2 in the Figure 6.45(g). Now, for the first time, we actually print something, the word ANN. Then we execute statement 3, which calls PRINT
again (Figure 6.45(h); note the different return number in the last environment). Once again we exit PRINT immediately, erasing the last
environment, and start executing statement 4 in the ANN environment;
that is, we also exit that procedure immediately. This leaves us about to
execute statement 2 in the environment of Figure 6.45(i). At this point
we write BOB, the second word printed, and call PRINT for BOB's
RCHILD (Figure 6.45(j)). As before, we call PRINT again for the NIL
left child, print CAL, call PRINT for the NIL right child, and then exit
the CAL environment. At this point we have printed ANN, BOB, and
CAL and are ready to execute statement 4 in the BOB environment,
that is, exit, leaving us ready to execute statement 2 in the environment

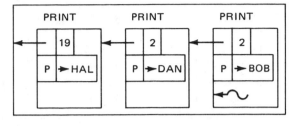

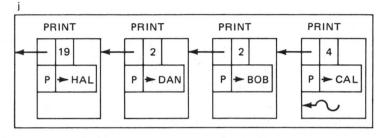

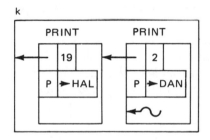

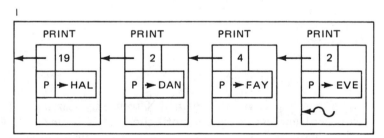

FIGURE 6.45 i–l

of Figure 6.45(k). We now print DAN and execute statement 3, which calls PRINT with P pointing to FAY, which in turn calls PRINT with P pointing to EVE, giving us Figure 6.45(l).

As before, we print EVE, come back and print FAY, go forward and print GIG, and finally find ourselves back in the DAN environment ready to execute statement 4. This causes us to exit the DAN environm

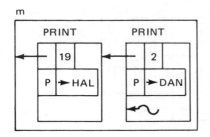

n

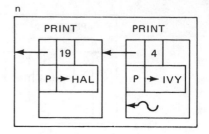

FIGURE 6.45 m–n

ment and execute statement 2 in the environment of Figure 6.45(m). Thus the DAN environment is exited, HAL is printed, and PRINT is called for HAL's RCHILD (Figure 6.45(n)), and so on. This probably seems excessively complicated to you; but this process is not intended to be done in every case. It is intended to convince you that recursion works, so that you do not *have* to go through this in every case.

Note that the creation and deletion of environments looks a lot like a stack situation. In fact, recursion is implemented in languages like Pascal using stacks.

For completeness, we end this section by describing what happens when we have more than one variable of the same name. Of course, we cannot have two variables with the same name declared in the same environment, but we can have something like

```
    . . .
VAR X: REAL;
    . . .
PROCEDURE MMM;
    VAR X: REAL;
    BEGIN (* MMM *)
        . . .
        X := 12.8
    . . .
```

Pascal determines which variable named X to use by starting in the current environment and working out until the first X is reached. That is the one used. Thus any Xs in larger environments become invisible. If we have a main program which includes

```
    . . .
X := –3.5;
MMM;
X := X + 1
    . . .
```

the environments are as shown in Figure 6.46.

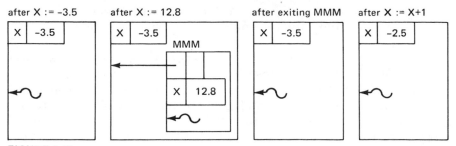

FIGURE 6.46

    The Pascal WITH statement, which is convenient but not necessary in RECORD processing, can also be explained neatly using contour diagrams. As we will not use this statement in this book, I have relegated this description to Appendix D but commend it to the interested reader.

Exercises 6.3

    1. Draw a diagram representing the situation in program AAA if the main program calls CCC, which calls DDD, which then calls CCC again.
    2. What is printed by the program piece

```
VAR X: REAL;

PROCEDURE FFF;
   VAR X;
   BEGIN (* FFF *)
      X := X + 1; Y := Y + 1
   END;  (* FFF *)

BEGIN
   X := 0.25; Y := 24.1;
   FFF;
   WRITELN(X, Y)
      . . .
```

6.4   QUICKSORT: A RECURSIVE SORTING PROCEDURE

Quicksort, a procedure invented by C. A. R. Hoare, is the best known method for sorting large internal files. The idea is really quite simple; the surprising thing is that it works as efficiently as it does!
    The general scheme is to rearrange the file so that one element, more or less in the middle, is in its final position, where all records

with smaller keys are below it and all records with larger keys above it. This divides the file into two pieces which can then be sorted independently by the same process.

Since we will be sorting various pieces of the file, we postulate a program SORT(LO, HI) whose job it will be to sort our file between the indices LO and HI. We also need a function PARTITION(LO, HI) which returns an index, call it MID, such that the MID record is in its final position and, every record with lower index has smaller key and every record with higher index has higher key. Of course, PARTITION will have to do some rearranging of the file to do its work. If we assume we have PARTITION already, SORT(LO, HI) is easy:

```
IF (LO < HI) THEN (* OMIT TRIVIAL CASE *)
    BEGIN
        MID := PARTITION(LO, HI);
        SORT(LO, MID-1);
        SORT(MID+1, HI)
    END
```

The interesting part of quicksort is PARTITION, and we will look at it quite closely. The basic idea is to choose some record in the file, for example, the LOth one, and move all records with larger keys to the top end of the file and all records with smaller ones to the lower end. One way to do this would be to search from the bottom for a record with a larger key and from the top for a record with a smaller one and then interchange these two records. The process would continue from that point until the searches crossed each other. A better way is to search from the ends alternately and exchange as we go. The following version of PARTITION is not the most efficient, but is relatively non-mysterious. We assume a file with records R[K] of type RECTYPE with a key field R[K].KEY.

```
FUNCTION PARTITION(L, H: INTEGER): INTEGER;
        (* REORDER R[L .. H] SO THAT ONE ITEM IS IN ITS *)
        (* FINAL POSITION AND RETURN INDEX OF IT        *)
    VAR TEMP: RECTYPE;
    BEGIN (* PARTITION *)
        TEMP := R[L];  (* RECORD TO BE MIDDLE ONE *)
        WHILE (L < H) DO
            BEGIN
                WHILE (TEMP.KEY <= R[H].KEY) AND (L < H) DO
                    H := H - 1;  (* SEARCH DOWN FROM TOP *)
(* A *)         IF (L < H) THEN (* MORE TO DO *)
                    BEGIN
                        R[L] := R[H]; L := L + 1; (* MOVE *)
(* B *)                 WHILE (TEMP.KEY >= R[L].KEY) AND (L < H) DO
                            L := L + 1;  (* SEARCH UP *)
```

```
(* C *)                IF (L < H) THEN  (* MORE TO DO *)
                          BEGIN
                            R[H] := R[L] ; H := H – 1 (* MOVE *)
(* D *)                   END
                     END
               END;
         R[L] := TEMP;
         PARTITION := L  (* = H *)
   END;  (* PARTITION *)
```

Now let's convince ourselves that this program actually works. First let's take a specific example, a file with the twelve keys

$$35 \quad 28 \quad 18 \quad 80 \quad 93 \quad 73 \quad 99 \quad 84 \quad 16 \quad 23 \quad 77 \quad 27$$

In the trace of PARTITION that follows, the position in the program will be shown at the left, items that have moved will be boldfaced in their new position, and the place an item has left shaded until it is filled with another item. At the start of the WHILE (L < H) loop we

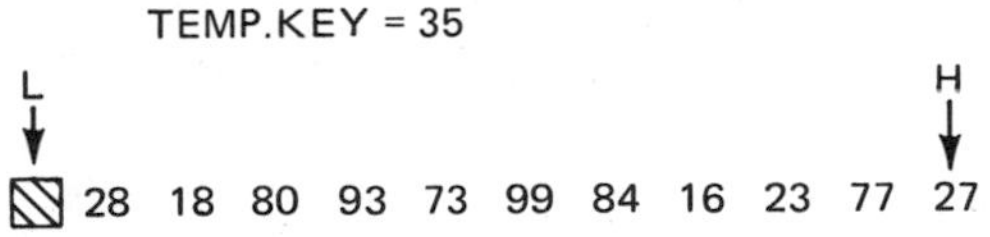

TEMP.KEY = 35

FIGURE 6.47

have Figure 6.47, and then, in turn, the lines of Figure 6.48. Finally,

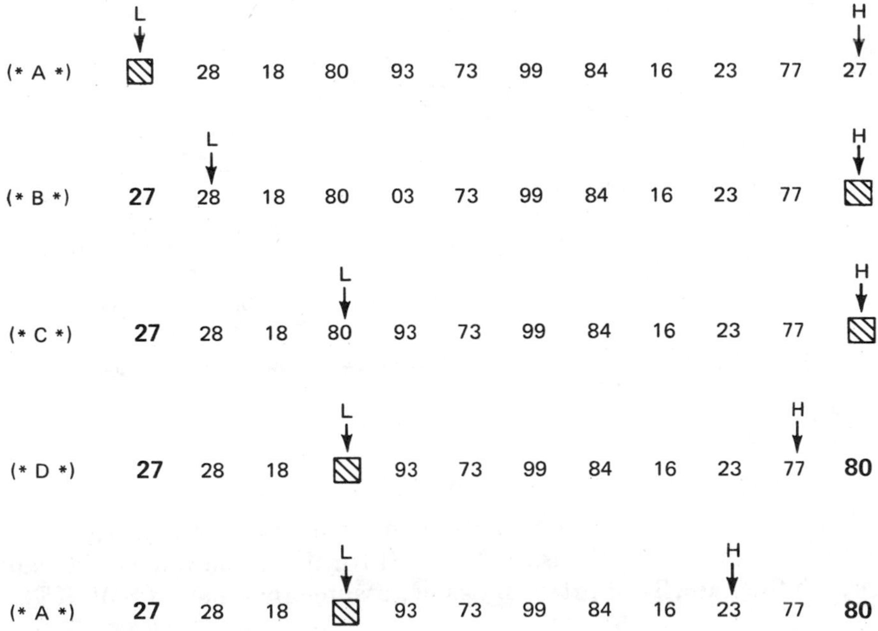

FIGURE 6.48

L   H
↓   ↓
(* B *)   **27** 28 18 **23** 93 73 99 84 16 ▨ 77 **80**

(* C *)   Same

L   H
↓   ↓
(* D *)   **27** 28 18 **23** ▨ 73 99 84 16 **93** 77 **80**

(* A *)   Same

L   H
↓   ↓
(* B *)   **27** 28 18 **23** **16** 73 99 84 ▨ **93** 77 **80**

(* C *)   Same

L   H
↓   ↓
(* D *)   **27** 28 18 **23** **16** ▨ 99 84 **73** **93** 77 **80**

L = H
↓
(* A *)   **27** 28 18 **23** **16** ▨ 99 84 **73** **93** 77 **80**

FIGURE 6.48 (continued)

we are left with Figure 6.49.

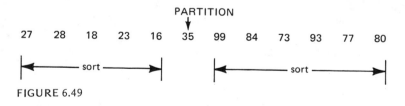

PARTITION
↓
27   28   18   23   16   35   99   84   73   93   77   80

|◄──── sort ────►| |◄──────── sort ────────►|

FIGURE 6.49

We can also apply the method of invariant relations first discussed in Section 3.3. We use LO and HI for the initial values of L and H, which they are. To shorten things, we assume that TK = TEMP.KEY.

The invariant relation for the main WHILE loop is as follows:

1. R[K].KEY <= TK for LO <= K < L.
2. TK <= R[K].KEY for H < K <= HI.
3. The original R[LO+1 .. HI] is rearranged in R[LO .. HI], less R[L].

We will abbreviate condition 3 by saying that R[L] is *empty* and picture R[L] shaded. Condition 3 means that if TEMP were put in R[L], the file would contain all its records, in some order. We picture the invariant relations as in Figure 6.50. The invariant relation is obviously valid when L = LO and H = HI; it does not say anything. We will verify that it remains true by seeing what has happened at the locations indicated by (* A *) to (* D *). At (* A *), just before the IF, we have Figure 6.51. At (* B *), we will have Figure 6.52. At (* C *), we will have Figure 6.53. And at (* D *), we will have Figure 6.54, which is just the original invariant relation back again; that is, the relation is indeed invariant, as advertised. The process terminates when L = H, and by the invariant relation we have Figure 6.55, which means that PARTITION does exactly what it is supposed to do. (For a complete version of a quicksort see Example 7.2.1.)

Now we will try to convince ourselves that, on the average, quicksort is a $O(n \log_2(n))$ method. PARTITION clearly looks at each item

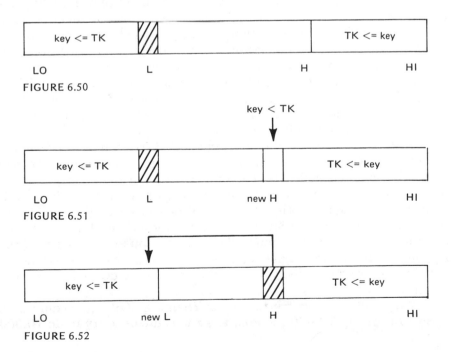

FIGURE 6.50

FIGURE 6.51

FIGURE 6.52

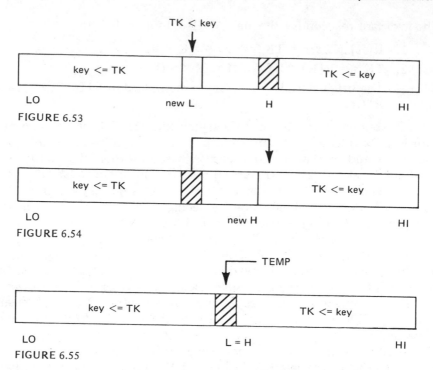

FIGURE 6.53

FIGURE 6.54

FIGURE 6.55

in the subfile exactly once, so it is O(length of subfile). Initially, it is $O(n)$. The file is divided into two pieces and each of them is partitioned, in time O(length of first piece) + O(length of second piece) = $O(n)$. These pieces then become four and again the partitioning of these four adds up to $O(n)$. Thus sorting time is O(number of levels of partitioning $* n$). Assuming that each partition divides its subfile approximately in half, it will require $\log_2(n)$ levels of partitions to get down to files of length 1 by the halving principle. Thus time to quicksort "good" files should be $O(n \log_2(n))$.

In fact a more rigorous mathematical discussion shows that the *average* time for a quicksort is $O(n \log_2(n))$, and in fact it is faster than other $O(n \log_2(n))$ methods. The probem is that if we are very unlucky and the file is already sorted (or nearly so), we will have to do n levels of partitioning, and the time to sort will be $O(n ** 2)$. It is even worse if the file is in reverse order: there are still n levels but, further, at each partition the whole remaining file must be shifted down one. (The reason that the average time is fast is that, if files are chosen at random with all key orders equally likely, the bad orders do not occur very often.)

Worst of all, if we try to use the recursive SORT procedure on a "bad" file of say 10,000 records, this will cause us to try to do 10,000 levels of recursion, and it is hard to imagine a computer with enough memory to do this without dying. Thus sorting time will be $O(\text{infinity})$!

We can at least avoid the problem of not being able to sort a "bad" file at all. It will still take $O(n ** 2)$ time, but it will be done successfully. The following version of SORT never "recurses" more than $\log_2(n)$ levels (20 levels for $n = 1,000,000$) no matter how bad the file is.

```
PROCEDURE SORT(LO, HI: INTEGER);
        (* RECURSIVE PROCEDURE TO QUICKSORT R[LO .. HI] *)
    VAR MID: INTEGER;
    BEGIN (* SORT *)
        WHILE (LO < HI) DO (* ONLY RECURSE ON 1 SUBFILE *)
            BEGIN
                MID := PARTITION(LO, HI);
                IF (MID - LO) < (HI - MID) THEN
                    BEGIN (* RECURSIVE CALL FOR SHORTER SUBFILE *)
                        SORT(LO, MID - 1);
                        LO := MID + 1
                    END
                ELSE
                    BEGIN
                        SORT(MID + 1, HI);
                        HI := MID - 1
                    END
            END
    END; (* SORT *)
```

The reason that nesting is at most $\log_2(n)$ is that we always do the recursive call on the smaller subfile, that is, on a file at most half the size of the subfile we were called with. In at most $\log_2(n)$ steps, we get to a file with only one element and are done.

Exercises 6.4

1. For small files, whose length is less than some constant THRESHOLD (depending on the file, the computer, etc.), the insertion sort is faster than the quicksort (in Example 7.2.1, THRESHOLD = 19). Rewrite either version of SORT so that small files are sorted by an insertion sort procedure INSORT(LO, HI). You need not write INSORT.

2. Rewrite the tree printing program PRINT of Section 6.2 in the manner of the second version of SORT so that there is only one recursive call to PRINT.

3. Rewrite the second version of SORT without using recursion. Instead of the recursive call, push the two parameters onto an appropriate stack. The fundamental loop should be

```
set stack empty; LO := 1; HI := N;
```

```
WHILE (LO < HI) OR stack non-empty DO
   IF (LO >= HI) THEN
      pop stack into LO, HI
   ELSE
      PARTITION file, push limits of the smaller subfile onto the stack, and reset LO
      and HI to the limits of the larger subfile
```

6.5   INFIX TO RPN REVISITED

The conversion of infix to Polish (and, in fact, much more general
problems in compilers) lends itself to recursion because the definition
of infix expressions is recursive:

An *expression* is of the form term ± term ± term . . ..

A *term* is of the form factor */ factor */ factor . . ..

A *factor* is of the form variable or (expression).

(For simplicity we have allowed only +, -, *, and /, and no literals.
"*/" is to be read as "* or /.") A translator using the method of *recursive descent* works as follows: we have three procedures, EXPRES-
SION, TERM, and FACTOR. Each is assumed to read an infix expression of its type and print out its reverse Polish form. The fundamental
loop of EXPRESSION is

```
TERM;   (* writes out TERM in RPN *)
WHILE next char is + or – DO
   BEGIN
      save char and skip over it;
      TERM;   (* writes out second TERM in RPN *)
      write out saved char
   END;
```

The only problem is that EXPRESSION must call TERM, which must
call FACTOR, which must call EXPRESSION, and Pascal requires that
a procedure or function be defined before it is used. There is a loop-
hole. A subprogram can be declared first and its code given later. The
form is as follows for functions:

```
FUNCTION name (parameters): type; FORWARD;
   .
   .
other FUNCTIONS and PROCEDUREs
   .
   .
FUNCTION name;
   code for FUNCTION name
```

*In FORWARD declarations, parameter-
and function-type declarations appear
ONLY in the FIRST mention of the
subprogram.*

The "code for FUNCTION name" includes declarations for any locally
defined variables, subprograms, and so on.

EXAMPLE 6.5.1   Write a recursive descent program to translate
infix expressions to RPN. We will use an array and an enumerated type
to pick up character type as we have done before. We also now need
a procedure to read and skip over blanks, particularly if we have an
operating system that adds them to the ends of lines. The program is

```
(* EXAMPLE 6.5.1: INTORP2    *)
(* INFIX TO RPN CONVERSION  *)
(* USING RECURSIVE DESCENT *)

PROGRAM INTORP2(INPUT, OUTPUT);

CONST LOWORD = 0; HIGHORD = 127; (* LOWEST AND HIGHEST ORDS *)
      TAB = 9;  (* ORD OF THE ASCII TAB CHARACTER *)

TYPE   CHARTYPE = (BLANK,LETTER,ADDOP,MULOP,OTHER);

VAR   C: CHAR;  (* NEXT CHAR TO BE PROCESSED AND INDEX *)
      CLASS: ARRAY [CHAR] OF CHARTYPE;  (* TYPE OF CHARS *)

PROCEDURE EXPRESSION; FORWARD;

PROCEDURE READNB;
      (* SET GLOBAL C TO NEXT NON-BLANK CHAR IN INPUT *)
   BEGIN (* READNB *)
      IF EOLN THEN C := ' '
      ELSE
         REPEAT
            READ(C)
         UNTIL (CLASS[C] <> BLANK) OR EOLN
   END;  (* READNB *)

PROCEDURE FACTOR;
      (* PROCESS FACTOR = VBL OR ( EXPR ) *)
   CONST LPAREN = '('; RPAREN = ')';
   BEGIN (* FACTOR *)
      IF (C = LPAREN) THEN
         BEGIN  (* '(' EXPRESSION')'  *)
```

```
                    READNB;  (* SKIP OVER '(' *)
                    EXPRESSION;
                    IF (C <> RPAREN) THEN WRITELN('*** ) EXPECTED')
                    ELSE READNB  (* SKIP OVER ')' *)
            END
        ELSE
            IF (CLASS[C] = LETTER) THEN
                BEGIN
                    WRITE(C); READNB
                END
            ELSE WRITELN('*** VARIABLE EXPECTED')
        END;  (* FACTOR *)


PROCEDURE TERM;
        (* PROCESS TERM = FACTOR OPTIONALLY */ OTHER FACTORS *)
    VAR OP: CHAR;
    BEGIN (* TERM *)
        FACTOR;
        WHILE (CLASS[C] = MULOP) DO
            BEGIN
                OP := C;  (* SAVE * OR / *)
                READNB;  (* AND SKIP OVER IT *)
                FACTOR;
                WRITE(OP)
            END
    END;  (* TERM *)


PROCEDURE EXPRESSION:
        (* PROCESS EXPR = TERM OPTIONALLY +- OTHER TERMS *)
    VAR OP: CHAR;
    BEGIN (* EXPRESSION *)
        TERM;
        WHILE (CLASS[C] = ADDOP) DO
            BEGIN
                OP := C; READNB;
                TERM;
                WRITE(OP)
            END
    END;  (* EXPRESSION *)


BEGIN (* INTORP2 *)
        (* INITIALIZE CLASS *)
    FOR C := CHR(LOWORD) TO CHR(HIGHORD) DO CLASS[C] := OTHER;
    FOR C := 'A' TO 'Z' DO CLASS[C] := LETTER;
    CLASS[' '] := BLANK; CLASS[CHR(TAB)] := BLANK;
    CLASS['+'] := ADDOP; CLASS['-'] := ADDOP;
    CLASS['*'] := MULOP; CLASS['/'] := MULOP;
```

```
        READNB;  (* INITIALIZE C *)
        EXPRESSION;
        IF NOT EOLN THEN
            HALT('BADLY FORMED EXPRESSION');
        WRITELN
    END.  (* INTORP2 *)
```

Results of executing this program several times are:

```
    ? A+B*C
    ABC*+

    ? (A+B)*C
    AB+C*

    ? (A+B)/(C-D*E/F+G)
    AB+CDE*F/-G+/
```

Exercises 6.5

1. Add powers to the preceding program. Redefine factor as primary ^ primary ^ . . ., and primary = variable or (expression).

2. Alter EXPRESSION to allow for unary + and − (see Exercise 4.3.5). In RPN, the unary + is discarded and the unary − can be represented by ∼.

3. Another way to allow two procedures to call each other is to put one inside the other:

```
PROCEDURE P1;
    PROCEDURE P2;
        BEGIN (* P2 *)
            P1 can be called here as it has been declared
        END;  (* P2 *)
    BEGIN (* P1 *)
        P2 can be called here as it has been declared
    END;  (* P2 *)
```

(a) Show how EXPRESSION, FACTOR, and TERM can be arranged without using FORWARD so that the calls main → EXPRESSION → TERM → FACTOR → EXPRESSION are possible.

(b) Show that it is not possible to arrange the definitions of procedures A, B, and C so that each can call the other two without using FORWARD.

6.6   POSTSCRIPT: WHEN NOT TO USE RECURSION

There are many situations in which recursion *can* be used but should not be. Since recursion has a fair amount of hidden overhead, a rule of thumb is that if a nonrecursive version can be written which is very little longer than the recursive version, use the nonrecursive one.

EXAMPLE 6.6.1 $n!$ (read *n factorial*) can be defined by

$$n! = 1 \qquad \text{if } n = 0$$
$$= n*(n-1)!, \quad \text{if } n > 0$$

A recursive version of the factorial function would be

```
FUNCTION FACT(N: INTEGER): REAL;
     (* RETURNS N! COMPUTED RECURSIVELY *)
   BEGIN (* FACT *)
     IF (N = 0) THEN FACT := 1
     ELSE FACT := N * FACT(N - 1)
   END;  (* FACT *)
```

A more efficient version is

```
FUNCTION FACT(N: INTEGER); REAL;
     (* RETURNS N! COMPUTED WITH A LOOP *)
   VAR F: REAL;    (* ACCUMULATES N! *)
       I: INTEGER;  (* INDEX FOR N! COMPUTATON *)
   BEGIN (* FACT *)
     F := 1;
     FOR I := 2 TO N DO F := F * I;
     FACT := F
   END;  (* FACT *)
```

(FACT is made REAL because $n!$ grows very rapidly. 20! is on the order of 1E18. F is necessary in the second version because FACT := FACT * I would attempt to call FACT recursively.)

Exercises 6.6

1. The sequence $f(n)$ of *Fibonacci numbers* is defined by

$$f(n) = 1, \qquad\qquad n = 1 \text{ or } 2$$
$$= f(n-1) + f(n-2), \quad n > 2$$

The sequence starts 1, 1, 2, 3, 5, 8, 13, 21, ... Write recursive and nonrecursive versions of a function FIB(N) which computes the Nth Fibonacci number. Which version is preferable?

2. Write a recursive function POWER(X: REAL; N: INTEGER): REAL; whose value is X**N, computed as follows:

$$X ** N = \begin{cases} 1 \ / \ \text{POWER(X, -N)} & \text{if N} < 0 \\ 1 & \text{if N} = 0 \\ X & \text{if N} = 1 \\ \text{SQR(POWER(X, N DIV 2))} & \text{if N is even} \\ \text{SQR(POWER(X, N DIV 2))}*X & \text{if N is odd} \end{cases}$$

Programming Problems

6.1 Rewrite the program of Example 4.2.3 (the text insertion program) using a recursive PROCEDURE INSERT(VAR F: TEXT); (file parameters to subprograms must be VAR parameters). INSERT processes the text in one file. When a new $INSERT statement is encountered, do the RESET and call INSERT recursively.

6.2 Write a recursive procedure to solve the Towers of Hanoi puzzle. The puzzle consists of three pegs and a stack of disks with decreasing diameters on one of them (Figure 6.56). The problem is to transfer the disks, one at a time, from peg 1 to peg 2 in such a way that when a disk is transferred to any peg, the peg must

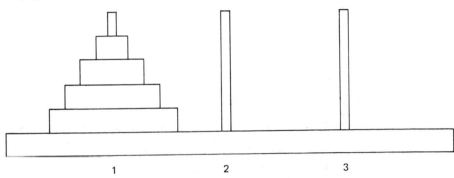

FIGURE 6.56

be empty or contain a larger disk. For example, to move two disks, move the small one to 3, the large to 2, and the small from 3 to 2. To move three disks, move the top 2 from peg 1 to peg 3, using the above procedure; move the largest to peg 2, and then move the smaller two from peg 3 to peg 2 again using the above procedure. At this point you probably recognize the recursion: To move n disks from peg i to peg j, do

Move $n - 1$ disks from peg i to the off peg.

Move nth disk from i to j.

Move $n - 1$ disks from off peg to peg j.

In moving the top $n - 1$ disks we can simply ignore the position of the nth since it is larger than the first $n - 1$. Your recursive procedure HANOI(I, J, N) should move N disks from peg I to peg J by printing the necessary instructions; for example,

MOVE DISK 5 FROM PEG 2 TO PEG 1

Test your program with N = 4.

6.3 Write a program which reads up to 1000 real numbers, terminated by −999, and prints their median (see Example 2.2.1 for the definition of median). To do this, write a recursive function FIND(K, LO, HI) which returns the index of the Kth smallest element in A[LO .. HI]. Use a copy of the M := PARTITION(LO, HI) function, which does some rearranging of A[LO .. HI] and sets M to the location of the M−LO+1st smallest entry in A[LO .. HI]. Done properly, A[I] ⩽ A[M]

$\leqslant$ A[J] when I $\leqslant$ M $\leqslant$ J so A[M] is the Mth largest item in A[1 . . N]. If there are
N numbers and N is odd, the median is at FIND(N DIV 2 + 1, 1, N), and if N is even,
it is the average of the entries at FIND(N DIV 2, 1, N) and (after this call has done
its work) FIND(1, N DIV 2 + 1, N).

6.4 The image of a two-dimensional object is to be digitized using

OBJ: PACKED ARRAY [1 . . M, 1 . . N] OF 0 . . 1;

with 1 representing where the object is, 0 where it isn't. Input to the program is in
the form of number-of-rows number-of-columns followed by the rows of 0s and 1s
representing the object. For instance a doughnut shaped object might be represented by

```
6   6
0  0  1  1  1  0
0  1  1  1  1  0
1  1  0  0  1  1
1  0  0  0  1  1
1  1  0  1  1  0
0  1  1  1  0  0
```

Write a program to read in such a representation of size up to say M, N = 20, and
determine if the object represented is a single connected object; i.e., is it possible
to get from any 1 to any other 1 by proceeding horizontally and vertically, passing
through 1s only. Thus the doughnut object above is connected, but

```
0  1
1  0
```

is not. Your program should proceed by finding a 1 at some position (I, J) and then
executing a recursive procedure REACH(I, J) which sets all the 1 positions reach-
able from (I, J) to 0. The figure was connected if there are no OBJ entries still set
to 1 when REACH is done. REACH(I, J) operates by setting OBJ[I, J] to 0 and
then executing REACH(P, Q) for the up to four adjacent positions containing 1s.

chapter 7

random numbers

7.1 INTRODUCTION

In this chapter we will be concerned with functions called *random-number generators*. Such functions have the property that each time they are invoked, they return a different value, the particular value *appearing* to depend purely on chance. The word "appearing" is emphasized because it is not possible to generate truly random numbers on a digital computer. Usually, each number in the sequence is obtained by performing some operation on the previous number in the sequence. Thus, far from being random, the random-number generators of which we speak produce a sequence of numbers which is (in principle) perfectly predictable and thus not random at all! The numbers *appear* to be random though, and this is sufficient for our purposes. To emphasize this state of affairs, we call them *pseudo-random* numbers.

There are many applications of random numbers to some of the most glamorous problems in computer science. Some of them are as follows:

1. *Sampling.* Rather than polling a whole population on some issue, a small sample may be polled. It is of course crucial that this sample be representative of the whole population. Most naive sampling methods (e.g., calling every hundredth name in the phone book) are biased to some extent. To avoid this, the population can be numbered in some way and a random-number generator used to choose a *truly* random sample. (See the card-dealing algorithm in Section 7.4.)

2. *Numerical Analysis (Monte Carlo methods).* Certain problems can be solved by averaging random results. The simplest such is a (very slow) method of computing the area of a plane figure. Points are chosen at random in a square containing the figure. If, say, 76% of these points lie in the figure itself and the square has area, say, of 400 units, we estimate the area of the figure at $0.76 * 400 = 304$ units.

3. *Simulation.* Many problems are inherently random. For example, arrival time and service time of customers at a bank or entry time and destination of cars in a road system. Problems of this type would be trivial if we could assume that, say, customers arrive exactly every 5 minutes and require exactly 10 minutes each for service (two clerks, no waiting). Unfortunately, there tend to be clots, and in complicated situations one cannot compute an answer simply. Rather than building a road or a bank and trying it out, we can *simulate* many possibilities using computers and random numbers. A number of languages (SIMSCRIPT, GPSS, SIMULA) have been invented for this purpose, but it is not too hard to simulate simple problems in Pascal, as we will see in Section 7.6.

4. *Testing computer programs.* Random numbers are an excellent way to generate data in large quantities and (perhaps) with fewer biases than human-generated data. Examples will be given in Section 7.2 and Chapter 8.

5. *Games.* Computers can be programmed to play games of chance, with random-number generators taking care of things like rolling dice or shuffling cards (see Section 7.4). Random numbers can also be used in choosing strategies, for instance, when to bluff in poker.

Throughout this book we will assume the existence of a separate (pseudo) random-number generating function RANDOM, which should be available in some form at most installations. In most Pascals such a function can be referenced by including the declaration

```
FUNCTION RANDOM: REAL; EXTERN;
```

in the usual place for function declarations. (The keyword is EX-TERNAL in some versions.) See Appendix C if your system does not have such a function. We will go into the properties of a standard RANDOM function in Section 7.3.

7.2 APPLICATION TO SORTING

We do not need to know much about the RANDOM function to apply it to problems in sorting.

EXAMPLE 7.2.1   Write programs comparing sorting speeds of various methods on files of random numbers of various sizes. We will test the insertion sort (Section 3.5), the selection sort (Exercise 3.5.2), the bubble sort (Exercise 2.2.1), and the quicksort (Section 6.4). We use a function CLOCK which is built in in some systems and which returns the number of milliseconds of CPU time used by the program so far. Some experiments showed that on the computer used (a CDC Cyber 174) files of 15 or 20 items required only 1 to 5 clock ticks, which does not really allow for accurate estimates (the time can depend on where in the clock's cycle we started, what the particular mix of jobs was in the system at the time, etc.). Some of these problems can be ironed out by sorting several files and averaging the times. We will sort enough files to make the total number of items sorted about 1000 (or more).

We start with quicksort. In addition to file length and sorting time, we will also print sorting time/$n*\ln(n)$, which should be roughly constant if quicksort is a $O(n*\log_2(n))$ method, since $\ln(n)/\log_2(n)$ is constant ($= \ln(2)$). The sorting part of the program is just as in Section 6.3. There is also a loop to check to see if the file(s) are actually sorted.

```
(* EXAMPLE 7.2.1: QUICK        *)
(* QUICKSORT RANDOM FILES OF *)
(* VARIOUS SIZES               *)

PROGRAM QUICK(INPUT, OUTPUT);

CONST MAXFILE = 10000;    (* LARGEST FILE TO SORT *)
      NUMER   = 1000;     (* NO. OF FILES TO SORT * SIZE = NUMER *)
```

```
VAR    X: ARRAY [1 .. MAXFILE] OF REAL;  (* FILE(S) TO SORT *)
       SIZE,                    (* LENGTH OF FILE(S) TO SORT *)
       REPS,                    (* NUMBER OF FILES THAT SIZE TO SORT *)
       C, I,                    (* COUNTERS *)
       CPUTIME: INTEGER; (* CPUTIME IN MILLISECONDS *)
       AVTIME: REAL;      (* = CPUTIME / REPS, IN MILLISECONDS *)
       GOOD: BOOLEAN;     (* INDICATOR FOR SORT TEST *)


FUNCTION RANDOM; REAL; EXTERN;


FUNCTION PARTITION(L, H: INTEGER): INTEGER;
       (* REARRANGES A[L .. H] AND RETURNS M SUCH THAT     *)
       (* A[M] COMES AFTER A[L .. M-1] AND BEFORE A[M+1 .. H] *)
    VAR TK: REAL;  (* TEMPORARY *)
    BEGIN (* PARTITION *)
       TK := X[L];
       WHILE (L < H) DO
          BEGIN
             WHILE (TK <= X[H] ) AND (L < H) DO
                H := H – 1;
             IF (L < H) THEN
                BEGIN
                   X[L] := X[H] ; L := L + 1;
                   WHILE (TK >= X[L] ) AND (L < H) DO
                      L := L + 1;
                   IF (L < H) THEN
                      BEGIN
                         X[H] := X[L] ; H := H – 1,
                      END
                END
          END;
       X[L] := TK; PARTITION := L
    END;  (* PARTITION *)


PROCEDURE SORT(LO, HI: INTEGER);
       (* QUICKSORT A[LO .. HI] *)
    VAR MID: INTEGER;
    BEGIN (* SORT *)
       IF (LO < HI) THEN
          BEGIN
             MID := PARTITION(LO, HI);
             SORT(LO, MID–1);
             SORT(MID+1, HI)
          END
    END;  (* SORT *)

BEGIN (* QUICK *)
    WRITELN('WRITE IN SIZES OF FILES TO SORT, ENDING WITH 0');
```

```
READ(SIZE);  (* FIRST SIZE *)
WRITELN; WRITELN('TIMING DATA ON QUICKSORT'); WRITELN;
WRITELN('        SIZE     TIME(MS)     TIME/SIZE*LN(SIZE))');
WRITELN;

WHILE (SIZE > 0) AND (SIZE <= MAXFILE) DO
    BEGIN
        REPS := NUMER DIV SIZE; IF (REPS < 1) THEN REPS := 1;
        FOR I := 1 TO SIZE*REPS DO X[I] := RANDOM;
            (* GENERATE RANDOM FILES *)
        I := 1;  (* POINTER TO START OF CURRENT SUBFILE *)
        CPUTIME := CLOCK;  (* STARTING TIME *)
        FOR C := 1 TO REPS DO
            BEGIN
                SORT(I, I+SIZE-1);
                I := I + SIZE
            END;
        CPUTIME := CLOCK - CPUTIME; (* TOTAL TIME *)
        I := 1; GOOD := TRUE;  (* TEST SORTS *)
        WHILE (I < SIZE * REPS) AND GOOD DO
            BEGIN
                GOOD := (X[I] <= X[I+1]) OR (I MOD SIZE = 0);
                I := I + 1
            END;
        AVTIME := CPUTIME / REPS;
        IF GOOD THEN
            WRITELN(SIZE, AVTIME:10:2, AVTIME/(SIZE*LN(SIZE)):15:6)
        ELSE WRITELN(SIZE, '  UNSUCCESSFUL');
        READ(SIZE)
    END
END.  (* QUICK *)
```

When this program was run on a CDC Cyber 174, the results were as
follows:

```
WRITE IN SIZES OF FILES TO SORT, ENDING WITH 0
? 15 16 17 18 19 20 25 50 100 500 1000 5000 10000 0

TIMING DATA ON QUICKSORT
```

SIZE	TIME(MS)	TIME/(SIZE*LN(SIZE))
15	1.65	0.040657
16	1.92	0.043266
17	1.95	0.040450
18	2.16	0.041587
19	2.21	0.039531
20	2.38	0.039723

25	3.10	0.038523
50	7.75	0.039621
100	17.90	0.038869
500	116.00	0.037331
1000	270.00	0.039087
5000	1559.00	0.036608
10000	3312.00	0.035960

The main program for the insertion, selection, and bubble sorts is similar. Since these are $O(n ** 2)$ methods, we divide by size $** 2$ instead of size*ln(size). Also in the insertion sort, we add a 0th entry to X for the sentinel, and because of sentinels in the multiple file situation, the order checking loop will not work, so it is deleted. The results on a Cyber 174 were:

WRITE IN SIZES OF FILES TO SORT, ENDING WITH 0
? 15 16 17 18 19 20 25 50 100 500 1000 0

TIMING DATA ON INSERTION SORT

SIZE	TIME(MS)	TIME/SIZE**2
15	1.45	0.006465
16	1.71	0.006678
17	1.90	0.006562
18	2.07	0.006397
19	2.27	0.006286
20	2.52	0.006300
25	3.60	0.005760
50	13.55	0.005420
100	51.00	0.005100
500	1164.00	0.004656
1000	4621.00	0.004621

and

WRITE IN SIZES OF FILES TO SORT, ENDING WITH 0
? 15 25 50 100 1000 0

TIMING DATA ON SELECTION SORT

SIZE	TIME(MS)	TIME/SIZE**2
15	2.58	0.011448
25	6.80	0.010880
50	26.05	0.010420
100	99.80	0.009980
1000	9732.00	0.009732

and

WRITE IN SIZES OF FILES TO SORT, ENDING WITH 0
? 15 25 50 0

TIMING DATA ON BUBBLE SORT

SIZE	TIME(MS)	TIME/SIZE**2
15	3.26	0.014478
25	8.73	0.013960
50	34.60	0.013840

Note that we did not sort really large files with the insertion, bubble, and selection sorts. This is because a file of 1000 items requires about 5 seconds to insertion sort, so a file of 10,000 items would require about 5 * 10 ** 2 = 500 seconds = 8 minutes, whereas the quicksort of such a file only takes 3+ seconds! Note also that, for files of this particular type, insertion sorting is preferable for size ≤ 18 and quicksorting for size > 18. Finally, the selection sort is inferior to both of these methods for files of all sizes, and the bubble sort is worst of all.

Exercise 7.2

Assuming that pointers require at most as much storage as real numbers, which would you expect to be faster, an address table sort using the insertion sort or an address table sort using the selection sort?

7.3   PROPERTIES OF PSEUDO-RANDOM-NUMBER GENERATORS

Most computer languages have a random-number generating function with properties similar to the RANDOM which will be discussed here. Note first that a single random number is meaningless. It is impossible to tell by looking at it whether a single number is random or not. A whole sequence must be looked at in order to observe random behavior.

As we have said, a pseudo-random-number generator usually generates each number in the sequence by applying some arithmetic function to the previous number in the sequence. A typical method is

next number := (A * last number + C) MOD M

where A, C, and M must be carefully chosen for the particular computer. Thus, when the first number, called the *seed* is known, the rest of the sequence is determined. Normally, random-number generators start with the same seed each time the program is run. This is useful for debugging purposes because it means that results are consistent from run to run. When this is not desired, it is usually possible to *randomize* the random-number generator by choosing a more or less random seed. This is usually some low-order bits from the time clock, which is fairly random from run to run. What should *not* be done is to randomize more than once in a program! These randomizations will probably come at more or less of a fixed time apart, so there may be some relationship between the numbers before and after the second randomization.

Another thing to keep in mind is that all pseudo-random-number generators eventually repeat their sequence. This is because any computer can represent only finitely many numbers, so eventually a single number must be repeated. But when this happens, all future numbers are computed starting from that number, so the whole sequence repeats. This does not cause difficulties in small problems, because a generator will generally produce several million numbers at least before it starts to repeat.

To use a random-number generator, we must not only know that its values appear random, we must know their *distribution*, that is, what values are assumed and with what relative frequencies. The most commonly used is the *uniform distribution* in which each value assumed is assumed about the same number of times. I say "about" because in truly random situations it is very unlikely that we will get *exactly* the expected distribution of numbers. In fact, if we did, we should be suspicious of our random-number generator. The sequence of numbers, 1, 2, 3, 4, 5, 1, 2, 3, 4, 5, . . . certainly is uniformly distributed, but it is not what one would call random.

Most standard pseudo-random-number generators, like RANDOM, produce values which are uniformly distributed between 0 and 1. To be more precise,

$$0 \leqslant \text{RANDOM} < 1$$

and if $0 \leqslant x \leqslant y \leqslant 1$, then

$$x \leqslant \text{RANDOM} < y, \qquad y - x \text{ of the time}$$

For example, RANDOM is between 0.25 and 0.5 one fourth of the time. (Whether the inequalities at the ends are $<$ or $\leqslant$ is insignificant, because the probability that RANDOM actually equals a specific number is very small. The fact that RANDOM is never 1, however, will prove useful.)

Once we have a function like RANDOM, it is easy to generate functions with other distributions.

EXAMPLE 7.3.1 Write a function which produces uniformly distributed random numbers X with $A \leqslant X < B$:

```
FUNCTION RAND: REAL;
        (* RAND IS UNIFORMLY DISTRIBUTED A <= RAND < B *)
    BEGIN (* RAND *)
        RAND := A + (B–A) * RANDOM
    END;  (* RAND *)
```

One sees immediately that when RANDOM is 0, RAND is A, and that when RANDOM is near 1, RAND is near A + (B–A) = B.

EXAMPLE 7.3.2   Write a function DIE which simulates the rolling of one die (die is the singular of dice). We assume that each of the faces numbered 1 to 6 occurs equally often, that is, a uniform distribution. Note that

$$0 \leqslant \text{RANDOM} < 1/6 \qquad \text{1/6th of the time}$$
$$1/6 \leqslant \text{RANDOM} < 2/6 \qquad \text{1/6th of the time}$$
$$2/6 \leqslant \text{RANDOM} < 3/6 \qquad \text{1/6th of the time}$$
$$3/6 \leqslant \text{RANDOM} < 4/6 \qquad \text{1/6th of the time}$$
$$4/6 \leqslant \text{RANDOM} < 5/6 \qquad \text{1/6th of the time}$$
$$5/6 \leqslant \text{RANDOM} < 1 \qquad \text{1/6th of the time}$$

so

$$0 \leqslant 6 * \text{RANDOM} < 1 \qquad \text{1/6th of the time}$$
$$1 \leqslant 6 * \text{RANDOM} < 2 \qquad \text{1/6th of the time}$$
$$2 \leqslant 6 * \text{RANDOM} < 3 \qquad \text{1/6th of the time}$$
$$\text{etc.}$$

so

$$\text{TRUNC}(6*\text{RANDOM}) = 0 \qquad \text{1/6th of the time}$$
$$\text{TRUNC}(6*\text{RANDOM}) = 1 \qquad \text{1/6th of the time}$$
$$\text{TRUNC}(6*\text{RANDOM}) = 2 \qquad \text{1/6th of the time}$$
$$\cdots$$
$$\text{TRUNC}(6*\text{RANDOM}) = 5 \qquad \text{1/6th of the time}$$

Thus the following function works:

```
FUNCTION DIE: INTEGER;
        (* DIE GIVES 1 . . 6 UNIFORMLY RANDOMLY *)
    BEGIN (*DIE *)
        DIE := 1 + TRUNC(6 * RANDOM)
    END;  (* DIE *)
```

EXAMPLE 7.3.3   Write a function RNDINT(M, N) which produces an integer uniformly distributed from M to N (inclusive). A little thought gives us the following generalization of Example 7.3.2:

```
FUNCTION RNDINT(M, N: INTEGER): INTEGER;
    (* M <= RNDINT <= N *)
  BEGIN (* RNDINT *)
    RNDINT := M + TRUNC((N - M + 1)*RANDOM)
  END;  (*RNDINT *)
```

The + 1 may be a little surprising. This is because there are in fact
N – M + 1 integers from M to N, inclusive. (For example, there are
two integers from 0 to 1, inclusive.)

For our final example we will demonstrate a simple-minded way
in which nonuniform distributions can be gotten. We will discuss a
more sophisticated method for a particular nonuniform distribution in
Section 7.5.

EXAMPLE 7.3.4 Write a function FUNNYR which produces random numbers equal to 5.5 for 24% of the time, 7.6 for 36% of the
time, and uniformly distributed, not necessarily integer valued, from
10 to 12 the rest (40%) of the time. The function is

```
FUNCTION FUNNYR: REAL;
    VAR X: REAL;  (* SAVES RANDOM NUMBER *)
    BEGIN (* FUNNYR *)
      X := RANDOM;
      IF (X < 0.24) THEN FUNNYR := 5.5
      ELSE
          IF (X < 0.60) THEN FUNNYR := 7.6
          ELSE FUNNYR := 5 * X + 7
    END; (* FUNNYR *)
```

We could not write

```
  IF (RANDOM < 0.24) THEN . . .
  ELSE
      IF (RANDOM < 0.60) THEN . . .
      ELSE FUNNYR := 5 * RANDOM + 7
```

because each mention of RANDOM causes a new random number to be
computed! The mysterious formula $5 * X + 7$ is derived as follows:
the final ELSE case is for $0.60 \leq X < 1$. To increase the range from
0.40 to $2 = 12 - 10$, multiply by 5, giving us $3 \leq 5 * X < 5$, so $10 \leq 5 * X + 7 < 12$.

Exercises 7.3

1. About what percentage of the time would you expect RANDOM to be
between 0.37 and 0.55?

2. Write a function RF which produces pseudo-random numbers uniformly
distributed with $0 < RF \leq 1$.

3. Write a function TOSS which simulates the toss of a true coin. TOSS returns the CHAR 'H' or 'T' depending on the outcome of the coin toss.

4. Write a function FUNR which generates pseudo-random numbers with FUNR = 18 for 20% of the time, = 2.3 for 44% of the time, = –5.6 for 16% of the time, and = 1.2 the remaining 20% of the time.

5. Write a pseudo-random function LETTER: CHAR which produces each of the twenty-six letters of the alphabet about equally often. You should write a function which works with any character set.

7.4 GAMES

In this section we will show how random numbers can be applied to the games of craps and blackjack. In the process, we will show how a deck of cards can be shuffled and a random sample chosen.

EXAMPLE 7.4.1 Simulate 1000 rolls of a pair of dice. Print out a histogram (bar chart) representing the number of times that each possible total 2 through 12 appears. We can use the function DIE from Example 7.3.2 and define ROLL := DIE + DIE (which is *not* the same as 2 * DIE. The latter is always even, the former not so).

There is some question as to what should be considered magic numbers and therefore defined as CONSTs. If it were possible to use constant *expressions* to define CONSTs or subscript limits, I would have no doubt about getting rid of all the magic numbers with something like

```
CONST LODIE=1; HIDIE=6; LOROLL=2*LODIE; HIROLL=2*HIDIE; (*ILLEGAL*)
```

As it is though, Pascal unfortunately does not allow this, so changing the dice would always require changing at least two constants. Rather than get this devious, we will simply not use CONSTs for these values; I do have mixed feelings, though. The program is

```
(* EXAMPLE 7.4.1: DICE        *)
(* DRAW HISTOGRAM OF 1000 *)
(* SIMULATED DICE TOSSES.   *)

PROGRAM DICE(OUTPUT);

CONST NTRIALS = 1000; (* NUMBER OF ROLLS OF THE DICE *)
        MAXBAR = 58;     (* MAXIMUM LENGTH OF A HISTOGRAM BAR *)

VAR   CT: ARRAY [2 .. 12] OF INTEGER;  (* COUNTS OF RESULTS *)
        ROLL,              (* VALUE OF PSEUDO ROLL *)
        N: INTEGER;      (* ROLL COUNTER *)
```

```
FUNCTION RANDOM: REAL; EXTERN;

FUNCTION DIE: INTEGER;
        (* SIMULATED ROLL OF 1 DIE *)
     BEGIN DIE := 1 + TRUNC(6*RANDOM) END;

BEGIN  (* DICE *)
   FOR ROLL := 2 TO 12 DO CT[ROLL] := 0;
   FOR N := 1 TO NTRIALS DO
      BEGIN  (* ROLL AND COUNT ROLLS *)
         ROLL := DIE + DIE;
         CT[ROLL] := CT[ROLL] + 1
      END;
   FOR ROLL := 2 TO 12 DO
      BEGIN  (* PRINT OUT HISTOGRAM *)
         WRITE(ROLL:3,' ');
         FOR N := 1 TO CT[ROLL] *MAXBAR/CT[7] DO WRITE('*');
         WRITELN
      END
END.  (* DICE *)
```

When the program was run, the following results were obtained:

```
 2  ************
 3  ****************
 4  *****************************
 5  ************************************
 6  **************************************
 7  ********************************************************
 8  **************************************
 9  ***********************************
10  ****************************
11  ******************
12  ******
```

We multiplied CT[ROLL] by MAXBAR/CT[7] when printing the histogram to make sure that all the bars fit on the page. A little probability theory (see Section 7.5) tells us that we would expect to roll 7 most often, so we have guaranteed that the 7 bar fits on the page, as well as all the others, which are presumably shorter. As 7 occurs about one sixth of the time, you may wonder why we did not just roll the dice only MAXBAR*6 times. The reason is that the more rolls we do, the more the irregular effects of randomness are smoothed out. Even so, those who know a little probability will realize that the *theory* says we should expect the histogram to be perfectly symmetric with respect to the 7 bar, and it is not. In truly random situations, we should not expect to get *exactly* what the theory says, only something fairly close.

EXAMPLE 7.4.2   Write a program to simulate the dealer's play in the game of blackjack. In this game, an ordinary pack of 52 playing cards is used. Each player is dealt one face up and one face down. The purpose of the game is to get a card point total as close as possible to 21 without going over it. For the purposes of counting, an ace counts as either 1 or 11 and all face cards count as 10. When it is his turn to play, a player can request more face up cards until he is satisfied with his hand or until he goes over 21 (busts). In casinos the dealer, who is a casino employee, plays her hand open (after everyone else) with a fixed strategy to avoid suspicion of spies or collusion. One such strategy is to take more cards if her point total is 16 or less and to "stay," that is, take no more cards, if her point total is 17 or greater.

It would be extremely complicated to simulate blackjack in all its detail, so we will simply simulate the dealer's play and find the percentage of time he busts and what his average count is on nonbust hands.

The most interesting part of the program is the handling of the deck. Since we are only interested in the numerical value of cards, our deck will be an array of 52 integers, four 2's, four 3's, . . ., four 9's, sixteen 10's, and four 11's (representing aces). The order of items in the array is considered to be their order in the deck. Shuffling takes place when fewer than five cards remain. (Once again, as before, we will treat a deck as being relatively stable and not use magic numbers to represent it so that we do not end up with too many CONSTs for easy understanding.)

The shuffling algorithm is from Knuth, vol. 2, page 139 (see the Bibliography). It consists of choosing a random number between 1 and 52. The card at that position will be the new last card in the deck, and is exchanged with the current last card of the deck. This leaves us with the last card in position and 51 cards to be shuffled. We continue the process by choosing a random number from 1 to 51 and letting that card be the second last, and so on. This method of shuffling can also be used to pick a random sample. To choose m things from n things, we start out as if we were shuffling the n things, but do the picking only m times. The last m items resulting are our random sample.

The one remaining item to be discussed is how we handle aces, which can be counted in two ways. The answer is that we always count an ace as 11 if we can, and keep an integer ACEAS11 to tell us how many times this has been done (it can be done only twice). Then when we run over 21 this variable can be checked and, if nonzero, we can recount an ace as 1.

The program is

(* EXAMPLE 7.4.2: BLACK   *)

```
(* SIMULATE A BLACK-JACK *)
(* DEALER'S STRATEGY        *)

PROGRAM BLACK(OUTPUT);

CONST NTRIALS = 1000;        (* NUMBER OF HANDS *)
      HITME = 16;            (* TAKE ANOTHER CARD IF COUNT <= THIS *)
      SHUFFLEPOINT = 47; (* SHUFFLE WHEN THIS MANY CARDS DEALT *)

VAR   DECK: ARRAY [1 . . 52] OF INTEGER; (* REPRESENTS CARD DECK *)
      NCARD,                 (* NEXT CARD TO BE DEALT *)
      K,                     (* INDEX *)
      PTCT,                  (* POINT COUNT OF CURRENT HAND *)
      NONBUSTTOT,            (* TOTAL COUNT OF NON-BUST HANDS *)
      ACEAS11,               (* NUMBER OF ACES COUNTED AS 11 *)
      LOSSCT: INTEGER;   (* NUMBER OF BUST HANDS *)

FUNCTION RANDOM: REAL; EXTERN;

PROCEDURE SHUFFLE;
      (* SHUFFLE PSEUDO-DECK *)
    VAR I, J, T: INTEGER;
    BEGIN (* SHUFFLE *)
       FOR J := 52 DOWNTO 2 DO
          BEGIN
             I := TRUNC(J*RANDOM)+1   (* 1 <= I <= J *)
             T := DECK[I];  (* INTERCHANGE DECK[I] *)
             DECK[I] := DECK[J];  (* AND DECK[J] *)
             DECK[J] := T
          END;
       NCARD := 1
    END;  (* SHUFFLE *)

FUNCTION DEAL: INTEGER;
      (* DEAL NEXT CARD, SHUFFLING IF NECESSARY *)
    BEGIN (* DEAL *)
       IF (NCARD > SHUFFLEPOINT) THEN SHUFFLE;
       IF (DECK[NCARD] = 11) THEN ACEAS11 := ACEAS11 + 1;
       DEAL := DECK[NCARD] ; NCARD := NCARD + 1
    END;  (* DEAL *)

BEGIN  (* BLACK *)
         (* INITIALIZE DECK MYSTERIOUSLY *)
   FOR K := 1 TO 40 DO
      DECK[K] := (K + 7) DIV 4;  (* GIVES VALUES 2,2,2,2, *)
         (* 3, 3, 3, 3, 4, . . ., 11, 11, 11, 11 *)
   FOR K := 41 TO 52 DO DECK[K] := 10;  (* FACE CARDS *)
   NCARD := SHUFFLEPOINT+1;  (* FORCES INITIAL SHUFFLE *)
```

```
      NONBUSTTOT := 0; LOSSCT := 0;
      FOR K := 1 TO NTRIALS DO
          BEGIN   (* PLAY ONE HAND *)
              ACEAS11 := 0; PTCT := DEAL; (* DEAL FIRST CARD *)
              REPEAT
                 PTCT := PTCT + DEAL;
                 IF (PTCT > 21) AND (ACEAS11 > 0) THEN
                     BEGIN (* THIS WORKS IF WE CAN DO IT *)
                         ACEAS11 := ACEAS11 - 1;
                         PTCT := PTCT - 10
                     END
              UNTIL (PTCT > HITME);
              IF (PTCT > 21) THEN LOSSCT := LOSSCT + 1
              ELSE NONBUSTTOT := NONBUSTTOT + PTCT
          END;

      WRITELN('DEALER BUSTED ', LOSSCT * 100 / NTRIALS:1:2,
          '% OF THE TIME');
      WRITELN('AVERAGE POINT COUNT OF NON-BUST HANDS WAS ',
          NONBUSTTOT/(NTRIALS - LOSSCT):1:3)
      END;  (* BLACK *)
```

The results of executing this program were

```
DEALER BUSTED 29.10% OF THE TIME
AVERAGE POINT COUNT OF NON-BUST HANDS WAS 18.965
```

Exercises 7.4

1. How should the program of Example 7.4.2 be modified so that the dealer takes another card on a "soft 17," a point count of 17 with an ace counted as 11?

2. Write a procedure CHOOSE(M) which randomly chooses and prints M elements from an array A[1 .. N].

7.5   PROBABILITY AND THE EXPONENTIAL DISTRIBUTION

Before we introduce the exponential distribution, we need some facts about probability. First some definitions. An *event* is a set of some of the possible outcomes of an experiment. We will denote events by capital letters A, B, C, ... We say an event A *occurs* if the outcome of the experiment is in the set of outcomes A.

Example: The experiment is rolling two dice. The 36 possible outcomes are $(1, 1)$, $(1, 2)$, $(1, 3)$, $(1, 4)$, $(1, 5)$, $(1, 6)$, $(2, 1)$, . . ., $(6, 5)$, $(6, 6)$. The event "a total of 7 is rolled" is the set of 6 outcomes $(1, 6)$, $(2, 5)$, $(3, 4)$, $(4, 3)$, $(5, 2)$, $(6, 1)$.

A *probability function* is a function which might be declared in Pascal as P(A: event): REAL;. We think of $P(A)$ as the fraction of the time that the event A occurs. P satisfies the following properties:

1. $0 \leqslant P(A) \leqslant 1$ for all events A.
2. If an event S must occur, then $P(S) = 1$.
3. If an event N cannot occur, then $P(N) = 0$.
4. Two events are *mutually exclusive* if both cannot occur simultaneously. (The events "a total of 6 is rolled" and "a total of 8 is rolled" are mutually exclusive. The events "a total of 6 is rolled" and "one die is 3" are not mutually exclusive.) If $A1$, $A2, \ldots, An$ are all mutually exclusive then

$$P(A1 \text{ or } A2 \text{ or } \ldots \text{ or } An) = P(A1) + P(A2) + \cdots P(An)$$

Several useful facts can be derived from properties 1 to 4:

If A is any event, let not(A) be all outcomes not in event A. Then A and not(A) are mutually exclusive and "A or not(A)" is certain to occur, so

$$1 = P(A \text{ or not}(A)) = P(A) + P(\text{not}(A))$$

and we have property 5.

5. $P(\text{not}(A)) = 1 - P(A)$.

Now suppose that the outcomes of an experiment consist of n mutually exclusive events $A1$, $A2, \ldots, An$, and that all these events are equally likely; that is, $P(Ai) = P(Aj)$ for all i and j. Then

$$1 = P(A1 \text{ or } A2 \text{ or } \ldots \text{ or } An) = P(A1) + P(A2) + \cdots + P(An)$$
$$= P(Ai) + \cdots + P(Ai) = nP(Ai)$$

so $P(Ai) = 1/n$ for all i. If B is an event consisting of m of the Ai's, then $P(B) = m/n$. Hence, property 6.

6. If an experiment has n equally likely outcomes and B consists of m of them, then $P(B) = m/n$.

Example: Assuming the 36 outcomes of rolling a pair of dice are equally likely, P(a total of 7 is rolled) = 6/36 = 1/6.

A very good question is, "why is this set of events considered equally likely?" Why not consider the rolls of (4, 3) and (3, 4) the same? This would give us a total of 21 rolls, three of which total 7, and P(a total of 7 is rolled) = 3/21 = 1/7. Which is correct? The ultimate answer is that there is no way of telling from the mathematics alone. Intuition and reasoning can help, but the only way to determine which (if either) is correct is to determine which correctly describes the real-world situation. In fact, the first method, with 36 equally likely outcomes, is the correct one.

The final law we will discuss concerns independent events: Two events are *independent* if the probability of either occurring does not depend on whether the other occurs.

7.   If A and B are independent events, then $P(A$ and B both occur) $= P(A)P(B)$.

The most frequent use of independent events is *independent trials*. An experiment is repeated in such a way that the outcome of each trial (experiment) is independent of the outcomes of any other trials. If $A1, A2, \ldots, An$ are events in a single experiment and we assume independent trials, the probability of $A1$ on the first trial, $A2$ on the second, $\ldots, An$ on the nth is $P(A1)P(A2) \ldots P(An)$.

Example: The probability of *not* rolling 7 on either of two successive rolls of two dice is $(1 - 1/6) * (1 - 1/6) = 25/36$.

A *random variable* is a number associated with each outcome of the experiment. The *expected value* of a random variable is the *sum* of all terms of the form

$v * P(v$ occurs), $\quad$ v a value of the random variable

The *law of large numbers* of probability theory says that if we repeat an experiment many times (independent trials) the average value that the random variable takes gets closer and closer to the expected value.

Example: Consider again the rolling of two dice and let the random variable be the sum of the numbers rolled. The outcome 2 can occur in one way, $(1, 1)$. The outcome 3 can occur in two ways, $(1, 2)$ and $(2, 1)$. The outcome 4 can occur in three ways, $(1, 3), (2, 2)$, and $(3, 1)$, and so on. Thus the expected (or average) value of a roll is $2 * 1/36 + 3 * 2/36 + 4 * 3/36 + 5 * 4/36 + \cdots = 252/36 = 7$ (surprise!).

Example: We compute the expected number of comparisons for finding an item X in an array of n items using the linear search. The random variable is the number of comparisons, so the expectation is

$1 * P(1 \text{ comp}) + 2 * P(2 \text{ comps}) + \cdots + n * P(n \text{ comps})$

If all positions are equally likely, then each probabilty is $1/n$ and the expected value is

$1 * 1/n + 2 * 1/n + \cdots + n * 1/n = (1/n)(1 + 2 + \cdots + n)$

which, by the triangle principle, is $(1/n)n(n + 1)/2 = (n + 1)/2$. On the other hand, suppose that all items are not equally likely and suppose that the file has been arranged so that the more likely items come earlier. Suppose further that the probability of the kth item occurring is $2 ** -k$ and that the probability of X not being in the file at all is $2 ** -n$ (to make probabilities add up to 1). Then the expectation is

$$1 * 2 ** -1 + 2 * 2 ** -2 + \cdots + (n -1) * 2 ** -(n -1) + n * (2 ** -n + 2 ** -n)$$

which by Knuth, volume 1, Exercise 16 of Section 1.2.3, is seen to be less than 2.

We now introduce the *exponential distribution*. It is a good approximation for many naturally occurring phenomena, such as the random arrival of persons in a queue or service times for such persons. The random value of interest will be a number between 0 and infinity, which will be interpreted in various ways, say as the time between arrival of customers or the service times of customers. As you might expect, although very large values are possible, the larger the value, the less likely it is to occur (see Example 7.5.1).

To fix our ideas, consider a sequence of random numbers $r1, r2,$ . . ., rn, . . ., which are the times between arrivals of successive customers $c1, c2,$ . . ., cn (see Figure 7.1). The exponential distribution of r's satisfies the property that the probability of arrivals within any

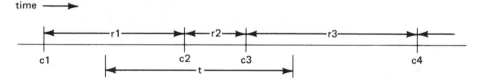

FIGURE 7.1

time interval depends only on the length of the interval and not on where it is or what has taken place in previous time intervals (e.g., customers are not discouraged by lines, and there is no variation as to time of day). The reader interested only in results can now skip to the Summary just before Example 7.5.1.

Let for instance $Po(t)$ be the probability of no arrivals within time t. The event "no arrivals for time $t1 + t2$" is the same as "no arrival for $t1$" and then "no arrival for $t2$." Since these are independent events,

$$Po(t1 + t2) = Po(t1)Po(t2)$$

It is also obviously the case that $Po(0) = 1$ (the certain event) and a little elementary calculus (see Exercise 7.5.4) shows that any reasonably well behaved function satisfying these properties is of the form

$$Po(t) = e ** (-mt)$$

with e as usual the base of natural logarithms, 2.71828. . ., and $m >$ 0. ($m = 0$ corresponds to the trivial case where there are no arrivals.)

We now want to show that if r is exponentially distributed as above, then $e ** (-mr)$ is *uniformly* distributed. Let a and b be numbers between 0 and infinity, $a \leqslant b$, and r be an exponentially distributed random number. We want to compute the probability that $a \leqslant r \leqslant b$. But this is the compound of two independent events: "no arrivals for time a" followed by "1 or more arrivals for time $b - a$." $P(1$ or more arrivals for time $b - a) = 1 - P($no arrivals for time $b - a)$ $= 1 - Po(b - a)$. Hence

$$P(a \leqslant r \leqslant b) = Po(a)(1 - Po(b - a))$$
$$= e ** (-ma) - e ** (-mb)$$

$a \leqslant r \leqslant b$ is equivalent to $e ** (-mb) \leqslant e ** (-mr) \leqslant e ** (-ma)$, so letting $x = e ** (-mb)$, $y = e ** (-ma)$, we have

$$P(x \leqslant e ** (-mr) \leqslant y) = y - x$$

that is, $e ** (-mr)$ is uniformly distributed as desired! $0 \leqslant 1 - e ** (-mr) < 1$, so $1 - e ** (-mr)$ looks just like a standard pseudo-random-number generator. Therefore, we can simulate the exponential distribution by solving $1 - e ** (-mr) = $ RANDOM for r. This gives $r = -\ln(1 - $ RANDOM$)/m$.

We now know how to generate an exponentially distributed sequence of pseudo-random numbers, but do not yet know the meaning of m. To do this, we give an informal argument requiring a little calculus. The reader who wishes to avoid the argument can skip to the Summary.

Let dt be an infinitesimally small quantity (nonrigorously, dt is a quantity so small that $dt ** 2 = 0$). Then

$$P(t \leqslant r \leqslant t + dt) = e ** (-m(t + dt)) - e ** (-mt)$$
$$= e ** (-mt) (e ** (-m\ dt) - 1)$$

If we plug $-m\ dt$ into the power series for e, we get $e ** (-m\ dt) = 1 -m\ dt + 0 - \cdots = 1 - m\ dt$, so $P(t \leqslant r \leqslant t + dt) = -me ** (-mt)\ dt$. The expected value of r is the sum of all terms of the form $t * P(t \leqslant r \leqslant t + dt)$, and such infinite sums of infinitesimals are found using integrals, in this case the integral from 0 to ∞ of $-mt\ e ** (-mt)\ dt$. When this integral is computed, the result is that the expected value of r is $1/m$.

Summary: The formula

$$-LN(1 - RANDOM)/M$$

generates exponentially distributed pseudo-random numbers with mean interarrival time $1/M$ and mean number of arrivals per unit of time M. The last fact follows from the fact that if the mean time between arrivals is X, we would expect T/X arrivals in a time interval of length T.

We finish up this section by making a histogram of an exponential distribution to see what it looks like.

EXAMPLE 7.5.1 Print out a histogram (see Example 7.4.1) for exponentially distributed pseudo-random numbers with mean interarrival time of 2. Also print out the actual average interarrival time.

In theory such a histogram would contain infinitely many bars, but the bars for large r will be very small, so we will only print out 30 of them. It seems reasonable to make the bars correspond to intervals of 0.20. The program is

```
(* EXAMPLE 7.5.1: EXPDIST      *)
(* PRINT HISTOGRAM OF          *)
(* EXPONENTIAL DISTRIBUTION *)

PROGRAM EXPDIST(OUTPUT);

CONST NBARS = 30;            (* NUMBER OF BARS IN CHART *)
      NTRIALS = 1000;        (* TOTAL NUMBER OF RAND NUMS *)
      BARINTRVL = 0.20;      (* INTERVAL IN A SINGLE BAR *)
      INTERMEAN = 2.0;       (* MEAN INTERARRIVAL TIME *)
      MAXBAR = 48;           (* APPROX MAXIMUM BAR LENGTH *)

VAR   CT: ARRAY[1 .. NBARS] OF INTEGER;  (* COUNTS *)
      R,                     (* EXPON DISTRIBUTED RANDOM NUMBER *)
      SUM,                   (* SUM OF THE R'S *)
      SCALE,                 (* TO SCALE BARS TO PAGE SIZE *)
      ARRSPERUNIT: REAL;     (* ARRIVALS PER TIME UNIT *)
      I,K: INTEGER;          (* MISCELLANEOUS COUNTERS, ETC. *)

FUNCTION RANDOM; REAL: EXTERN;

BEGIN (* EXPDIST *)
   SUM := 0; ARRSPERUNIT := 1/INTERMEAN;
   FOR K := 1 TO NBARS DO CT[K] := 0;
   FOR I := 1 TO NTRIALS DO
      BEGIN
         R := -LN(1 - RANDOM)/ARRSPERUNIT;
         SUM := SUM + R;
         K := TRUNC(R / BARINTRVL) + 1;
```

```
            IF (K <= NBARS) THEN CT[K] := CT[K] + 1
        END;
    WRITELN('AVERAGE = ', SUM/NTRIALS:1:5,
        ' FREQUENCY DISTRIBUTION IS . . .'); WRITELN;
    SCALE := MAXBAR/CT[1];
    FOR I := 1 TO NBARS DO
        BEGIN
            WRITE(I*BARINTRVL:4:2, '  ');
            FOR K := 1 TO ROUND(SCALE * CT[I]) DO
                WRITE('=');
            WRITELN
        END
END.  (* EXPDIST *)
```

The line SCALE := MAXBAR/CT[1] is to keep bars from running off the page and is based on the (mistaken) assumption that the first bar is the longest. The results of running this program are

```
AVERAGE = 2.05072 FREQUENCY DISTRIBUTION IS . . .

0.20  =================================================
0.40  ===================================================
0.60  ===========================================================
0.80  ===========================================
1.00  ===============================================
1.20  =======================================
1.40  =================================
1.60  ============================
1.80  ==================================
2.00  ============================
2.20  =====================
2.40  ===========================
2.60  ===================
2.80  ==============
3.00  ====================
3.20  ====================
3.40  ==========
3.60  ===============
3.80  =========
4.00  ======
4.20  ======
4.40  =======
4.60  ==========
4.80  ====
5.00  ====
5.20  ===
5.40  =====
5.60  ===
5.80  ==
6.00  ==
```

Exercises 7.5

1. Two dice are rolled. What is the probability that (a) a total of 11 is rolled; (b) a total of 7 or 11 is rolled?

2. Two dice are rolled. Show that the expected value of "larger result – smaller one" is 35/18.

3. What is the probability of flipping a coin three times and getting three successive heads?

4. (Requires calculus) Show that $Po(t) = e ** (-mt)$ for some $m \geqslant 0$ as follows:

(a) Use $Po(t1 + t2) = Po(t1)Po(t2)$ to show that $Po'(t) = Po'(0)Po(t) = -mPo(t)$, $m = -Po'(0)$.

(b) Show that $Po(t) = ce ** (-mt)$ using part (a). (*Hint:* Integrate Po'/Po.)

(c) Using properties of probability and part (b), show that $c = 1$ and $m \geqslant 0$.

7.6 SIMULATION

Many naturally occurring random phenomena are closely modeled by the exponential distribution. In this section we will talk about one of them, the *single server queue*. In this situation, customers arrive at various times to be served by the single server. Arrival times and service times are randomly distributed, here, we assume, with an exponential distribution. When the server is busy with another customer, arriving customers wait in line. We wish to determine the customer's average total service time, including waiting time.

It is shown in queueing theory that if arrivals are exponentially distributed at A per unit of time and service times are exponentially distributed at S per unit of time, then when equilibrium is reached in the system the average time for waiting and service is $1/(S - A)$. Thus, if customers arrive at the rate of 10 per hour and are served at the rate of 12 per hour, we have $A = 10$, $S = 12$, and an average total service-and-wait time of $1/(12 - 10) = \frac{1}{2}$ hour.

EXAMPLE 7.6.1 Find by simulation average total service-and-wait time for a single-server queue with average interarrival time of 3.0 and average service time of 2.0, both exponentially distributed. (In this case, $A = \frac{1}{3}$, $S = \frac{1}{2}$, so we would expect an average service-and-wait time of $1/(\frac{1}{2} - \frac{1}{3}) = 6.0$. The program uses a variable NEXTARRIVE to tell us when the next arrival will occur and a variable CLOCK to tell us when all the previous arrivals will have been served. To find out when the current arrival will be served, there are two cases: (1) NEXTARRIVE $<$ CLOCK means that one or more people are in the system when the current arrival happens. Total service-and-wait time is actual service time + CLOCK – NEXTARRIVE (the time for waiting in line). (2) NEXTARRIVE $\geq$ CLOCK means that there is no waiting. CLOCK is updated to NEXTARRIVE and total service-and-wait time is actual service time. In both cases, actual service time is added to CLOCK to make it ready for the next customer.

The program is

```
(* EXAMPLE 7.6.1: SSQUEUE          *)
(* SIMULATE SINGLE-SERVER QUEUE *)

PROGRAM SSQUEUE(INPUT, OUTPUT);

VAR  NTRIALS,        (* NUMBER OF SIMULATIONS *)
     NCUST,          (* NUMBER OF CUSTOMERS PER SIM *)
     T,              (* TRIAL INDEX *)
     C: INTEGER;     (* CUSTOMER INDEX *)
     ARRMEAN,        (* MEAN INTERARRIVAL TIME *)
     NEXTARRIVE,     (* TIME OF NEXT ARRIVAL *)
     SERVMEAN,       (* MEAN SERVICE TIME *)
     SERVTIME,       (* SERVICE TIME FOR A CUST. *)
     WAIT,           (* TOTAL WAIT TIME *)
     CLOCK: REAL;    (* SIMULATED CLOCK *)

FUNCTION RANDOM: REAL; EXTERN;

FUNCTION REXP(INTERMEAN: REAL): REAL;
     (* GENERATE EXPONENTIALLY DISTRIBUTED PSEUDO- *)
     (* RANDOM NUMBERS WITH EXPECTED VAL INTERMEAN *)
   BEGIN (* REXP *)
     REXP := – INTERMEAN * LN(1 – RANDOM)
   END;  (* REXP *)

BEGIN (* SSQUEUE *)
   WRITELN('NUMBER OF CUSTOMERS PER TRIAL:'); READ(NCUST);
   WRITELN('NUMBER OF TRIALS:'); READ(NTRIALS);
   WRITELN('AVERAGE INTERARRIVAL TIME:'); READ(ARRMEAN);
   WRITELN('MEAN SERVICE TIME:'); READ(SERVMEAN);

   FOR T := 1 TO NTRIALS DO
     BEGIN
         NEXTARRIVE := 0; (* ARRIVAL OF FIRST CUSTOMER *)
         CLOCK := REXP(SERVMEAN); (* HIS SERVICE TIME *)
         WAIT := CLOCK; (* AND HIS TOTAL SERVICE TIME *)
         FOR C := 2 TO NCUST DO
           BEGIN
               NEXTARRIVE := NEXTARRIVE + REXP(ARRMEAN);
               IF (NEXTARRIVE < CLOCK) THEN
                   WAIT := WAIT + CLOCK – NEXTARRIVE
```

```
                        (* ADD TIME TILL CLERK FREE *)
                ELSE CLOCK := NEXTARRIVE;
                        (* NO WAITING OVER SERVICE TIME *)
                SERVTIME := REXP(SERVMEAN);
                CLOCK := CLOCK + SERVTIME;
                WAIT := WAIT + SERVTIME
            END;
          WRITELN('TRIAL   ', T:1, ': AVERAGE TOTAL WAIT = ',
            WAIT / NCUST:1:5)
        END
    END.  (* SSQUEUE *)
```

The program was run with the following results:

```
NUMBER OF CUSTOMERS PER TRIAL:
? 500
NUMBER OF TRIALS:
? 3
AVERAGE INTERARRIVAL TIME:
? 3.0
MEAN SERVICE TIME:
? 2.0
TRIAL 1: AVERAGE TOTAL WAIT = 6.55206
TRIAL 2: AVERAGE TOTAL WAIT = 5.03060
TRIAL 3: AVERAGE TOTAL WAIT = 6.02090
```

Note that the redeclaration of CLOCK, a built-in function, works.

Exercise 7.6

In a single-server queue situation with exponential distribution, what is the expected waiting time if, on the average (a) customers arrive every 15 minutes and require 10 minutes to be served, and (b) customers arrive every 10 minutes and require 15 minutes to be served.

Programming Problems

7.1 Write a program to simulate 1000 crap games and print the percentage of times won (should be about 49%). The rules of the game are as follows: roll two dice. If the total is 2, 3, or 12, you lose immediately. If the total is 7 or 11, you win immediately. Otherwise the total rolled becomes your "point." Keep rolling until your point is rolled (you win) or a 7 is rolled (you lose). This constitutes one game. While checking out your program, use 100 games instead of 1000 to save computer time.

7.2 Write a computer program to simulate a queue situation with two servers. Assume that there are two lines and that the customer chooses the shorter one. Test the program as in Example 7.6.1 with average interarrival time of 1.5 and average service time of 2.0, both exponentially distributed (this is essentially twice as many customers and twice as many servers, but the same service time).

7.3 Write a computer program to sort 100 random files of the form

```
F: ARRAY [1 .. 15] OF
           RECORD
             KEY: REAL;
             FILLER: ARRAY [1 .. N] OF REAL
           END;
```

using random KEYs and various N's. Sort the same files using insertion (Example 3.5.1) and selection (Exercise 3.5.2) sorts, and try to determine for what value of N (if any) selection becomes better than insertion.

7.4 Write a program to generate random six-letter passwords for accounts on a time-sharing system. To make the passwords (more or less) pronounceable and thus easier to remember, observe the following rules:

(a) Two consecutive consonants are not allowed

(b) "aa," "ii," and "uu" are not allowed

(c) Three consecutive vowels are not allowed.

Choose letters in order, all letters having equal probability except for those that may be forbidden in a particular position.

chapter 8

hash-table searching

8.1 HASH TABLES

Looking back at the binary search, it would seem that there could not possibly be a faster method for searching large files. This is true as long as decisions are made based only on key *comparisons*. However, in this chapter we will meet a method which is in fact $O(1)$! Finding any item in the table will take only two or three looks (on the average) no matter how big the table is.

The basic idea of the method is simple: rather than looking at the whole table to find where something is, we apply a function to the key which tells us where to go in the file immediately. A trivial example of this technique is the way arrays are accessed: A[I] can be found directly by computing with the value I rather than a search being needed (although this has not stopped some programmers from doing such a search anyway).

When a location is computed from a key, an attempt is usually made to "smear" the keys out evenly across a range of values (the table indices). This is often done by cutting up and recombining pieces of the key, and for this reason the whole technique is often called *hashing* and the function used is called the *hashing function*.

A fundamental problem with hashing may already have occurred to you. Typically, there may be millions of different possible key values and perhaps only a few hundred table entries, which means that in many cases the hashing function applied to two different keys will take us to the same place (as we say, "hash to the same value"). This is called a *collision*, and the method of dealing with collisions is called *collision resolution*. Thus there are two decisions to be made: (1) how is the hashing function to be computed, and (2) how are collisions to be handled.

The first problem is the easier because there is one simple class of techniques which always produces acceptable results. One simply extracts an integer number from the key in some manner and then takes its remainder MOD the table size. To get a good spread of hash values, the table size should be a prime number (a number divisible only by 1 and itself). Otherwise, the hash value tends to depend on only part of the key. If the key is numeric, extracting a number is easy, and if it is alphabetic, the numeric representation of the characters is used. This is quite easy in most languages, which allow you to change types with no effort, whether you want to or not, but in Pascal the type change must be made explicit. One possibility for an array KEY of CHARs is

```
ORD(KEY[1]) * MULT + ORD(KEY[2])
```

MULT can be chosen a power of 2, which gives very fast multiplication on some Pascals. If, say, the machine in use has eight-bit characters, then defining MULT as 256 would have the effect of simply sliding KEY[1] left and placing it next to KEY[2], then interpreting the whole thing as an integer.

The problem of collision resolution is much more interesting. The simplest technique is to consider each entry in the table as a pointer to the start of a linked list of all items with the same hash value. If there are T slots in the table and N items in the file to be searched, we would expect that each list would have about N/T items, so it would require no more than about N/T comparisons on the average to find any item. To keep this number of comparisons down, we simply increase T (another example of trading storage for speed).

For instance, if we never expect to deal with files of more than 1000 items, we could start with a table of 337 initial list pointers (337 is prime) and expect about three comparisons per search, assuming that our hashing function spread things out reasonably well.

EXAMPLE 8.1.1 Construct a hash table for the German-to-English number problem using linked lists for collision resolution. This problem is really too small to be a worthwhile application of hashing techniques, but it has the advantage of being small enough that we can easily view the entire table that is built.

Picking a table size of 7, the program becomes:

```
(* EXAMPLE 8.1.1: HASH1   *)
(* HASHING WITH LINKED   *)
(* COLLISION RESOLUTION *)


PROGRAM HASH1(INPUT, OUTPUT);

CONST   MULT=256;       (* = 2**BITS PER CHAR *)
        TABLEN=7;       (* LENGTH OF INITIAL POINTER TABLE *)
        TM1=6;          (* := TABLEN – 1 *)

TYPE    PTRTONODE = ^NODE;
        NODE = RECORD GER, ENG: ALFA; LINK: PTRTONODE END;

VAR     TABLE: ARRAY [0 .. TM1] OF PTRTONODE; (* INITIAL POINTERS *)
        FOUND: BOOLEAN;   (* TO TERMINATE LINKED LIST SEARCH *)
        P: PTRTONODE;     (* RUNNING LIST POINTER *)
        H,                (* HASH VALUE *)
        N,                (* NUMBER OF ITEMS LOOKED UP *)
        COMPS: INTEGER;   (* TOTAL NUMBER OF COMPARISONS *)
        GWORD,            (* GERMAN WORD SOUGHT *)
        EWORD: ALFA;      (* CORRESPONDING ENGLISH WORD *)

FUNCTION HASH(X: ALFA): INTEGER;
    (* RETURNS HASH INDEX OF X *)
  BEGIN (* HASH *)
      HASH := (MULT*ORD(X[1]) + ORD (X[2])) MOD TABLEN
  END; (* HASH *)
BEGIN (* HASH1 *)
    FOR H := 0 TO TABLEN–1 DO TABLE[H] := NIL;

    WRITELN('ENTER GERMAN WORDS, TERMINATING WITH ****');
    READLN(GWORD); N := 0; COMPS := 0;
    WHILE (GWORD <> '****          ') DO
        BEGIN
            N := N + 1; H := HASH(GWORD); P := TABLE[H];
            FOUND := FALSE; COMPS := COMPS + 1;
            WHILE (P <> NIL) AND NOT FOUND DO
                BEGIN
                    COMPS := COMPS + 1;
                    IF (P^.GER = GWORD) THEN FOUND := TRUE
```

```
                ELSE P := P^.LINK
            END;
        IF FOUND THEN WRITELN('THE ENGLISH IS  ', P^.ENG)
        ELSE
            BEGIN
                WRITELN('WHAT IS THE ENGLISH FOR THAT',
                    ' (X FOR ERROR)');
                READLN(EWORD);
                IF (EWORD <> 'X             ') THEN
                    BEGIN
                        NEW(P); P^.GER := GWORD; P^.ENG := EWORD;
                        P^. LINK := TABLE[H] ; TABLE [H] := P
                    END
            END;
        READLN(GWORD)
    END;

    IF (N > 0) THEN WRITELN('AVG NUMBER OF COMPARES WAS ',
        COMPS/N:1:3);
    FOR H := 0 TO TABLEN-1 DO
        BEGIN (* PRINT OUT TABLE OF LINKED LISTS *)
            WRITE(H:2); P := TABLE[H] ;
            WHILE (P <> NIL) DO
                BEGIN
                    WRITE(' --> ', P^.GER );
                    P := P^.LINK
                END;
            WRITELN
        END
END. ( *HASH1 *)
```

When the program was run, the ten German numbers were entered by hand as follows:

```
ENTER GERMAN WORDS, TERMINATING WITH ****
? EINS
WHAT IS THE ENGLISH FOR THAT (X FOR ERROR)
? ONE
? ZWEI
WHAT IS THE ENGLISH FOR THAT (X FOR ERROR)
? TWO
? TROIS
WHAT IS THE ENGLISH FOR THAT (X FOR ERROR)
? X
? etc.
```

and then various sample lookups were performed, ending with

```
? ZEHN
```

```
THE ENGLISH IS TEN
? * * * *
AVERAGE NUMBER OF COMPARISONS WAS 2.048
   0
   1 -- > FUNF
   2 -- > ZEHN        -- > SECHS
   3 -- > NEUN
   4 -- > VIER        -- > DREI
   5 -- > ACHT
   6 -- > SIEBEN      -- > ZWEI      -- > EINS
```

Several remarks are in order:

1. COMPS is augmented both inside and outside the search loop so that the comparison that fails and ends the search loop is also counted; that is, COMPS is the number of times the WHILE condition is tested.

2. Hash tables are clearly highly useful for files which are highly volatile; they are fast to search and it is easy to add (and delete) items from the file.

3. On the other hand, it is generally quite difficult to set up a hash table by hand and therefore it is usually re-created, as in the preceding, from scratch each time the program is run. This is no problem in what is one of the most common applications of hash tables: tables of symbols in programming language translators. Usually, such tables consist of at most a few predefined symbols, the rest being particular to the program being translated, and thus the table must be constructed more or less from scratch anyway.

Returning to the general problem of collision resolution, a hash table may also be in the form of a linear array of entries, saving the space necessary for pointers. This method is called *open addressing* and requires a different method of collision resolution. For the moment, we consider the simplest method, *linear collision resolution.* In this method, we assume that it is possible to tell if a table entry is empty or not, and that there is always at least one empty table entry (to stop a linear search). The hashing function tells us where to start a linear search, which ends when the desired item is found (success) or an empty entry is found (failure). The table is treated like a circular queue, with the beginning entry immediately following the end one.

EXAMPLE 8.1.2 Write a program to do the German-to-English translation using a hash table with open addressing and linear collision resolution. We will need a table which is at least one larger than the number of items (to guarantee an empty entry). We choose a table size of 13 since, as we will see later, it is a good idea to have the table a fair amount larger than necessary (again trading storage for time). We say that a table entry is empty if it has a German part which is all blanks. The program is

```
            (* EXAMPLE 8.1.2: HASH2            *)
            (* HASHING WITH OPEN ADDRESSING  *)


     PROGRAM HASH2(INPUT, OUTPUT);

     CONST   MULT=256;         (* = 2**BITS PER CHAR *)
             TABLEN=13;        (* HASH TABLE LENGTH *)
             TM1=12;           (* = TABLEN - 1 *)


     TYPE    ENTRY=RECORD GER, ENG: ALFA END;


     VAR     TABLE: ARRAY [0 . . TM1] OF ENTRY; (* HASH TABLE *)
             H,                (* VALUE OF HASH *)
             N,                (* NUMBER OF WORDS LOOKED UP *)
             COMPS,            (* TOTAL NUMBER OF COMPARISONS *)
             CT: INTEGER;      (* NUMBER OF USED SLOTS IN TABLE *)
                               (* CAN BE AT MOST TABLEN - 1 *)
             GWORD,            (* GERMAN WORD TO LOOK UP *)
             EWORD: ALFA;  (* CORRESPONDING ENGLISH WORD *)

     FUNCTION HASH(X:ALFA); INTEGER;
             (* RETURNS HASH OF X *)
         BEGIN (* HASH *)
             HASH := (MULT*ORD(X[1]) + ORD(X[2])) MOD TABLEN
         END; (* HASH *)

     BEGIN (* HASH2 *)
         FOR H := 0 TO TABLEN–1 DO TABLE[H] .GER := '

         WRITELN('ENTER GERMAN WORDS, TERMINATING WITH ****');
         READLN(GWORD); N := 0; COMPS := 0; CT := 0;
         WHILE (GWORD <> '****        ') DO
             BEGIN
                 N := N + 1; COMPS := COMPS + 1;
                 H := HASH(GWORD);
                 WHILE (TABLE[H] .GER <> GWORD) AND
                     (TABLE[H] .GER <> '          ') DO
                     BEGIN
                         COMPS := COMPS + 1; H := H + 1;
                         IF (H = TABLEN) THEN H := 0
                     END;
```

```
                    IF (TABLE[H].GER = GWORD) THEN
                        WRITELN('THE ENGLISH IS   ', TABLE[H].ENG)
                    ELSE
                        BEGIN
                            WRITELN('WHAT IS THE ENGLISH FOR THAT',
                                '  (X FOR ERROR)');
                            READLN(EWORD);
                            IF (EWORD <> 'X              ') THEN
                                BEGIN
                                    IF (CT >= TABLEN-1) THEN
                                        WRITELN('TABLE FULL')
                                    ELSE
                                        BEGIN
                                            CT := CT + 1;
                                            TABLE[H].GER := GWORD;
                                            TABLE[H].ENG := EWORD
                                        END
                                END
                        END;
                    READLN(GWORD)
                END;

        IF (N > 0) THEN WRITELN('AVERAGE NUMBER OF COMPARISONS WAS ',
            COMPS/N:1:3);
        FOR H := 0 TO TABLEN-1 DO
            BEGIN
                WRITE(H:2);
                IF (TABLE[H].GER <> '              ') THEN
                    WRITE('     ', TABLE[H].GER, HASH(TABLE[H].GER):4);
                WRITELN
            END
    END. (* HASH2 *)
```

After words were entered as before, the final output produced was

```
AVERAGE NUMBER OF COMPARISONS WAS 1.900
 0    ZWEI      0
 1    FUNF      0
 2    VIER      2
 3    SIEBEN    1
 4    ACHT      2
 5    EINS      5
 6    DREI      5
 7    NEUN      4
 8    ZEHN      8
 9
10    SECHS    10
11
12
```

(The fact that the last entries of the table are empty is coincidental.)

Note that the hashing function takes us to our destination immediately for ZWEI, VIER, EINS, ZEHN, and SECHS, and that two probes are required for FUNF and DREI, three for SIEBEN and ACHT, and four for NEUN.

With tables this small, no useful comparison can be made between the two methods we have used. In general, in terms of storage used, the linked method requires extra space for the links, whereas open addressing requires unused table entries. However, the first method uses only as much storage as is actually needed for the particular table searched, while in the open-addressing method a fixed area of storage must be given over to the table which is large enough to accommodate any table desired.

It is generally difficult to predict the average number of comparisons necessary in open addressing. We will resort instead to simulations with random numbers. It will turn out that in open addressing the key to determining search time is not the table size, but a quantity a called the *load factor*, which is defined by

$$a = \text{load factor} = \text{table entries in use/table size}$$

It is generally the case that if $a \leqslant 0.75$ the performance of the method cannot be significantly improved by making the table larger, and that as long as $a \leqslant 0.90$, performance is at least satisfactory.

EXAMPLE 8.1.3 Simulate performance of hashing with open addressing and linear collision resolution for various combinations of table size and load factor. The particular keys are unimportant, so we will start with the *value* of the hashing function. Since it is desirable that that be uniformly distributed between 0 and (table size - 1), we will simply generate such numbers with a pseudo-random-number generator. Another simplifying assumption will be that all keys occur about equally often so that we can simulate trying all searches by merely doing one per key. Thus we will generate $N = $ (load factor) $*$ (table size) random numbers and consider that each of them belongs to a different key, so all that the searching will involve is finding an empty entry to put the new key into. The program is

```
(* EXAMPLE 8.1.3: HASH3              *)
(* RANDOM SIMULATION OF HASHING *)
(* WITH OPEN ADDRESSING AND         *)
(* LINEAR COLLISION RESOLUTION     *)

PROGRAM HASH3(INPUT, OUTPUT);
```

```
CONST    MAXTABSIZE=9999; (* MAXIMUM HASH TABLE SIZE *)
         ARBITRARY=10; (* LIMIT ON NUM OF LOADS, TABLE SIZES *)

TYPE     USETYPE=(OCCUPIED, FREE); (* FOR TABLE ENTRIES *)

VAR      TAB: PACKED ARRAY [0 . . MAXTABSIZE] OF USETYPE;
             (* HASH TABLE *)
         TABSIZE: ARRAY [1 . . ARBITRARY] OF INTEGER; (* TABLE SIZES *)
         LOADFACTOR: ARRAY [1 . . ARBITRARY] OF REAL;
                     (* LOAD FACTORS *)
         NTS,           (* NUMBER OF TABLE SIZES *)
         NLF,           (* NUMBER OF LOAD FACTORS *)
         ITS,           (* INDEX TO TABSIZE ARRAY *)
         ILF,           (* INDEX TO LOADFACTOR ARRAY *)
         TS,            (* TABSIZE[ITS] *)
         N,             (* ENTRIES USED = TS * LOADFACTOR[ILF] *)
         I,             (* TAB ENTRY COUNTER *)
         COMPS: INTEGER;   (* NUMBER OF COMPARISONS *)

FUNCTION RANDOM: REAL; EXTERN;

BEGIN (* HASH3 *)
   (* READ IN LOADFACTORS AND TABLE SIZES *)
   WRITELN('NUMBER OF LOAD FACTORS:'); READ (NLF);
   WRITELN('ENTER LOAD FACTORS:');
   FOR ILF := 1 TO NLF DO READ(LOADFACTOR[ILF]);
   WRITELN('NUMBER OF TABLE SIZES:'); READ(NTS);
   WRITELN ('ENTER TABLE SIZES:')
   FOR ITS := 1 TO NTS DO READ(TABSIZE[ITS]);

   WRITELN; WRITELN('AVERAGE NUMBER OF COMPARISONS . . .'); WRITELN;
   WRITE('LOAD   ':9);
   FOR ILF := 1 TO NLF DO WRITE(LOADFACTOR[ILF] :7:2);
   WRITELN; WRITELN(' SIZE');

   FOR ITS := 1 TO NTS DO
      BEGIN (* WRITE LINE FOR TABSIZE[ITS] *)
         TS := TABSIZE[ITS]; WRITE(TS:6, '      ');
         FOR ILF := 1 TO NLF DO
            BEGIN (* COMPUTE AVG COMPS FOR ONE PAIR *)
               N := TRUNC(LOADFACTOR[ILF] *TS);
               FOR H := 0 TO TS-1 DO TAB[H] := FREE;
               COMPS := 0;
               FOR I := 1 TO N DO
                  BEGIN (* LOOK UP ONE ENTRY *)
                     H := TRUNC(TS*RANDOM); COMPS := COMPS + 1;
                     WHILE (TAB[H] = OCCUPIED) DO
```

```
                    BEGIN (* ADVANCE TO NEXT ENTRY *)
                      H := H + 1; COMPS := COMPS + 1;
                      IF (H = TS) THEN H := 0
                    END;
                  TAB[H] := OCCUPIED
                END;
              WRITE(COMPS/N:7:2);
            END;
          WRITELN
        END
END. (* HASH3 *)
```

The results of a sample run were

NUMBER OF LOAD FACTORS:
? 5
ENTER LOAD FACTORS:
? 0.5 0.75 0.9 0.95 0.99
NUMBER OF TABLE SIZES:
? 3
ENTER TABLE SIZES:
? 503 997 9973

AVERAGE NUMBER OF COMPARISONS . . .

LOAD SIZE	0.50	0.75	0.90	0.95	0.99
503	1.39	2.49	3.73	6.43	13.12
997	1.55	2.73	4.39	9.76	19.00
9973	1.54	2.55	5.86	9.47	23.33

Notice that, except for minor variations perhaps due to chance, the number of comparisons seems to depend mostly on the load factor. (In real life, I would expect the number of comparisons to go up a little faster than this because I would not expect a real hashing function to give as even a spread of values.) Recall also that the expected number of comparisons with the binary search and a table of 500, 1000, of 10,000 items would be about 9, 10, and 13, respectively.

(The remainder of this section can be skipped on first reading.)

Linear collision resolution has an important flaw: table entries tend to cluster together as the table fills up, which causes a long linear search. By a "cluster" we mean an adjacent set of filled table entries. Since a bigger cluster is in effect a bigger target, the odds are that if you hit a cluster you will hit a big one, and with linear collision resolution no matter where you hit in the cluster, you add to the length of the search for *all* the items in the cluster.

One solution to this problem is instead of searching H, H + 1,

H + 2, . . . , as in linear resolution, search H, H + 1, H + 4, H + 9, . . . ,
H + I**2, . . . , a method called *quadratic collision resolution.* Now
clusters do not make as much sense intuitively, but a long search chain
from H would look like Figure 8.1, while if another item hashes to, say,
K = H + 4, then there will be little overlap in the sequences searched
(see Figure 8.2).

An important question concerning quadratic resolution is just
which entries of the table will it reach. Conceivably, it might only look

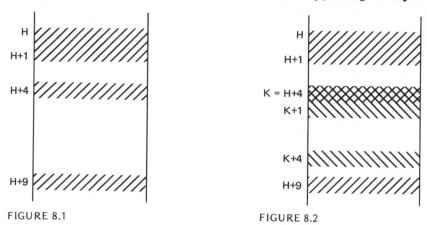

FIGURE 8.1   FIGURE 8.2

at a few entries in the table before the sequence repeats itself. In fact, it
is easy to see that when the table size is prime we will cover at least half
the table, and that is enough.

The successive values searched are H, (H+1) MOD TABSIZE,
(H+4) MOD TABSIZE, . . . , (H+I**2) MOD TABSIZE, . . . , so we
could start by asking when it can happen that

$$(*)\ (H+I**2)\ MOD\ TABSIZE = (H+J**2)\ MOD\ TABSIZE$$

There seems no point in considering I or J ⩾ TABSIZE, as there are
only TABSIZE entries in the table. Hence we assume I < J ⩽ TABSIZE.
Formula (*) can only happen if J**2 - I**2 is divisible by TABSIZE.
As J**2 - I**2 = (J - I) * (J + I), if TABSIZE is prime, then TABSIZE
must divide J - I or J + I, and since it cannot divide J - I (< TAB-
SIZE), it must divide J + I. This means that J + I ⩾ TABSIZE, and
hence J ⩾ TABSIZE/2. Therefore, the first TABSIZE/2 values of H,
H + 1, H + 4, . . . , give us all different entries in our table, so quadratic
searching takes us through half of the table, at least. Since that already
represents a sizable length for a search, we will simply agree that the table is full when we get that far and have not found an empty slot. (Although this could happen with the table actually only half-full, in
practice it seldom happens unless the table is very nearly full.)

Before presenting a program, it is worth considering how (H+I**2) MOD TABSIZE can be generated easily. Note that

$$(H + (I+1)**2) - (H + I**2) = 2*I + 1$$

That is, successive squares differ by successive odd numbers. Also note that I will become $\geq$ TABSIZE/2 exactly when $2*I + 1$ becomes $>$ TABSIZE. In the following implementation we will keep an integer D whose value is the next odd integer. To get from the last probe location H := (H + I**2) MOD TABSIZE to the next, we merely add D to H and take the result MOD TABSIZE. For the last operation we do not need a division, because if H $<$ TABSIZE and D $\leq$ TABSIZE, then certainly H + D - TABSIZE $<$ TABSIZE.

EXAMPLE 8.1.4 Simulate performance of hashing with open addressing and quadratic collision handling. The program is the same as in Example 8.1.3 except that an integer variable D is declared and the search loop "LOOK UP ONE ENTRY" becomes

```
H := TRUNC(TS * RANDOM);
COMPS := COMPS + 1; D := 1;
WHILE (TAB[H] = OCCUPIED) AND (D <= TS) DO
    BEGIN
        H := H + D; D := D + 2; COMPS := COMPS + 1;
        IF (H >= TS) THEN H := H - TS
    END;
IF (D > TS) THEN
    WRITELN('TABLE FULL')
ELSE TAB[H] := OCCUPIED
```

When this program was run with data as in Example 8.1.3, the results were

AVERAGE NUMBER OF COMPARISONS . . .					
LOAD	0.50	0.75	0.90	0.95	0.99
SIZE					
503	1.36	1.95	2.79	3.27	3.84
997	1.50	2.04	2.83	3.27	4.60
9973	1.42	1.95	2.71	3.39	5.02

Quite a dramatic improvement, for a minimum of effort!

Exercises 8.1

1. Assuming you are given a HASH function and table structure as in Example 8.1.1, write code to read a German word X and delete its entry from the table.

2. Consider the problem of deleting entries from an open addressing table.

You cannot simply mark the entry empty. For instance, in the German number table, if DREI were deleted and its entry set to empty, we then could not find NEUN anymore as it would still hash to 4, but the search would stop at the empty entry 6. Suggest a method for handling such deletions successfully.

3. Write a program which takes as input an integer N and which produces as output the smallest prime number $\geqslant N/0.9$. What is such a program good for?

4. The method used here for constructing a hashing function would not be very good for a table of variable names in a compiler, as programmers often have many variable names which start with the same two characters: SUM1, SUM2, and so on. Suggest possible improvements on the method given here.

8.2 AN APPLICATION:
FINITE-STATE MACHINES

In this section we will develop a program which reads numbers up to 999 in words and prints their numerical value. Various inputs will be allowed, such as ONE HUNDRED SEVEN, ONE OH SEVEN, and ONE HUNDRED AND SEVEN. Making a table of number words and finding values for individual words is a straightforward application of hashing techniques. The interesting part of the program is interpreting combinations of number words, whose meanings vary with context. Consider, for instance, SEVENTY FIVE and FIVE SEVENTY. Organization is a real problem here, and often the best way to solve problems of this type is to use the finite state machine approach.

A *finite-state machine* is a collection of nodes (called *states*) with an arrow leaving each node for each possible input that can be encountered at that node. To operate the machine, we start at a particular node, called the START state, and read an input and follow the arrow labeled with that input to the next state, where we read the next input and continue the process. Typically, we also perform some auxiliary computations during the process. The state we end in can be used to determine whether we processed input in a legal sequence.

As an example, let's look at a finite-state machine to process numbers of the form ±XXX.XXX, where the sign is optional and there may be arbitrarily many digits on either side of the decimal point. All we will do here is check numbers for correct form; it is an easy matter to add code to accumulate their numeric values at the same time.

The problem is to allow the sign only once and at the beginning, to allow the decimal point only once and to require at least one digit. We could number the states (from 0, say) but in a language like Pascal it is much more useful to create an enumerated type with values to name the nodes with. Figure 8.3 is a machine for numbers with state names written beside the nodes. If, for instance, we are in the START

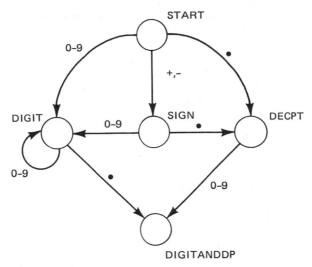

FIGURE 8.3

state, a digit 0-9 takes us to the DIGIT state, a decimal point to DECPT, and a + or - sign to SIGN. As is often the case, we will also postulate a state ERROR into which we will go in case of an illegal input in any state, but we will not show it or all its arrows in the diagram. The input +12.34 would take us through the states START, SIGN, DIGIT, DIGITANDDP, DIGITANDDP, and the input .12. takes us through the states START, DECPT, DIGITANDDP, DIGITANDDP, ERROR. If we end in states DIGIT or DIGITANDDP, the number is properly formed. It is easy to write a program to simulate the actions of this finite-state machine. We can declare a

```
VAR STATE: (START,DIGIT,SIGN,DECPT,DIGITANDDP,ERROR);
```

to keep track of which state we are in and process each input character through a CASE statement on STATE. The finite-state machine to read numbers ±XXX.XXX then might be realized as follows (remember that all we are doing is checking for proper form).

```
STATE := START; READ(C);
WHILE (C <> ' ') DO
    BEGIN
        CASE STATE OF
    START:  IF (C >= '0') AND (C <= '9') THEN STATE := DIGIT
            ELSE IF (C = '+') OR (C = '-') THEN STATE := SIGN
            ELSE IF (C = '.') THEN STATE := DECPT
            ELSE STATE := ERROR;
    DIGIT:  IF (C = '.') THEN STATE := DIGITANDDP
            ELSE IF (C < '0') OR (C > '9') THEN STATE := ERROR;
```

```
   SIGN:  IF (C >= '0') AND (C <= '9') THEN STATE := DIGIT
            ELSE IF (C = '.') THEN STATE := DECPT
            ELSE STATE := ERROR;
   DECPT:  IF (C >= '0') AND (C <= '9') THEN
                STATE := DIGITANDDP
            ELSE STATE := ERROR;
DIGITANDDP: IF (C < '0') OR (C > '9') THEN STATE := ERROR;
   ERROR: (* DO NOTHING *)
      END; (* OF CASE STATE *)
      READ(C)
   END; (* OF WHILE C <> ' ' *)
CASE STATE OF
START,SIGN,DECPT,ERROR: WRITELN('BAD NUMBER');
      DIGITANDDP,DIGIT: WRITELN('GOOD NUMBER')
END
```

Now let's construct the finite-state machine for our number-word reading problem. In the intitial START state there are several possibilities:

1. The digits ONE-NINE can either be the entire number or can be followed by HUNDRED, OH, or a number from TEN to NINETY NINE. We will let state DIGIT deal with these possibilities.

2. The numbers TEN-NINETEEN must be complete numbers. We let state DONE indicate that no more input is allowed.

3. TWENTY, THIRTY, . . . , NINETY can either be complete numbers or can be followed by a digit. Let state UMPTY be the state of looking for a digit or nothing.

Any other input causes state ERROR. We will not show it in the diagram to avoid confusion. To begin with we have Figure 8.4. Now look at DIGIT. In this state we could encounter HUNDRED (which must be followed by AND or ONE-NINETY NINE), which takes us to a

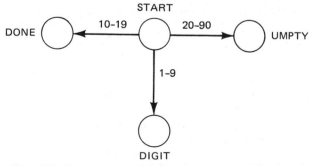

FIGURE 8.4

new state HUNDRED; OH (which can only be followed by a digit ONE-NINE), which takes us to state OH; or TEN-NINETEEN, which takes us to state DONE; or TWENTY-NINETY, which takes us to UMPTY. Thus the arrows from DIGIT are as in Figure 8.5.

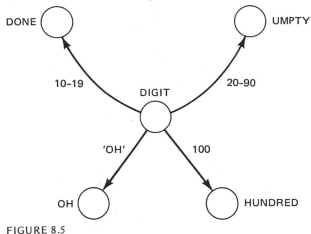

FIGURE 8.5

In DONE the occurrence of anything is an error, and in UMPTY the digits ONE-NINE take us to DONE. In state OH it is also the case that the digits ONE-NINE take us to DONE and that nothing else is legal. States UMPTY and OH are not the same though, because it is legal to end in UMPTY but not in OH. Finally, in HUNDRED, 1–19 takes us to DONE, 20–90 to UMPTY, and AND to a new state ANDS (we cannot call it AND as that would conflict with the reserved word AND), which is just like HUNDRED except that 'AND' is not allowed and it is not legal to end in state ANDS (ONE HUNDRED AND is not a legal number). Figure 8.6 gives the complete diagram of the finite-state machine (omitting ERROR).

EXAMPLE 8.2.1 Turn the finite-state machine of Figure 8.6 into a program. There are a couple of problems left to solve, generally concerned with the Pascal language rather than the program itself. The first and easier is the matter of table initialization. This is awkward in Pascal, so we have chosen to do so by reading table data from a file. And what better file than the program text itself! Thus the data serve as a comment at the beginning of the program text and are unlikely to get lost, strayed, or stolen. Special conventional values are given to AND and OH, and we will put those in as CONSTs ANDVAL and OHVAL to make them easy to remember.

A much more serious problem is the usual Pascal headache, input. When writing this program I first considered requiring the user to use

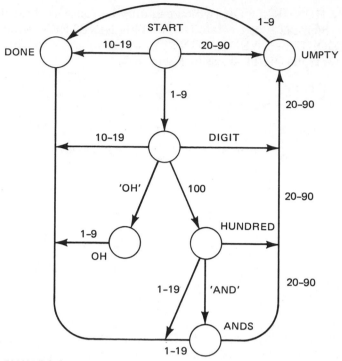

FIGURE 8.6

special tricky forms of input, but finally decided that at this point in the book it was time to pick a reasonable input format, and *then* worry about how to implement it. The format chosen is that each number (in words, perhaps several words each) shall appear on a separate line and that the program shall be terminated by a line consisting of four asterisks: ****.

One problem is that words can be terminated by regular blanks or EOLN blanks, and in the latter case we have to be careful not to read that blank and lose the EOLN indication. On the other hand, the operating system or the user might put extra blanks at the end of the line, and we want this to register correctly as an end of line. To take care of this we will write a

FUNCTION EOLNS: BOOLEAN;

which skips to the next nonblank or end of line in INPUT and returns the value of EOLN. A problem here is that, if we READ a character to see if it is blank, then we cannot reread it later to use it in a word. We could maintain a "last character read" variable, but this delicacy is certainly to be avoided if possible. Here, finally, Pascal's I/O comes to

236

the rescue, and its habit of reading ahead, which has proved such a bother, now is a help. As we shall see in greater detail in Section 9.1, if F is any file variable, then F acts like a pointer to the next record to be read; that is, in the case of INPUT, INPUT^ is the next character to be read. Also highly useful is the built-in procedure GET(file-variable), which in the case of a TEXT file advances to the next character in the file but does not read it into a character variable. READ(F, C) is equivalent to C := F^ ; GET(F).

The code to process one line is

```
WHILE NOT EOLNS DO
    BEGIN
        read word X;
        process word X
    END;
cleanup;
READLN (* to prepare for next line of input *)
```

To repeat this until '****' is read, we can include '****' in our number word table and put a transition arrow from START to a new state STOP in our finite-state machine on '****'. The outline of the whole main loop is

```
REPEAT
    STATE:= START;
    process one line (as above)
UNTIL STATE = STOP
```

We can write a procedure RWORD to read words, and it becomes particularly simple as EOLNS guarantees that there are no leading blanks to skip over. On the other hand, if we do skip blanks and pass the file as a parameter, we can use the same procedure to read table initialization! F^ and GET(F) as described previously can also be profitably used.

Finally, since we go into the ERROR state and print an error message so many places, that is done in a separate procedure, SETERROR. The complete program is

```
        (* EXAMPLE 8.2.1: NUMWRDS       *)
        (* READ NUMBERS IN ENGLISH AND *)
        (* PRINT THEIR NUMERIC VALUE    *)


    (* NUMWDS DATA: ONE 1 TWO 2 THREE 3 FOUR 4 FIVE 5 SIX 6
        SEVEN 7 EIGHT 8 NINE 9 TEN 10 ELEVEN 11 TWELVE 12
        THIRTEEN 13 FOURTEEN 14 FIFTEEN 15 SIXTEEN 16 SEVENTEEN 17
        EIGHTEEN 18 NINETEEN 19 TWENTY 20 THIRTY 30 FORTY 40
        FIFTY 50 SIXTY 60 SEVENTY 70 EIGHTY 80 NINETY 90
        HUNDRED 100 AND 900 OH 999 **** –1 *)
```

```
PROGRAM NUMWRDS(INPUT, OUTPUT, NUMWDS);

CONST   TABLEN = 39;  (* HASH TABLE SIZE *)
        TM1 = 38;        (* = TABLEN – 1 *)
        MULT = 256;      (* = 2**BITS PER CHAR *)
        ANDVAL = 900;(* VALUE GIVEN TO 'AND' *)
        OHVAL = 999;  (* VALUE GIVEN TO 'OH' *)
        STOPVAL = –1; (* VALUE GIVEN TO '****' *)


TYPE    ENTRY = RECORD WD: ALFA; VAL: INTEGER END;


VAR     TABLE: ARRAY [0 .. TM1] OF ENTRY; (* OPEN ENTRY HASH
               TABLE *)
        NUMWDS: TEXT;        (* THIS VERY FILE *)
        W: ALFA;               (* THE WORD READ BY RWORD *)
        STATE: (START,DONE,UMPTY,DIGIT,OH,HUNDRED,
               ANDS,ERROR,STOP); (* STATE MACHINE STATES *)
        H,                     (* INDEX INTO HASH TABLE *)
        V,                     (* LOOKED UP VALUE OF W *)
        TOT: INTEGER;        (* ACCUMULATED VALUE OF NUMBER *)

FUNCTION EOLNS: BOOLEAN;
     (* SKIP TO NEXT NONBLANK OR EOLN AND RETURN EOLN *)
   BEGIN (* EOLNS *)
     WHILE (INPUT^ = ' ') AND NOT EOLN DO GET(INPUT);
     EOLNS := EOLN
   END; (* EOLNS *)


PROCEDURE SETERROR;
     (* PRINT ERROR MESSAGE AND SET STATE TO ERROR *)
   BEGIN (* SETERROR *)
     IF (STATE <> ERROR) THEN (* ONLY DO IT ONCE *)
        BEGIN
           WRITELN(W, '  <- - ERROR'); STATE := ERROR
        END
   END; (* SETERROR *)


PROCEDURE RWORD(VAR F: TEXT);
     (* READ NEXT WORD FROM FILE F INTO GLOBAL W *)
   VAR I: INTEGER;
   BEGIN (* RWORD *)
     W := '          ';
     WHILE (F^ = ' ') DO GET (F);
     I := 0;
     REPEAT
        I := I + 1;
        IF (I <= 10) THEN W[I] := F^;
        GET(F)
```

```
            UNTIL (F^ = ' '); (* NOTE: EOLN TEST AUTOMATIC *)
            IF (I > 10) THEN SETERROR
        END; (* RWORD *)

FUNCTION LOOKUP: INTEGER;
    (* DO HASH-TABLE LOOKUP ON W AND *)
    (* RETURN INDEX OF ENTRY FOUND    *)

    VAR HI: INTEGER; (* HASH INDEX *)

    FUNCTION HASH: INTEGER;
            (* RETURN HASH OF W *)
        BEGIN (* HASH *)
            HASH := (MULT*ORD(W[1]) + (ORD(W[2])) MOD TABLEN
        END; (* HASH *)

    BEGIN (* LOOKUP *)
        HI := HASH;
        WHILE (TABLE [HI].VAL <> 0) AND (TABLE[HI].WD <> W) DO
            BEGIN
                HI := HI + 1;
                IF (HI = TABLEN) THEN HI := 0
            END;
        LOOKUP := HI
    END; (* LOOKUP *)

BEGIN (* NUMWRDS *)
        (* INITIALIZE TABLE *)
    FOR H := 0 TO TABLEN–1 DO
        TABLE[H].VAL := 0; (* INDICATES ENTRY EMPTY *)
    RESET(NUMWDS); (* THIS VERY FILE *)
    REPEAT RWORD(NUMWDS) UNTIL (W = 'DATA:           ');
    RWORD(NUMWDS);
    REPEAT
        H := LOOKUP; (* HERE, H POINTS TO AN EMPTY ENTRY *)
        TABLE[H].WD := W; READ(NUMWDS, TABLE[H].VAL);
        RWORD(NUMWDS)
    UNTIL (W = '*)

    REPEAT
        STATE := START;
        WHILE NOT EOLNS DO
            BEGIN
                RWORD(INPUT); V := TABLE[LOOKUP].VAL;
                IF (V = 0) THEN SETERROR;
                CASE STATE OF
                START: BEGIN
                            TOT := V;
```

```
                         IF (V = STOPVAL) THEN STATE := STOP
                         ELSE IF (V < 10) THEN STATE := DIGIT
                         ELSE IF (V < 20) THEN STATE := DONE
                         ELSE IF (V < 100) THEN STATE := UMPTY
                         ELSE SETERROR
                      END;
             DIGIT: BEGIN
                         TOT := 100 * TOT;
                         IF (V < 10) THEN SETERROR
                         ELSE IF (V < 100) THEN
                            BEGIN
                               TOT := TOT + V;
                               IF (V < 20) THEN STATE := DONE
                               ELSE STATE := UMPTY
                            END
                         ELSE IF (V = 100) THEN STATE := HUNDRED
                         ELSE IF (V = OHVAL) THEN STATE := OH
                         ELSE SETERROR
                      END;
             DONE: SETERROR;  (* ANY INPUT ILLEGAL HERE *)
        UMPTY, OH: IF (V < 10) THEN
                         BEGIN TOT := TOT + V; STATE := DONE END
                      ELSE SETERROR;
       ERROR, STOP: (* DO NOTHING *);
   HUNDRED, ANDS: IF (V = ANDVAL) AND (STATE = HUNDRED) THEN
                         STATE := ANDS
                      ELSE
                         BEGIN
                            TOT := TOT + V;
                            IF (V < 20) THEN STATE := DONE
                            ELSE IF (V < 100) THEN STATE := UMPTY
                            ELSE SETERROR
                         END;
                END;  (* OF CASE STATEMENT *)
            END;  (* OF LINE PROCESSING *)
       CASE STATE OF     (* CLEANUP *)
                      STOP, ERROR: ; (* DO NOTHING *)
       DIGIT,DONE,HUNDRED,UMPTY: WRITELN('VALUE IS ', TOT:1);
                      AND, OH: WRITELN('ERROR; MORE INPUT EXPECTED')
            END;  (* OF CLEANUP CASE *)
         READLN  (* TO PREPARE FOR NEXT LINE *)
      UNTIL (STATE = STOP)
   END.  (* NUMWRDS *)
```

Exercises 8.2

1. In the finite-state machine for numbers of the form ±XXX.XX, why must states DECPT and DIGITANDDP be different states?

2. Add code to the program which implements the finite-state machine for numbers of the form ±XXX.XX so that the numerical value of this number is stored in VAL. [*Hint:* Keep four variables, SIGN, WHOLE, FRACT, and MULT. SIGN is ±1. When a digit to the left of the decimal point is encountered, we do WHOLE := 10∗WHOLE + ORD(C) - ORC('0'). When a digit to the right of the decimal point is encountered, we do FRACT := 10 ∗ FRACT + ORD(C) - ORD('0') and MULT := MULT/10. If done properly, when we are finished, VAL := SIGN ∗ (WHOLE + MULT ∗ FRACT).]

3. Alter the finite-state machine for numbers of the form ±XXX.XX so that there can be arbitrarily many blanks before and after the (optional) sign, but no blanks elsewhere.

4. Alter the finite-state machine for numbers so that it accepts numbers of the form ±XXX.XXE±XX, where the E part is optional and, if present, its sign is optional.

8.3   SUMMARY OF SEARCHING METHODS

For easy reference, the four searching methods we have discussed in this book are listed here along with their big Oh estimates for a file of size n, with the advantages and disadvantages of each.

1. *Linear search:* $O(n)$; fast on small files; easy to program; uses no extra space; can be used on files which are not randomly accessible, such as external files and linked lists.

2. *Binary search:* $O(\log_2(n))$; faster than linear on larger files; uses no extra memory; file must be sorted and randomly accessible; best for relatively static files.

3. *Binary search tree:* $O(\log_2(n))$; gives sort and binary search simultaneously; good for volatile tables; uses extra memory for links and, if you are unlucky, you can end up with a linear search.

4. *Hashing:* $O(1)$; search time independent of table size; good for volatile tables; uses extra memory and leaves data in otherwise meaningless order.

Programming Problems

8.1   Write a text processing program which takes its input from the TEXT file TFILE and copies it to OUTPUT, with the exception that "text variables" are converted to their numeric value. A text variable consists of one or more letters and digits and is declared by the first occurrence of the line

%name=value

were "%" is in column 1, "name" is the variable name, and "value" is the initial value of "name," an integer. Such a line is not copied to the output. The value of "name" is substituted for the occurrence of %name% or %+name% anywhere in the text. In the case of %+name%, 1 is added to "name" before its value is printed. For example,

TFILE:

```
%CH=0
                    Chapter %+CH%
%SECT=0
%CH%.%+SECT% — — — — — — — —
— — — — — — — — — — — — — —
%CH%.%+SECT% — — — — — — — —
— — — — — — — — — — — — — —
                    Chapter %+CH%
%SECT=0
%CH%.%+SECT% — — — — — — — —
— — — — — — — — — — — — — —
etc.
```

which produces

```
                    Chapter 1
1.1 — — — — — — — — — — — — — —
— — — — — — — — — — — — — — —
1.2 — — — — — — — — — — — — — —
— — — — — — — — — — — — — — —
                    Chapter 2
2.1 — — — — — — — — — — — — — —
— — — — — — — — — — — — — — —
etc.
```

Write a program to process such files. Use a hash table to store text variables and their values. (Note that such a program can be made much more impressive: translations of numbers into roman numerals and letters as well as assignments with arbitrary expressions for values.)

8.2 Write a program using the finite-state machine approach which reads a polynomial in the form

$$c_1 X^{\wedge} e_1 \pm c_2 X^{\wedge} e_2 \pm \cdots \pm c_{n-1} X \pm c_n$$

where $c_1, \ldots, c_n$ and $e_1, e_2, \ldots$ are unsigned integer constants and $\pm$ means that a + or a - sign is allowed. Any or all terms may be missing and internal blanks are allowed. Store your polynomial coefficients in C: ARRAY [1 . . 100] OF INTEGER, with the $c_i X^{\wedge} e_i$ coefficient stored in C[e_i]. Then accept real numbers X, stopping on $X = -99$, and print the value of the polynomial for X (see Exercise 1.9.2 c).

8.3 Two TEXT files F1 and F2 contain up to 1000 words each, with each word on its own line and at most 10 characters long. Write a program to find and list all words which are in both files.

Method 1 (wrong): For each item in F2, search F1 linearly. This requires roughly 500 * 1000 = 500,000 probes of F1.

Method 2 (right): Read F1 into a hash table with, say, 1117 entries. Look up each item in F2 in this table. If each entry and look takes an average, say of 3 probes, the program will require a total of 3 * 2000 = 6000 probes, less than 1/80th of method 1.

(If your storage is limited, assume smaller files and make the hash table smaller.)

chapter 9

sequential file processing

When processing "external" files, that is, files which cannot be contained entirely in the computer's main memory, programs tend to take much longer because they are dependent on devices moving at mechanical rather than electronic speed, and as a result the proper choice of algorithm can be even more important than on purely internal problems. This subject has been studied intensively for 80 or 90 years (for card processing even before there were digital computers), so we can barely hope to scratch the surface of the subject in one chapter. I do hope to be able to give you some feeling for it, though.

9.1 NON-TEXT FILES IN PASCAL

Up to now all the files we have used have been of type TEXT, on which the READ and WRITE procedures can be used. Some versions of Pascal *restrict* READ and WRITE to TEXT files and require the use of somewhat more primitive procedures GET and PUT on files of other types. GET and PUT can also be used on TEXT files and, as we saw in Example 8.2.1, in some applications are more convenient than READ and WRITE (and more efficient) even when the latter operations are available. It is the purpose of this section to introduce GET and PUT and related operations.

First, let's go back to what a Pascal file is; our discussion of TEXT files, which are somewhat odd, may have obscured this. A file in Pascal is an arbitrarily long sequence of records each of the same Pascal data type (which may or may not be the Pascal type RECORD). A file is referred to in a Pascal program by a file *variable*, which is declared in the VAR section via a statement like

    filevariable: FILE OF recordtype;

(A TEXT file is a FILE OF CHAR, with the line structure tacked on.) The name "filevariable" need have no relationship to the actual external name of the file (if any), which might vary from run to run or even within a run, and might contain characters which are illegal in a Pascal variable name. The actual external file name is associated with filevariable through the PROGRAM statement or RESET, REWRITE, or OPEN statements (see the following or Appendix B).

All files in standard Pascal are *sequential*, in the sense that they must be accessed from the beginning, in order. An active file has a notion of *current position*. When a file is being written, that position is always just beyond the last record written, so that records are always written at the end of the file. When a file is being read, the current position can be anywhere in the file, but you must get there by starting at the beginning and reading through all the intervening records. Writing also must start at the beginning of the file (which, when writing, is also the end), so it is not possible to rewrite *part* of a file.

Although they may seem limited, in fact the standard Pascal file facilities closely resemble the operations available on (simple) tape files, and also the way in which disk files operate most efficiently. As a result, there are a large number of important file-handling methods for such files, and the study of a few of them is more than enough to occupy us here.

Suppose now for the purpose of discussion that we have defined

    F: FILE OF sometype;

In some respects, F acts like a ^sometype; F points to the current record in the file. F^ is sometimes called a "window" into the file, and is of type sometype. F^ either contains the record read at the last file-read operation or the contents to be written at the next file-write operation. F^ is in fact a *buffer*. Note though that F is not a normal variable, and in particular is not a normal pointer variable! NEW cannot be applied to F, and F by itself cannot be on either side of an assignment or comparison (though F^, which is "normal," can).

The window, F^, is advanced sequentially through the file using the GET (for reading) or PUT (for writing) built-in procedures. To read a file, we commence by executing

RESET(F)

(about which more later). This has the effect of setting the file's current position at the first record and reading that record into F^ (we always read one ahead). The contents of F^ can be removed and manipulated the same way as if F were a pointer. The current position of F is advanced by executing

GET(F)

Thus the processing of a file consists of repeated executions of

process F^; GET(F)

If READ is applicable to the file F, and X is a variable of type 'some-type,' then READ(F, X) is equivalent to X := F^; GET(F). By using GET instead of READ, much data movement can sometimes be avoided. When F^ advances beyond the end of the file, the built-in function EOF(F) becomes TRUE and the contents of F^ become unpredictable, but *they can be used without causing a runtime error* (unlike using P^ when the pointer P is NIL). This is often very convenient. (As we saw in Example 8.2.1, GET is sometimes preferable to READ because with GET, EOF becomes true *after* we attempt to read a nonexistent record, while with READ this happens when the nonexistent record will be the *next* read, so EOF becomes true with a record still to process in the latter case.)

To write a file, we execute

REWRITE(F)

This (re)creates F as an empty file and makes F^ what will become the first record when the current position of F is advanced, via

PUT(F)

After REWRITE or PUT, the contents of F^ are unpredictable until something is put into it. The writing of a file consists of repeating the code

put data into F^; PUT(F)

EOF(F) is always true of a file being written. If WRITE is applicable to the file F, then WRITE(F, X) is equivalent to F^ := X; PUT(F).

To read F after you have written it, you must RESET it, which sets the window F^ back to the beginning of the file. You may only READ or GET a file after RESETing it, until a REWRITE is done on it, and then you may only WRITE or PUT the file until a RESET is done.

EXAMPLE 9.1.1   R1, R2, and R3 are assumed to be variables of type 'sometype'. In Figure 9.1, we show the effect of writing them into a file F and then reading them back into variables S1, S2, and S3, also of 'sometype'. When we are done, we have S1 = R1, S2 = R2, and S3 = R3. (*Note:* In some nonstandard Pascal systems, the operation CLOSE(F) must be done before the RESET operation. In some sys-

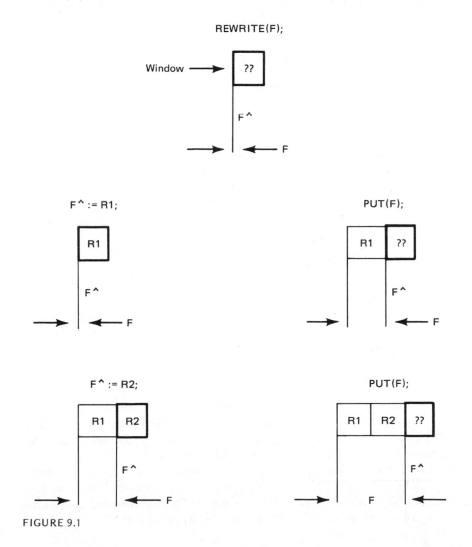

FIGURE 9.1

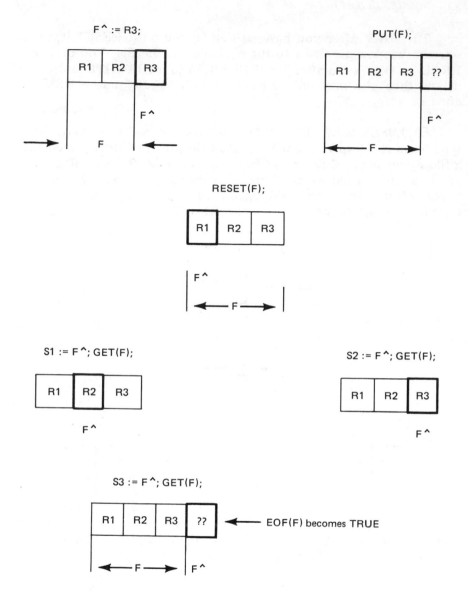

FIGURE 9.1 (continued)

tems, the external name of the file must be specified in the RESET and REWRITE operations, as in RESET(F, '[1234] XAMPL/PASSWD= MINE'), and in some other systems this operation is divided among two instructions, a RESET as we originally had and an OPEN operation. Because of the nature of some operating systems, the EOF indication may not be reliable: the operating system writes several logical records in one physical record and will allow you to "GET" unused space after the last logical record. For more detail, see Appendix B.)

248

Exercises 9.1

1. Write a program to read real numbers from the terminal, stopping on -99, and print the mean of the data read.

2. Write a program to read a FILE OF REAL as in Exercise 1 (stopping on EOF), and compute and print the mean of the data read.

9.2   GROUP TOTALS

In this section we will develop a method for attacking problems like the following: Over some standard period, say a month, a store sells various items, receives items into stock from its wholesalers, and has customer returns. These occur in a more or less random sequence, which might be expressed in tabular form as in the following table.

Stock Number	Transaction	Amount
A004–32	Sale	10
32ZB–12	Sale	15
A005–21	Return	8
32ZB–12	Receipt	100
B002–13	Sale	12

We want to prepare a summary report listing the net movement of each item for the period.

The first problem is to get all the transactions on the same item together. There are several possible solutions depending on the nature of the data:

1. If the stock numbers are in fact numbers in some small range, say 1 . . 1000, we could define an array

NETMOVE: ARRAY [1 . . 1000] OF INTEGER;

initialize it to 0, and then go through the file of changes once, updating the appropriate NETMOVE entry for each file record.

2. Even if the stock numbers are arbitrary character strings, as in the table, if there are few enough of them to fit into main memory, we can make a hash table to contain the item numbers and their net movements.

Let's suppose (realistically) that there are too many items to fit in memory at once. A simple-minded solution would be to save the first stock number from the file and then go through the entire file, picking out all occurrences of that item and getting a net total, then starting all over again with the second item, and so on. This method presents two major difficulties: (1) how to keep track of items we have already processed and (2) the time required to read the entire file over and over again. Something of a solution to both problems could be obtained by copying the unused items onto an auxiliary file on each pass through the data, and then, on the next pass, using the previous auxiliary file instead of the original input. To avoid an excessive number of files, one simply alternates between two auxiliary files. This method is still very slow, though. Suppose we have 10,000 items and a file of 100,000 transactions. Then, on the average, the first time through we would read 100,000 items, the second time, 99,990, the third, 99,980, and so on, for a total of $10 + 20 + \cdots + 99,990 + 100,000$ items, which is $10(1 + 2 + \cdots + 10,000) = 10 * 10,000 * 10,001/2$, about 5E8, by the triangle principle. This is still equivalent to reading the entire file 5,000 times!

In fact the normal solution to this problem is to do *more* than we need to: sort the file using stock number as key. This just incidentally puts all items with the same stock number together on the file, and the net movement problem can be solved with one final pass through the file! But how long will sorting take? In the next section we will show that under quite conservative assumptions the whole problem, net movement and all, can be done in 12 passes through the file! *And* when we are done, we can print a report in sorted order, making it much easier to use.

To give you another idea of the time savings of sorting, if we assume that it takes 1 millisecond to read a record (which is quite fast), then the first method, without sorting, will take about 6 *days*, while the second, with sorting, will take about 20 *minutes*.

Returning to our original problem, let's now suppose that our input file is sorted. Our troubles are not over though; we still need an algorithm to process the file. If done incorrectly, such a program can be rather messy. Our approach here comes from an excellent book by M. A. Jackson, which, unfortunately for Pascal fans, uses the COBOL language (see Bibliography).

In what follows, a "group" will mean all the records with the same item number (key). The fundamental loop of the program is

```
RESET(transactionfile);
WHILE NOT EOF(transactionfile)DO
    BEGIN
        Process next group
    END
```

The code for "Process next group" is

```
Initialize group;
WHILE record is in group DO
```

```
BEGIN
    Process record;
    GET(transactionfile)
END;
Do output for group
```

The key problem is in the "record is in group" idea. If we are not careful, we will have to treat the first or last record of each group as special, and/or treat the first or last record of the file as special. Done correctly though, the solution is simple: To initialize group processing, save the item number of the first record in, say, CURITEMNO. The "record in group" condition becomes

```
(transactionfile^.ITEMNO = CURITEMNO) AND NOT EOF (transactionfile)
```

Here we used the fact that evaluating transactionfile^ is not an error even if EOF(transactionfile) is true.

EXAMPLE 9.2.1 Write a program to print a net movement report. Given the preceding discussion, the program is now straightforward.

```
(* EXAMPLE 9.2.1: GROUPS          *)
(* DO GROUP TOTALS ON SORTED  *)
(* FILE TRANSF                    *)

PROGRAM GROUPS(TRANSF, OUTPUT);

TYPE TREC = RECORD ITEMNO: ALFA;
                   TRTYPE: (SALE, RECEIPT, RETURN);
                   AMOUNT: INTEGER END;

VAR TRANSF: FILE OF TREC; (* THE TRANSACTION FILE,      *)
                         (* SORTED ON KEY ITEMNO       *)
           NETMOVE: INTEGER;   (* NET MOVEMENT IN A GROUP  *)
           CURITEMNO: ALFA;    (* ITEM NO OF CURRENT GROUP *)

BEGIN (* GROUPS *)
    RESET(TRANSF);
    WRITELN(' ITEM NO       NETMOVEMENT'); WRITELN;

    WHILE NOT EOF(TRANSF) DO
        BEGIN (* PROCESS NEXT GROUP *)
            CURITEMNO := TRANSF^.ITEMNO;  (* INITIALIZE GROUP *)
            NETMOVE := 0;
            WHILE (TRANSF^.ITEMNO=CURITEMNO)
                AND NOT EOF(TRANSF) DO
                BEGIN (* PROCESS RECORD IN GROUP *)
                    CASE TRANSF^.TRTYPE OF
                        SALE: NETMOVE := NETMOVE+TRANSF^.AMOUNT;
```

```
RECEIPT, RETURN: NETMOVE := NETMOVE-TRANSF^.AMOUNT
        END;
      GET(TRANSF)
    END;  (* PROCESS RECORD IN GROUP *)
  WRITELN(CURITEMNO,NETMOVE)
 END  (* PROCESS GROUP *)
END.  (* GROUPS *)
```

The beauty of this method is that it generalizes easily to the case of groups within groups.

EXAMPLE 9.2.2 Suppose for instance our transaction file also has a "store code" field and, within a given item, the file is sorted by store code; then we can give the net movement of each item in each store, as well as a total net movement for each item in all stores. The program to do this is, in outline,

```
WHILE NOT EOF(TRANSF) DO
    BEGIN  (* process ITEM *)
      Save ITEMNO;
      WHILE same ITEMNO AND NOT EOF DO
          BEGIN (* process STORE within ITEM *)
            Save STORECODE
            WHILE same ITEMNO AND same STORECODE AND NOT EOF DO
                BEGIN
                    Process Record;
                    GET(TRANSF)
                END;
            Print Store total
          END;  (* process STORE within ITEM *)
      Print Item total
    END;  (* process ITEM *)
```

Exercises 9.2

1. Assume that TRANSF in Example 9.2.1 is terminated by a record whose ITEMNO is a sentinel, say **********. Show what changes to program GROUPS are necessary.

2. Why can't the third WHILE statement of Example 9.2.2 omit the "same ITEMNO" test?

3. Assume that TREC has a field STORECODE of two CHARacters, and that TRANSF is sorted properly. Complete the program outline of Example 9.2.2 to give a program which produces output of the following type:

ITEM NO	STORE	STORE TOTAL	ITEM TOTAL
AX-1342-WW			
	DK	1324	

MM	424
XX	-123

1625

B2-4232-00

DK	544
EF	23
MM	-111
XX	79

535

etc.

4. Suppose that our transaction file also has a DEPTNO field, and that the file is sorted by DEPTNO and within DEPTNO, by ITEMNO, and within ITEMNO, by STORECODE. Develop an outline program as in Example 9.2.2 for three-level group processing.

9.3 MERGING

At first thought, it may not be at all obvious how one can manage to sort a file when it is not possible to access it randomly. We will build a method out of repeated use of a simpler technique known as *merging*, in which two (or more) files which are already in order are "shuffled together" to make a single ordered file. Once we understand merging, the principle of the *merge sort* is simple. With merging, we can, for instance, merge two ordered files each of length K into a single ordered file of length $2K$. Hence to sort a file of N records, we start by considering it as a collection of N files of 1 record each, in order. Merging pairs of these files gives us $(N + 1)$ DIV 2 ordered "files" of length 2, and merging again gives $(N + 3)$ DIV 4 ordered 'files' of length 4. By the halving principle, we need merely repeat this process $\log_2(N)$ times to obtain a sorted file.

In this section we will ignore the sorting process as a whole and concentrate on merging two already sorted files. This can be done with only enough main-memory storage to hold one record from each input file. We diagram the process for two input files as follows. Initially the situation is like Figure 9.2. At each stage of the program, we pick the record in main memory with the smallest key, write it to the output file, and read a new record from the corresponding input file. Applying this method to Figure 9.2, the first few steps of the process are as in Figure 9.3.

The fundamental loop for a merge program on two or more files is:

```
WHILE at least two files aren't at EOF DO
    BEGIN
```

```
        Pick file Fj such that Fj^ has the smallest
             key of the files not at EOF;
        Write Fj^ out to the output file;
        GET(Fj)
    END;
Copy the rest of the single remaining file to the output
```

When we try to fill in the details though, things get a little messy. Keeping track of which files are used up is a chore if there are more than two files to merge (if there are only two, we stop merging when the first of them runs out). Also, the copy statement at the end can be a little unpleasant as it must be applicable to any of the files being merged.

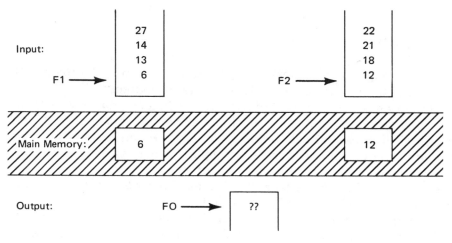

FIGURE 9.2

Both of these problems can be taken care of neatly, along with the problem mentioned in Section 9.1 in which some Pascals cannot determine end of file accurately, by putting a *sentinel* record at the end of each file with an impossibly large key. If we call this key SENTINEL, then the fundamental loop of a program to merge files F1, . . ., FN into an output file F0 would be

```
WHILE (F1^.KEY < SENTINEL) OR (F2^.KEY < SENTINEL) OR ... DO
    BEGIN
```

```
Get the Fj having the smallest Fj^.KEY;
   F0^ := Fj^; PUT(F0); GET(Fj)
END
```

with no extra bookkeeping or copying at the end required!

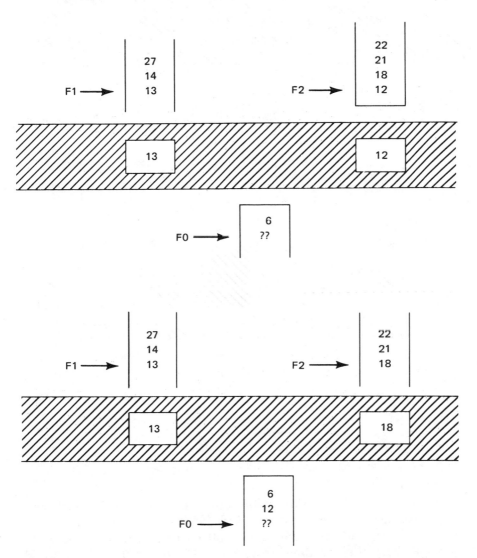

FIGURE 9.3

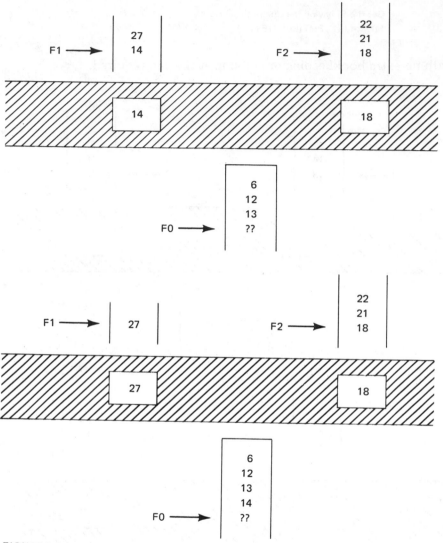

FIGURE 9.3 (continued)

EXAMPLE 9.3.1 Print a table of corresponding Fahrenheit and Celsius (centigrade) temperatures. Arrange it so that all the whole-number Celsius readings from –10 to 50 occur and that all the even-numbered Fahrenheit readings from 10 to 100 occur. The table should be in two columns, one for each temperature scale, and the tempera-tures in each column should be increasing.

Method: Since this is a section on merging, we will create two files of corresponding Fahrenheit and Celsius temperatures, one with even-numbered Fahrenheit readings and the other with whole-numbered Celsius readings. We will then merge them into a single table. As sentinel, we will use a Fahrenheit value of 9999, and since it does not really matter which temperature scale we use for key, we will arbitrarily pick Fahrenheit. (Recall that the formula for converting Celsius to Fahrenheit is $°F = 1.8°C + 32$.) The program is

```
(* EXAMPLE 9.3.1: MERGE *)
(* PRINT MERGED CELSIUS*)
(* VS FAHRENHEIT TABLE *)

PROGRAM MERGE(OUTPUT);

CONST SENTINEL=9999;     (* ENDS OF FILES *)
       FREEZEF=32        (* FREEZING IN FAHRENHEIT *)
       CTOF=1.8;         (* CEL TO FAHR CONVERSION FACTOR *)
       LOF=10; HIF=100;  (* FAHRENHEIT LIMITS      *)
       FINTERVAL=2;      (* FAHRENHEIT INTERVAL *)
       LOC=-10; HIC=50;  (* CELSIUS LIMITS         *)
       CINTERVAL=1;      (* CELSIUS INTERVAL       *)

TYPE   TEMPREC=RECORD FAHR, CEL: REAL END;

VAR    T: INTEGER        (* 'NICE' TEMP FOR FILE GENERATION *)
       FC, CF: FILE OF TEMPREC; (* FILES TO BE MERGED *)

BEGIN (* MERGE *)
   REWRITE(FC); T := LOF;
   WHILE (T <= HIF) DO
      BEGIN (* GENERATE EVEN FAHRENHEITS FILE *)
          FC^.FAHR := T;
          FC^.CEL := (T - FREEZEF)/CTOI;
          PUT(FC);
          T := T + FINTERVAL
      END;  (* GENERATE EVEN FAHRENHEITS FILE *)
   REWRITE(CF); T := LOC;
   WHILE (T <= HIC) DO
      BEGIN (* GENERATE WHOLE CELSIUS FILE *)
          CF^.CEL := T;
          CF^.FAHR := T * CTOF + FREEZEF;
          PUT(CF);
          T := T + CINTERVAL
      END;  (* GENERATE WHOLE CELSIUS FILE *)
   FC^.FAHR := SENTINEL; PUT(FC); RESET(FC);
   CF^.FAHR := SENTINEL; PUT(CF); RESET(CF);

   WRITELN('      FAHRENHEIT      CELSIUS');
   WRITELN('      — — — — — — — — — — — — —');
```

```
      WRITELN;

      (* NOW, MERGE FILES *)

      WHILE (FC^.FAHR < SENTINEL) OR (CF^.FAHR < SENTINEL) DO
         IF (FC^.FAHR <= CF^.FAHR) THEN
            BEGIN   (* FAHRENHEIT SMALLER *)
               WRITELN(FC^.FAHR:13:1, FC^.CEL:14:1);
               IF (FC^.FAHR = CF^.FAHR) THEN
                  GET(CF); (* DON'T REPEAT A LINE *)
               GET(FC)
            END
         ELSE
            BEGIN (* CELSIUS SMALLER *)
               WRITELN(CF^.FAHR:13:1, CF^.CEL:14:1);
               GET(CF)
            END;  (* OF MERGE LOOP, TOO *)
   END.  (* MERGE *)
```

The files to be merged look like

CF			FC		
FAHR	CEL		FAHR	CEL	
14.0	−10.0		10.0	−12.2	
15.8	−9.0		12.0	−11.1	
17.6	−8.0		14.0	−10.0	
19.4	−7.0		16.0	−8.9	
. . .			. . .		
9999	xxx		9999	xxx	

and the start of the output looks like

FAHRENHEIT	CELSIUS
— — — — — — — — — — — —	
10.0	−12.2
12.0	−11.1
14.0	−10.0
15.8	−9.0
16.0	−8.9
17.6	−8.0
. . .	

Note that since FC and CF are temporary ("scratch") files, they need not be listed in the PROGRAM statement.

Exercises 9.3

1. It is not really necessary to use files in Example 9.3.1. Rewrite MERGE with CF and FC as variables of type ^TEMPREC, and procedures GETCF and

GETFC to replace GET(CF) and GET(FC) which use the previous contents of CF^ and FC^ to generate the equivalent of the next record.

2. In the general loop for a merge, the test (F1^.KEY < MAXKEY) OR (F2^.KEY < MAXKEY) OR . . . can be combined with the computation of the Fj which minimizes Fj^.KEY. How?

3. A kilometer is 0.62137 miles and a knot (nautical mile) is 1.15193 miles. Write a program to construct a table of equivalent kilometers, knots, and miles in increasing order with whole-number values for kilometers between 0 and 20, miles between 0 and 12, and knots between 0 and 10.

9.4   MERGE SORTING EXTERNAL FILES

As we saw at the start of Section 9.3, we can sort a file of N records by merging through the whole file $\log_2(N)$ times. Since each merging pass treats each record in the file once, this is a $O(N \log_2 (N))$ method. This basic method can be improved considerably. It is usually possible to put several records in main memory at once, and we can sort these pieces by internal methods, greatly increasing the overall speed of the sort. This is the method which we will consider in detail in this section.

First we must define the concept of a *run*. A run in a file is a sequence of records whose keys are in order. In terms of the preceding method, we start with runs of length 1; one merge produces runs of length 2; a second, runs of length 4; and each succeeding merge essentially doubles the lengths of the runs of the preceding stage. We are done when the file consists of exactly one run.

If we assume that main memory will hold K records at once (in addition to the sorting program itself), then by sorting these K records with an internal method such as quicksort, we can assume that we start with runs of K records rather than only one. This reduces the number of passes through the file to about $\log_2(N/K) + 1 = \log_2(N) - \log_2(K) + 1$. (The +1 is for the initial pass to form the runs.) Of course, we have increased the internal processing time, but the decreased number of passes more than compensates for this. (Knuth, volume 3, pages 254-258, gives a very clever method whereby runs of average length $2K$ can be produced initially! See the Bibliography.)

Returning for a moment to the example of Section 9.2, where we wished to sort a file with 100,000 records, let us assume that 100 of these records will fit in memory at once for internal sorting. Then in the first pass through the file we can create 1000 runs of 100 records each. In $\log_2(1000)$, about 10, more passes, we can sort the file. This gives the 11 passes promised in Section 9.2 (not including the final pass to produce group totals).

There are still some serious bookkeeping questions to be answered. We will do that as well as demonstrate the method on an example of more manageable size: a file with 14 records and internal storage capable of holding 3 at a time.

Step 1: Produce runs (see Figure 9.4). Runs are shown separated by |. It would be difficult to merge the first and second runs if they were on the same file, as here, so we need to distribute the runs out

Input File:

| 8 | 14 | 12 | 36 | 24 | 7 | 15 | 2 | 5 | 1 | 18 | 19 | 13 | 6 | ◄—— start |

Output File:

start ——►

| 6 | 13 | 19 | 1 | 5 | 18 | 2 | 7 | 15 | 12 | 24 | 36 | 8 | 14 |

FIGURE 9.4

between *two* (or more) files so we can merge the first runs from each, then the second, and so on. In fact, there is no reason why we cannot do this at the same time we are computing the runs. We use two output files and the first run goes to the first file, the second to the second file, the third back to the first file again, and so on. If we end on the first output file, we can put a phony run on the second output file and be assured that we have the same number of runs on each file.

Step 1a: Now let's rewrite Step 1 with this in mind, now using "s" to represent a sentinel record written to terminate runs (Figure 9.5).

Step 2: Merging pairs of runs onto a single output file would give Figure 9.6.

Step 2a: Once again, to continue merging we would have to distribute output runs onto separate files, but once again this can be done as part of the merge step, sending merged runs to two output files alternately. Hence we replace Figure 9.6 with Figure 9.7, where we have again equalized the number of runs on both output files.

Step 3: Continuing the process, we have Figure 9.8.
Step 4: And, finally, Figure 9.9.
In this example, we chose to use two input and two output files. The resulting program is called a *two-way merge.* Three-way, four-way, and so on, merges are of course possible, but generally an *N*-way merge requires 4*N* I/O devices for maximum efficiency. This is true even of disk files, as placing two files on the same disk will cause a lot

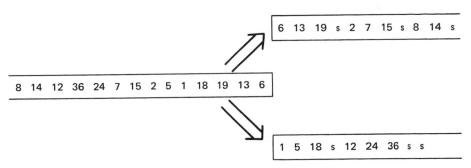

FIGURE 9.5

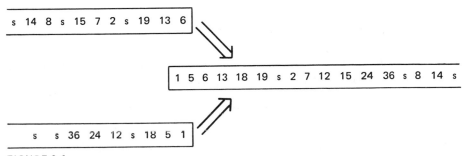

FIGURE 9.6

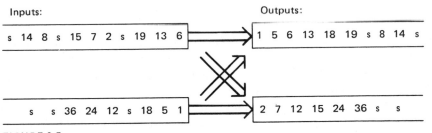

FIGURE 9.7

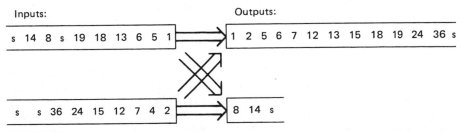

FIGURE 9.8

Inputs:

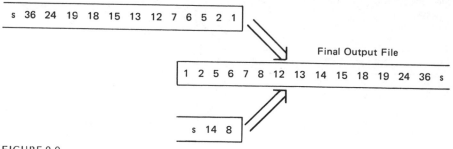

FIGURE 9.9

of disk arm motion seeking back and forth between them. We will restrict ourselves to two-way merges here.

EXAMPLE 9.4.1   Write a program to do a two-way merge sort on external files. The overall outline of the program is

> Read input file and sort it into runs;
> Merge-sort runs

To do a two-way merge, we need four files and must flip back and forth between pairs of them, alternately considering a pair as the input files or as the output files. One simple way to do this is to define an array of files:

MF: ARRAY [1 .. 2, 1 .. 2] OF recordtype;

We keep two indices, INP and OUT, such that, at any time, the input files are MF[INP,1] and MF[INP,2] and the output files are MF-[OUT,1] and MF[OUT,2]. At the end of each pass through the data, INP and OUT can be interchanged.

A difficulty with this method is that when the sorting procedure is done, we will end up with the final sorted file on MF[OUT,1], but in standard Pascal this can only be a temporary file existing for the life of the program as there is no way in standard Pascal to specify an external name for a subscripted internal file. In Pascals which allow one to specify external file names dynamically via RESET or REWRITE, there is no problem; the program simply creates four external files and tells the user which one the output is on when it is done (although this may leave the user a cleanup job to get rid of the other three files).

Here though we will treat the final sorting pass as a special case, with output file specified by the user, instead of MF[OUT,1]. We can determine when the last pass is about to occur by keeping track of the number of runs in a variable called NRUNS, and when this number is 2, we know to do the special final pass. Thus "Merge-sort runs" is the fundamental loop

```
WHILE (NRUNS > 2) DO
    BEGIN
        NRUNS := (NRUNS+1) DIV 2; (* NRUNS AFTER THIS PASS *)
        Merge NRUNS pairs of runs from input files to output files;
        Swap input and output files
    END;
Merge 2 runs from input files to user-supplied output file
```

Since merging is done in two places, it seems reasonable to make it a PROCEDURE with one parameter, the output file. To make the procedure as simple as possible, we set it up to merge just one pair of runs, and let the main program take care of repeating it. The merging procedure is then

```
PROCEDURE MERGERUNPAIR(VAR F: filetype);
    VAR N: INTEGER;
    BEGIN (* MERGERUNPAIR *)
        WHILE (MF[INP,2] ^.KEY < SENTINEL) OR (MF[INP,2] ^.KEY
            < SENTINEL) DO
        BEGIN
            IF (MF[INP,1] ^.KEY < MF[INP,2] ^.KEY) THEN N := 1
            ELSE N := 2;
            F ^ := MF[INP,N] ^;
            PUT(F); GET(MF[INP,N] )
        END;
        Write out sentinel on F;
        Skip over sentinels in MF[INP, 1 .. 2]
    END;  (* MERGERUNPAIR *)
```

Pascal Pointer 25 > *FILE parameters to subprograms must always be VAR parameters.*

"Merge NRUNS pairs of runs . . ." now becomes

```
CUROUT := 1;
FOR I := 1 TO NRUNS DO
    BEGIN
        MERGERUNPAIR(MF[OUT,CUROUT] );
        CUROUT := 3-CUROUT
    END
```

In an early version of this book, I dispensed with the variable CUROUT by noting that CUROUT = 2 − ORD(ODD(I)) [since if I is odd, ODD(I) is TRUE and ORD(ODD(I)) is therefore 1, and if I is even, ORD(ODD(I)) = ORD(FALSE) = 0]. This probably violates the Shirley

Temple principle and was a little less efficient but I thought: no matter. Well, if there is a principle more important than "Don't get cute," it is that if you must get cute at least be consistent in your cuteness. Applying this trick uniformly throughout the program, I found that the program was getting more and more complicated and less and less efficient, until I finally abandoned the trick as a bad idea. The vindication of principle! To further beat a dead horse, I later considered using Booleans instead of 1 . . 2 as subscripts for the files, but this produced a program that seemed excessively mysterious.

Now that we have the heart of the program fairly well squared away, let's return to the initial phase, sorting into runs. This is easily outlined as follows:

```
NRUNS := 0;
WHILE more input file DO
    BEGIN
        read a core load;
        sort internally;
        Write out core load;
        Write out sentinel;
        NRUNS := NRUNS + 1
    END;
```

We can use the same trick to alternate between output files. We will assume that the sort procedure exists externally (quicksort would be a good choice).

Only a few minor odds and ends remain to be cleaned up before giving the program. We will assume that the key is of type ALFA. To construct a sentinel, we need an ALFA variable all of whose characters are the largest possible value, and that depends on the character set in use. We will assume a machine with the ASCII set, in which case ORD(largest character) = 127. We also note that on any pass in which we end up with an odd number of runs we will have to write a dummy run consisting just of a sentinel record on the other output file, MF-[OUT,2]. As we end up writing sentinels at many different places, we will collect the code for this in a single place, a procedure PUT-SENTINEL. The program is

```
(* EXAMPLE 9.4.1: MERGESORT   *)
(* MERGE SORT INFILE LEAVING *)
(* RESULT ON OUTFILE          *)

PROGRAM MERGESORT(INFILE, OUTFILE, OUTPUT);

CONST MCL = 100;        (* MAX CORE LOAD *)
      MAXCHAR = 127;    (* = MAX ORD(CHAR) *)
```

```
TYPE  REC = RECORD KEY: ALFA (* . . . OTHER DATA *) END;
      MFILE = FILE OF REC;
      LOAD = ARRAY [1 . . MCL] OF REC;

VAR   INFILE, OUTFILE: MFILE; (* FINAL I/O FOR PROGRAM *)
      MF: ARRAY [1 . . 2, 1 . . 2] OF MFILE; (* WORK FILES *)
      NRUNS,   (* CURRENT NUMBER OF RUNS *)
      INP, OUT, (* CURRENT BANK OF INPUT, OUTPUT WORK FILES *)
      CUROUT, (* CURRENT OUTPUT FILE IN OUTPUT BANK OF FILES *)
      I, J: INTEGER; (* INITIALIZATION INDICES *)
      SENTINEL: ALFA;   (* LARGEST KEY *)
      A: LOAD; (* CORE LOAD TO BE SORTED FOR INITIAL RUNS *)

PROCEDURE SORT(VAR A: LOAD; SIZ: INTEGER); EXTERN;
      (* SORT A[1 . . SIZ] ON KEY FIELD *)

PROCEDURE PUTSENTINEL(VAR F: MFILE);
   BEGIN (* PUTSENTINEL *)
     F^.KEY := SENTINEL; PUT(F);
   END;  (* PUTSENTINEL *)

PROCEDURE MERGERUNPAIR(VAR F· MFILE);
      (* MERGE MF[INP,1 . . 2] INTO FILE F *)
   VAR N: INTEGER;
   BEGIN (* MERGERUNPAIR *)
      WHILE (MF[INP,1] ^.KEY < SENTINEL) OR (MF[INP,2] ^.KEY
            < SENTINEL) DO
         BEGIN (* OUTPUT SMALLER RECORD *)
            IF (MF[INP,1] ^.KEY < MF[INP,2] ^.KEY) THEN N := 1
            ELSE N := 2;
            F^ := MF[INP,N] ^;
            PUT(F); GET(MF[INP,N] )
         END;
      PUTSENTINEL(F);
      GET(MF[INP,1] ); GET(MF[INP,2] ) (* SKIP SENTINELS *)
   END;  (* MERGERUNPAIR *)

BEGIN (* MERGESORT *)
   FOR I := 1 TO 10 DO SENTINEL[I] := CHR(MAXCHAR);
   RESET(INFILE); REWRITE(MF[1,1] ); REWRITE (MF[1,2] );
   NRUNS := 0; CUROUT := 1;

   (* READ INPUT FILE AND SORT IT INTO RUNS *)

   WHILE (INFILE ^.KEY < SENTINEL) DO
      BEGIN
         (* READ A CORE LOAD *)
```

```
I := 0; (* NUMBER OF RECORDS READ *)
WHILE (I < MCL) AND (INFILE^.KEY < SENTINEL) DO
   BEGIN
      I := I + 1; A[I] := INFILE^; GET(INFILE)
   END:
SORT(A, I);
(* WRITE OUT CORE LOAD *)
FOR J := 1 TO I DO
   BEGIN
      MF[1,CUROUT] ^ := A[I] ; PUT(MF[1,CUROUT])
   END;
PUTSENTINEL(MF[1,CUROUT]);
NRUNS := NRUNS + 1; CUROUT := 3 - CUROUT
END;
IF (CUROUT = 2) THEN PUTSENTINEL(MF[1,CUROUT]);

(* SORT PAIRS OF RUNS *)

INP := 1;
WHILE (NRUNS > 2) DO
   BEGIN
      (* SWITCH INPUT AND OUTPUT BANK *)
      OUT := 3 - INP;
      RESET(MF[INP,1]); RESET(MF[INP,2]);
      REWRITE(MF[OUT,1]); REWRITE(MF[OUT,2]);
      NRUNS := (NRUNS + 1) DIV 2; CUROUT := 1;
      FOR I := 1 TO NRUNS DO
         BEGIN
            MERGERUNPAIR(MF[OUT,CUROUT]);
            CUROUT := 3 - CUROUT
         END;
      IF ODD(NRUNS) THEN PUTSENTINEL(MF[OUT,2]);
      INP := OUT
   END;

(* FINAL MERGE *)
RESET(MF[INP,1]); RESET(MF[INP,2]);
REWRITE(OUTFILE);
MERGERUNPAIR(OUTFILE)
END.   (* MERGESORT *)
```

9.5 SEQUENTIAL FILE UPDATE

We come finally to the classic of sequential file processing algorithms,
the *sequential file update*. The elements of the problem are a *master
file*, which could contain employee records, inventory, accounts receiv-

able, or whatever, and a set of *transactions*, which must be used to update the master file. Typical transactions are as follows:

1. *Add* a new record to the master file,
2. *Delete* an existing record from the master file.
3. *Update* an existing record in the master file.

In most applications, transaction 3 occurs most frequently.

Two problems present themselves immediately. The first is how to match up transactions with master file records, and the second is how to alter the master file if, as we assume, we cannot alter a record of a sequential file without rewriting the whole file.

These problems are solved together. To solve the second, the whole master file is rewritten. We take as input an *old master* and produce as output a *new master*, with unchanged records simply being copied from old to new master. As this process would be very time consuming if performed once for each transaction, transactions are *batched*; that is, all transactions for some fixed period of time, a day, week, or month, are collected for processing together. To make matching of transactions and master possible on one pass, we assume that the master file is ordered on a key. Applying the methods of this chapter, processing then consists of sorting the transaction file and merging it with the old master to produce the new master.

At this point, let's pause and consider what the transaction file must look like. We will assume a master file with a KEY field and a field to be updated, say a BALANCE field, and perhaps other fields. Transactions require different amounts of information depending on their type: all must contain the KEY of the record to be altered and an indication of their type (add, delete, or update), but after this, an add must have a complete record of information, an update just an amount by which BALANCE is changed, and a delete nothing further. This could be a problem-as Pascal requires that all records in a file be of the same type, but Pascal comes to our rescue by allowing us to declare *variants* in records. The first part of the record (possibly empty) has the same structure for all records, but this can be followed by a part with different data types for different cases. The general form is

```
RECORD fixed structure data declarations;
    CASE varianttype OF
        particularvariant1 : (data for particularvariant1);
        particularvariant2: (data for particularvariant2);

        . . .

        particularvariantn: (data for particularvariantn)
    END;
```

Note that

A RECORD with variant CASE has only one END, which ends both CASE and RECORD.

The "varianttype" is typically an enumerated data type. In our case it could be

TYPE TRANSTYPE = (ADD, DELETE, UPDATE);

and the three "particularvariants" would be ADD, DELETE, and UP-DATE, in any order. The programmer has a choice of whether or not to include a variable in the record of type "varianttype" to show which particular case of the variant holds. If, for instance, we wanted a variable TTP to tell us the TRANSTYPE of a record, we would use CASE TTP: TRANSTYPE OF . . ., and if we did not care, we would use CASE TRANSTYPE OF . . .. Declarations for the update program might look like

```
TYPE MREC = RECORD KEY: ALFA; BALANCE: REAL (* OTHER DATA *) END;
     TRANSTYPE = (ADD, DELETE, UPDATE);
     TREC = RECORD KEY: ALFA;
               CASE TTP: TRANSTYPE OF
               ADD: (NEWREC: MREC);
            DELETE: ( );
            UPDATE: (CHANGE: REAL)
            END;
```

(The empty DELETE variant is optional and is included so that a future reader of the program will not wonder if we forgot it.) If, say, TR were declared a variable of type TREC, then we could refer to its various parts by TR.KEY, TR.TTP, TR.CHANGE, TR.NEWREC.BALANCE, and so on. Note that there is nothing to keep you from altering TR.TTP so that it no longer correctly reflects the variant type, and there is nothing to stop you from accessing CHANGE in what is in fact an ADD record. It is up to the programmer to keep these things straight. Note also that when TR is declared, there is no way of knowing what its variant will be, so it will always be allocated an amount of storage sufficient for the largest variant. But if say, TRP were of type ^ TREC, we could execute NEW(TRP, DELETE), and Pascal might only allocate enough storage for a DELETE record.

Returning to the problem at hand, once we have sorted the transaction file, the merge-update is conceptually simple. To simplify matters, let us assume that the transaction file does not have more than one record with the same key. Multiple records with the same key could be handled with a somewhat more careful version of the program we are about to develop. The method is:

1. Read the first (next) transaction.

2. Read old master records and write them to the new master *until* we get one whose key is ⩾ the transaction key.

If the keys are equal, *delete* or *update* can be performed and *add* is an error. The situation when the keys are unequal is a bit more subtle. Since the master file record is the first with key ⩾ the transaction key, and since the keys are in increasing order, we know that there is no master file record with the given transaction key, so a delete or update is in error; and since all previous master file records have keys smaller than the transaction key, this is the place to output an add transaction to the new master file. Continuing with the program outline:

3. Process transaction and go back to 1.

The same reasoning holds for further transactions as their keys are in increasing order.

The preceding outline can be easily turned into a program:

```
WHILE more transactions DO
     BEGIN
         WHILE oldmaster key < transaction key DO
             transfer oldmaster record to newmaster and get next oldmaster record;
         Process transaction;
         Get next transaction
     END
```

This method is somewhat unesthetic though, as the loop may terminate with more old master records to be transferred, and a loop to handle this must be tacked on at the end. Making "WHILE more old master records DO . . ." the outer loop does not cure the problem either, as there may be transactions with keys beyond any master record key, and again an extra loop is required. The solution to the problem comes when we see that neither file controls the process by itself, but that the pair of files is processed simultaneously and processing ends when both are exhausted. Therefore, rather than having nested loops, we should have a single loop with a compound looping terminator (which more closely matches our other merging programs):

```
WHILE more transactions OR more master records DO
     IF old master key < transaction key THEN
         Transfer master record and get a new one
     ELSE
         BEGIN
             Process transaction;
             Get next transaction
         END
```

This outline assumes that old master and transaction file are both terminated by a SENTINEL record so that the key comparison will still work properly. Notice, too, that if we get to "Process transaction," there will be a real transaction to process. At that point old master key $>=$ transaction key, so if transaction key is the SENTINEL, so is old master key and the loop would have terminated before we got here.

EXAMPLE 9.5.1   A program to perform the merge update as in the preceding discussion is

```
(* EXAMPLE 9.5.1: MERGEUPDATE      *)
(* MERGE OLD MASTER FILE OM WITH *)
(* SORTED TRANSACTION FILE T TO    *)
(* PRODUCE NEW MASTER NM           *)

PROGRAM MERGEUPDATE(OM,NM,T,OUTPUT);

CONST MAXCHAR = 127; (* = MAX ORD(CHAR) *)

TYPE MREC = RECORD KEY: ALFA; BALANCE: REAL (* . . . *) END;
     TRANSTYPE = (ADD, DELETE, UPDATE);
     TREC = RECORD KEY: ALFA;
               CASE TTP: TRANSTYPE OF
                  ADD: (NEWREC: MREC);
                  DELETE: ( );
                  UPDATE: (CHANGE: REAL)
               END;

VAR   OM, NM: FILE OF MREC;  (* OLD, NEW MASTER FILES *)
      T: FILE OF TREC;          (* TRANSACTION FILE, SORTED *)
      SENTINEL: ALFA;           (* FOR IMPOSSIBLY LARGE KEY *)
      I: INTEGER;               (* USED TO SET SENTINEL *)

BEGIN (* MERGEUPDATE *)
   FOR I := 1 TO 10 DO SENTINEL[I] := CHR(MAXCHAR);
   RESET(OM); RESET(T); REWRITE(NM);

   WHILE (T^.KEY < SENTINEL) OR (OM^.KEY < SENTINEL) DO
      IF (OM^.KEY < T^.KEY) THEN
         BEGIN (* TRANSFER MASTER REC *)
            NM^ := OM^; PUT(NM); GET(OM)
         END
      ELSE
         BEGIN (* PROCESS TRANSACTION *)
            IF (OM^.KEY = T^.KEY) THEN
               BEGIN
                  CASE T^.TTP OF
                     ADD: WRITELN('BAD ADD AT  ', T^.KEY);
```

```
                    DELETE: ; (* NO TRANSFER *)
                    UPDATE: BEGIN
                              OM^.BALANCE :=
                                  OM^.BALANCE+T^.CHANGE;
                              NM^ := OM^; PUT(NM)
                          END
                    END;
                    GET(OM)
                END
            ELSE CASE T^.TTP OF
                    ADD: BEGIN
                              NM^ := T^.NEWREC; PUT(NM)
                        END;
            DELETE, UPDATE: WRITELN('NO RECORD   ', T^.KEY)
                    END;
                    GET(T)   (* GET NEXT TRANSACTION *)
                END (* PROCESS TRANSACTION *)
        END.   (* MERGEUPDATE *)
```

Exercise 9.5

The only case in the MERGEUPDATE loop in which we did not do a GET(OM) was on processing an ADD transaction. Why must we not do a GET(OM) here? Could this lead to an infinite loop?

Programming Problems

9.1 You are to write a program to prepare an index for a book. It is assumed that all references in the index are represented in a file RF by records consisting of 20 (PACKED) characters of text and an integer page number. You may assume that the file has already been sorted in order by text information and, within the same text information, in increasing order by page number. Thus the input file might start out like

ANVIL	24
ANVIL	36
AXE	12
AXE	108
AXE	144
BALL-BEARING	27
. . .	

from which you are to produce a listing as follows:

A

ANVIL 24, 36
AXE 12, 108, 144

B

BALL-BEARING 27

. . .

9.2 You are to write a program which takes as input arbitrarily many lines of text, each a name of a book or article, and produces a KWIC (Key Word In Context) index. In a KWIC index, each word in each title is considered to be a keyword (in actual applications, simple words like A, and THE, are not considered). The titles are printed arranged so that the keywords appear in a standard position, alphabetized. Assume that the input is two titles:

SURVEY OF PROGRAMMING CONCEPTS
CONCEPTS OF SURVEYING

Your program would first produce a file with keywords in standard positions:

|←   line start |←   keyword start

| SURVEY OF PROGRAMMING CONCEPTS
                        SURVEY   OF PROGRAMMING CONCEPTS
                     SURVEY OF   PROGRAMMING CONCEPTS
       SURVEY OF PROGRAMMING   CONCEPTS
                                        CONCEPTS OF SURVEYING
                      CONCEPTS   OF SURVEYING
                   CONCEPTS OF   SURVEYING

The next phase of your program merge-sorts this file, producing

       SURVEY OF PROGRAMMING   CONCEPTS
                                        CONCEPTS OF SURVEYING
                        SURVEY   OF PROGRAMMING CONCEPTS
                      CONCEPTS   OF SURVEYING
                     SURVEY OF   PROGRAMMING CONCEPTS
                                        SURVEY OF PROGRAMMING CONCEPTS
                   CONCEPTS OF   SURVEYING

Thus someone looking for articles in a particular area (for example, surveying) can quickly locate all articles with this or similar words in the title (a real KWIC index would also include other information, such as location of article).

Your program should assume that titles are at most 40 characters long. Input will be terminated by a line starting with four asterisks: ****. The records in the intermediate file to be sorted are PACKED ARRAY [1 . . 80] OF CHAR, the first 39 characters being title up to the keyword, the fortieth an obligatory extra blank for readability, and 41 . . 80 the keyword and subsequent words of the title. The key to be sorted on will be characters 41 . . 80. Your program should produce a listing of the sorted file as its final output.

(Note: A computer whose character set has the blank after the alphabet will give a slightly different ordering from the one above.)

chapter 10

real numbers

The fact that this chapter comes at the end of the book should not be taken as an indication of the importance of understanding real numbers and arithmetic. The position of this chapter is due more to the fact that there was no other convenient place to put it.

The reader has done enough programming by now that he or she would undoubtedly attest to the importance of real numbers, and has probably wondered more than once why we have to deal with any other type of number. Unfortunately, though, real numbers have the insidious property of doing exactly what you expect them to do 99.9% of the time so that the remaining 0.1% is a rude surprise. For example, if the program

```
PROGRAM BIGGERTHANONE(OUTPUT);

VAR X: REAL;
```

```
BEGIN (* BIGGERTHANONE *)
    X := 0.05;
    WHILE (X <= 1) DO X := X + 0.05;
    WRITELN(X)  (* SHOULD BE 1.05 *)
END.  (* BIGGERTHANONE *)
```

is run on a PDP-11, it produces the output

```
1.000000E+00
```

Does this mean that there is something wrong with Pascal or the PDP-11? Not at all. It is simply evidence of the inherent limitations of computer representation of real numbers. The purpose of this chapter is to explain such common anomalies connected with the use of real numbers. We will avoid the deeper problems that require extensive mathematical analysis.

10.1   FLOATING-POINT NUMBERS

To understand the vagaries of real numbers in computer programs, it is necessary to have some understanding of their representation inside the computer. This internal form is called *floating-point* numbers. It varies from machine to machine, but there are enough common features that we can give a general description here which is not too far different from any actual one.

The first thing to remember about real numbers in computers is that in general it would take infinitely many digits to represent the average real number exactly, and that a computer can use only finitely many digits. In fact, one or two computer words are generally used (32 to 64 binary digits) to represent one floating-point number. This is divided into a sign bit, an *exponent* part (generally 7 to 11 bits), and a *fraction* part (the remaining 24+ bits); as in Figure 10.1, where s

s	e1	...	en	f1	...	fm

FIGURE 10.1

is the sign of the fraction, e1 . . . en the exponent with the exponent's sign encoded in some way, and f1 . . . fm the fraction, interpreted as having a binary point (the binary equivalent of the decimal point) immediately to the left of f1. The value of this real number is

$$s\ 0.f1 \ldots fm * 2 ** e1 \ldots en$$

(The sign bit goes with the fraction even though it is usually physically separated from it.) Usually, the computer arranges it so that the fraction is *normalized;* that is f1 is 1. A nonzero real number can always be normalized: just shift the fraction to the left until f1 is 1, subtracting 1 from the exponent for each position shifted. The reason for normalization is that it gives the most possible room to show nonzero digits. (On IBM System 360/370 computers and some others the exponent is interpreted as a power of 16 rather than a power of 2, so a normalized number is a number with one of the first four digits of the fraction equal to 1. Such numbers are often said to be *base 16,* even though their parts are still encoded in binary.)

This brings us to the subject of *significant digits.* The number of significant digits in a real number is the number of digits from the first *nonzero* digit to the last *meaningful* digit. Assuming that only meaningful digits are written, each of the following has six significant digits

$$123456E+20 \qquad 0.00300021 \qquad -4256.33$$

Of course, computers generally represent significant *binary* digits, and when translated to decimal terms, this does not correspond to a whole number of significant decimal digits. Rather than worry about this, though, a good rule of thumb is that you can always count on at least six significant decimal digits. (Note though that the computer will give you these digits whether or not they are actually significant. If you perform a computation such as PI := 22/7 which is accurate to only three digits, the floating-point result would still appear to have at least six significant digits.)

The possible exponent range also does not translate exactly into decimal, but you can generally count on a range of at least 10 ∗∗ ±35.

To give simple examples involving floating-point numbers, we will use a decimal representation with four-digit fraction part and single-digit exponent in the form

$$\pm.NNNNe\pm N$$

To reflect the rigid format of internal representations, we will always write out all signs and digits and use a lowercase e instead of uppercase, but numerically we will consider such a number the same as ±0.NNNNE±N.

Every real number x has a nearest floating-point number fl(x), which we obtain by rounding x to four significant digits and normalizing. Thus

$$fl(34265) \quad = +.3427e+5$$
$$fl(-0.00949) = -.9490e-2$$

(Note that a 5 is always rounded up. If the exponent turns out to be less than -9, we say that fl(x) = +.0000e+0, and if the exponent is greater than +9, this is an error (overflow), and we will not consider that here.)

Every real number x, at least every one that is small enough, is represented internally in our hypothetical machine by fl(x). Note that if $x < y$, we can say only that fl(x) $\leq$ fl(y); for example,

$$\text{fl}(12345) = \text{fl}(12354.999999) = +.1235e+5$$

Exercises 10.1

1. Compute fl(-24.33), fl(0.00072565), fl(-0.00302), and fl(423.558).

2. What is the value of each of the following floating-point numbers, not using exponential notation: +.5323e+3, +.9090e-3, -.1233e+5, -.3326e-2.

Ordinary arithmetic operations applied to floating-point numbers usually produce results with more (or fewer) than four significant digits, so special operations are required which will produce results which are again floating-point numbers. We will call these operations [+], [-], [*], and [/]. They can be easily defined using the ordinary operations and fl; for example, x [+] y = fl($x + y$). But it is also instructive to give a more constructive description which is fairly indicative of how the computer actually performs the operations.

Addition, [+], is the most complicated. There are two cases.

Case 1: If the two numbers to be added have exponents differing by five or more (the number of significant digits here is four), then the smaller cannot effect the larger and the result is the operand with the larger exponent; for example,

$$+.2222e+8 \text{ [+] } +.9999e+2 = +.2222e+8$$

Case 2: If the exponents differ by four or less, the decimal point on the number with the smaller exponent is shifted left and its exponent increased until the exponents are the same. The numbers are then added (the CPU has room for the extra digits needed to develop the sum properly), rounded to four significant figures, and normalized. For example,

$$
\begin{aligned}
+.2153e+3 \text{ [+] } +.5136e+5 &= \text{fl}(0.2153\text{E}3 + 0.5136\text{E}5) \\
&= \text{fl}(0.002153\text{E}5 + 0.5136\text{E}5) \\
&= \text{fl}(0.515753\text{E}5) \\
&= +.5158e+5
\end{aligned}
$$

$$
\begin{aligned}
+.2153e+3 \text{ [+] } +.9983e+5 &= \text{fl}(0.002153\text{E}5 + 0.9983\text{E}5) \\
&= \text{fl}(1.000453\text{E}5) \\
&= +.1000e+6
\end{aligned}
$$

$$+.2431e+8 \; [+] \; -.2503e+8 = fl(-0.0072e+8)$$
$$= -.7200e+6$$

Notice that the last result still appears to have four significant digits but in fact the last two digits are meaningless, since, for instance, +.2431e+8 can represent anything from 0.24305E8 to 0.243149999E8. This loss of significance is typical when two nearly equal numbers are subtracted and will be discussed further in the next section.

Multiplication, [*], of real numbers is conceptually simpler than addition: just multiply the fractions, add the exponents, and round and normalize. Thus

$$+.2153e+3 \; [*] \; +.6148e+5 = fl(0.13236644E8)$$
$$= +.1324e+8$$

$$+.2106e-2 \; [*] \; +.3151e+4 = fl(0.06636006E2)$$
$$= +.6636e+1$$

Subtraction, [-], and division, [/], are similar to addition and multiplication, respectively.

Exercises 10.1, continued

3. Perform the following arithmetic operations:

$$+.5831e+3 \; [+] \; +.6714e+3 =$$
$$-.5831e+3 \; [+] \; +.6714e+3 =$$
$$-.3188e+5 \; [+] \; +.2242e-1 =$$
$$+.2242e+3 \; [+] \; +.2832e+1 =$$
$$-.9212e+8 \; [+] \; -.7877e+7 =$$
$$+.5111e+3 \; [*] \; +.2222e+2 =$$
$$+.3333e+5 \; [*] \; +.1111e-1 =$$

4. Why is it necessary to round *before* normalizing when $fl(x)$ is computed?

5. Find a floating-point number x such that $(x \; [+] \; x) / 2 \neq x$.

As we have seen, it is often the case that floating-point numbers which should not be equal are equal. What has even more disastrous consequences is when floating-point numbers which should be equal are not. In particular, some well-known laws of arithmetic are nonlaws of floating-point arithmetic. The associative laws $(a + b) + c = a + (b + c)$ and $(a * b) * c = a * (b * c)$ do not hold for floating-point operations, and neither does the distributive law $a * (b + c) = a * b + a * c$. For example,

$$(+.2000e+3 \; [+] \; -.2000e+3) \; [+] \; +.1111e+1 = +.1111e+1$$

+.2000e+3 [+] (−.2000e+3 [+] +.1111e+1)
    = +.2000e+3 [+] fl(−0.2000E3 + 0.001111E+3)
    = +.2000e+3 [+] fl(−0.198889E3)
    = +.2000e+3 [+] −.1989e+3
    = fl(0.0011E3)
    = +.1100e+1

(+.2000e−2 [∗] +.5000e+3) [∗] +.3333e+1
    = +.10000e+1 [∗] +.3333e+1 = +.3333e+1

+.2000e−2 [∗] (+.5000e+3 [∗] +.3333e+1)
    = +.2000e−2 [∗] fl(0.16665E4)
    = +.2000e−2 [∗] +.1667e+4 = +.3334e+1

+.5000e+1 [∗] (+.4001e+1 [+] −.4000e+1)
    = +.5000e+1 [∗] +.1000e−2 = +.5000e−2

+.5000e+1 [∗] +.4001e+1 [+] +.5000e+1 [∗] −.4000e+1
    = fl(0.20005E2) [+] fl(−0.2E2)
    = +.2001e+2 [+] −.2000e+2
    = fl(0.0001E2) = +.1000e−1

Exercises 10.1, continued

6. Compute

+.4000e+1 [∗] (+.4000e+1 [∗] +.4004e+1) =
(+.4000e+1 [∗] +.4000e+1) [∗] +.4004e+1 =

+.3000e+0 [∗] (+.6000e+3 [+] −.5999e+3) =
+.3000e+0 [∗] +.6000e+3 [+] +.3000e+0 [∗] −.5999e+3 =

+.6000e+5 [+] (−.6000e+5 [+] +.1234e+0) =
(+.6000e+5 [+] −.6000e+5) [+] +.1234e+0 =

+.3000e+1 [+] (−.3555e+1 [+] +.5555e+0) =
(+.3000e+1 [+] −.3555e+1) [+] +.5555e+0 =

10.2   RULES OF REALS

Based on the discussion of Section 10.1, we can explain the following
three rules for use of real variables in programming:

> ### The Real Rules:
>
> 1. Never test two real numbers for equality.
> 2. Try to add reals of similar size.
> 3. Try *not* to subtract reals of similar size.

These rules are oversimplified to make them easier to remember. We will spend the rest of this section treating each rule in considerably more detail.

Rule 1 follows from the principle that floating-point numbers are almost never equal, even when they should be. We have already seen numerous examples of this in the last section (where a [+] (b [+] c) was seen not always to be (a [+] b) [+] c, for instance). (Many of those examples also failed rule 2 or 3.)

There are several reasons why reals do not turn out to be equal when they should be.

1. With only finitely many digits of precision, the value of many reals cannot be exactly represented by floating-point numbers. This is not too surprising for PI, SQRT(2), or even 1/3; however, there are many reals that have finite decimal representations that do not have finite binary representations. This in fact explains why the program BIGGERTHANONE at the start of the chapter failed. 0.05 does not have a finite binary representation:

$$0.05 = 0.0000110011001100 \ldots (\text{base } 2)$$

(0.1 does not either, but it happens that on the PDP-11 with the particular Pascal used, rounding causes 0.1 to work "correctly" where 0.05 does not.)

At this point you might want to find out what numbers like 0.1 "really" are internally, and you might try to do so by printing them out. As we saw in BIGGERTHANONE, X printed as though it was exactly 1, even though we know that since the loop terminated, X must have been greater than 1. If we try a WRITELN(X:20) to get more digits of precision, we are doomed to failure also. Usually, when you get to the limit of the number of significant digits in a floating-point number, the output routines for them start producing garbage digits. The compiler writer can choose to either give you the garbage or round to the true number of significant digits and give you the extra digits as zeros, but in either case printing more digits does not usually give reliable results.

The solution to finding out how much X differs from 1 is to print X-1. The following program will give us various useful pieces of information:

```
PROGRAM FINDENDS(OUTPUT);

VAR SUM1, SUM2: REAL; N: INTEGER;

BEGIN (* FINDENDS *)
    SUM1 := 0; SUM2 := 0;
    FOR N := 1 TO 10 DO SUM1 := SUM1 + 0.1;
    FOR N := 1 TO 20 DO SUM2 := SUM2 + 0.05;
    WRITELN(10*0.1-1:1, SUM1-1:1, 20*0.05-1:1, SUM2-1:1)
END.    (* FINDENDS *)
```

The results of running this on a PDP-11 were

```
-6.0E-08 0.0E+00-6.0E-08 1.2E-07
```

and the results of running it on a Cyber 174 were

```
0  7.1E-015 0  7.1E-015
```

I was somewhat perplexed by the PDP-11 results because a little binary multiplication will show you that multiplying a base 2 floating-point 0.1 by 10 or 0.05 by 20 should always give you 1 exactly because of rounding (it will not give you 1 exactly for base 16 floating-point numbers). By looking at the floating-point numbers in binary, I determined that in fact this particular Pascal was not translating 0.1 correctly into binary (it was not rounding properly) so that in fact $0.1 \neq 1/10$ in this Pascal. This might be due to a defect in its translation algorithm, but it may also be due to the second reason for nonequality.

2. Approximations of results which require infinitely many steps, or at least many steps, are terminated before that number of steps are accomplished. This source of errors is of more interest in programs doing numerical analysis.

3. Error due to round-off. This, too, is more of a problem in numerical analysis but, as we saw in the last section, it can affect accuracy of even simple computations.

Given that we do not want to test two floating-point numbers for equality (or for inequality), how do we get around it? The solution in programs like BIGGERTHANONE is easy. If we are only concerned with X assuming the values 0.05, 0.10, and so on, the best solution is

```
FOR I := 1 TO 20 DO
    BEGIN
        X := I * 0.05; other processing
    END
```

If we really must use the WHILE form to stop, we use the fact that we are not really concerned with stopping at 1 exactly, merely stopping before 1.05. WHILE (X < 1.05) DO . . . is not satisfactory either though, as an X which prints as 1.05 might in fact be less than 1.05. The actual solution is to use

WHILE (X < 1.025) DO

This should work unless the computations are such that X can have really horrendous errors.

A different sort of problem is demonstrated by the standard Newton's method of finding square roots: To find the square root of X, we start with some initial guess S and then repeatedly replace S by (S + X/S)/2, which causes S to get closer and closer to the actual square root of X. How do we stop the process? You should realize by now that WHILE (SQR(S) <> X) DO . . . is not the way. In fact, if X were 2 and S were as close to SQRT(2) as possible, we would still have to get a lucky rounding to have S**2 = 2 exactly. The solution is to stop when SQR(S) is *close* to X, say WHILE (ABS(S*S - X) >= 1E-6) DO. But this is not satisfactory either. If we started with X = 1E-10 and S = 0, then we would stop immediately with a square root of 0, and if we started with X = 1E10, we would not stop until we had a square root with 16 digits of accuracy, an unlikely occurrence. Therefore, we should test for *relative* error, that is, the size of the error compared (in this case) to the size of X. We will stop when Error/X < 1E-6 (or some other small number). Repeated division could be avoided by testing for Error < X*1E-6 and computing the product only once. A reasonable program then would be

```
S := (* some guess, a reasonable one is *) (1 + X)/2;
TEST := X * 1E-6; (* or other allowable error *)
WHILE (ABS(S*S - X) >= TEST) DO
    S := (S + X/S)/2
```

To summarize, instead of testing for A = B (or A ≠ B) test for ABS(A - B)/B < some small number (or ≥ some small number). The small number should be of the order of 1E-n, where n is a little less than the number of significant digits the particular computer represents, perhaps a lot less if the computations are complicated and large errors can result.

Only the test for A = 0 remains to be discussed. Here we cannot divide by B (= 0) to get a relative error, so the best we can do is test for ABS(A) < some small number. How small that number is would have to be determined for each particular problem.

Turning now to rule 2, let us consider the effect of adding numbers of different size and how this might be avoided. The cause of the problem is easy to see. When we add two floating-point numbers whose exponents differ by quite a bit, then relatively few of the digits of the number with the smaller exponent participate in the result:

```
      +.nnnnnnnnnnnnn                    Exx
[+]   +.0000000mmmmmmmmmmmmmm           Exx
                  →|            |←  do not participate in sum
      _____

      +.ppppppppppppp                    Exx
```

If we must add two numbers of greatly different size, there seems to be no way to avoid it. And in fact there is not. The place where it can be avoided is in adding together *many* numbers of approximately the same size. If we do this by repeating something like SUM := SUM + X[I], this is all right when we start out, but after many X's have been added, SUM will be much different from X[I] in size and the sum will get less accurate. A solution to this problem is to split the sum of the X's up into several subsums and then add the subsums together.

EXAMPLE 10.2.1 The following program shows the effect of summing in two different ways:

```
(* EXAMPLE 10.2.1: TWOSUMS  *)
(* COMPARE SUMMING ALL AT *)
(* ONCE TO ADDING SUBSUMS  *)

PROGRAM TWOSUMS(OUTPUT);

CONST NTOSUM=10000;     (* NUMBER OF NUMBERS TO SUM *)
      PART = 100;       (* SIZE OF SUM PART *)
      D = 10;           (* SUM 1/D *)

VAR   SUM1,             (* SUM ALL AT ONCE *)
      SUM2,             (* SUM OF SUBSUMS *)
      SUBSUM,           (* SUM OF 'PART' NUMBERS *)
      TERM: REAL;       (* 1/D, THE SUMMAND *)
      N,                (* MAIN SUM INDEX *)
      I: INTEGER;       (* INDEX used to compute SUBSUM *)

BEGIN (* TWOSUMS *)
   TERM := 1/D;
   SUM1 := 0; SUM2 := 0;
      (* SIMPLE MINDED SUMMATION *)
   FOR N := 1 TO NTOSUM DO SUM1 := SUM1 + TERM;
      (* MORE SOPHISTICATED SUMMATION *)
   FOR N := 1 TO NTOSUM DIV PART DO
```

```
    BEGIN
      SUBSUM := 0;
      FOR K := 1 TO PART DO SUBSUM := SUBSUM + TERM;
      SUM2 := SUM2 + SUBSUM
    END;
   WRITELN(SUM1 - NTOSUM/D, SUM2 - NTOSUM/D)
  END.  (* TWOSUMS *)
```

When run on a PDP-11, this program produced the output

-9.710690E-02   6.103520E-05

(The second error is essentially the limit of the accuracy of this machine.)

Rule 3 also has an easy explanation: if two floating-point numbers have the same exponents and fractions whose first few digits are the same, then when subtracted the first few digits cancel out and we have fewer digits of precision:

$$
\begin{aligned}
& +.mmmmmmmpppppp \qquad \text{Exx}\\
&[-] +.mmmmmmmqqqqqq \qquad \text{Exx}\\
&\overline{}\\
& +.rrrrrr\,0000000\text{Eyy}
\end{aligned}
$$

Thus if $+.1111e+4$ is the internal representation of $0.11114E4$ and $+.1110e+4$ is the representation of $0.11095E4$, then

$$+.1111e+4\ [-]\ +.1110e+4 = +.1000e+1$$

which represents $0.19E1$; that is, the internal result has *no* digits of accuracy!

In Example 10.2.2 we will show a way of avoiding this problem in one particular computation. I must confess though that even in that simple algorithm it would not be obvious to me which method should be the most accurate. That is discovered by experimentation.

EXAMPLE 10.2.2 Write a program to compute the mean and standard deviation of N random numbers by two different methods. The first method is the one usually used to define the mean of $X[1 .. N]$. Compute

$$A = X[1] + \ldots + X[N] \text{ and } MEAN = A/N.$$

Then compute

$$V = [(X[1] - MEAN)**2 + \ldots + (X[N] - MEAN) ** 2]/(N-1)$$

and standard deviation $= SQRT(V)$.

The second method is what is usually called the *computational method*. It is algebraically equivalent to the first method and is called the computational method because it is easier to do by hand. In fact, we will see that it is the poorer choice if we are using a computer. To do this method, we compute A and MEAN as before, and also compute

$$B = X[1] ** 2 + \ldots + X[N] ** 2$$

Then the standard deviation is SQRT((N∗B − A∗A)/(N∗(N−1))).

In the following program, we pick our data in the form RANDOM + some fixed addend. Altering the addend will make the differences in method more evident. We also use the same basic set of random numbers for each test so that the results can be fairly compared. The program is

```
(* EXAMPLE 10.2.2: STDEV           *)
(* COMPUTE STANDARD DEVIATION *)
(* BY TWO DIFFERENT FORMULAS   *)

PROGRAM STDEV(INPUT, OUTPUT);

CONST MAXN = 1000;   (* MAXIMUM NUMBER OF DATA POINTS *)

VAR    R,               (* FIXED ARRAY OF RANDOM NUMBERS *)
       X: ARRAY [1 .. MAXN] OF REAL; (* DATA POINTS *)
       MEAN,           (* THE MEAN *)
       A,              (* SUM OF THE X'S *)
       B,              (* SUM OF SQUARES OF X'S *)
       V,              (* SUM FOR VARIANCE, FIRST METHOD *)
       STD1,           (* STANDARD DEVIATION, 1ST METHOD *)
       STD2,           (* STANDARD DEVIATION, COMP METHOD *)
       ADDER: REAL;(* BIAS FOR PSEUDO-RANDOM DATA *)
       N,              (* NUMBER OF NUMBERS TO PROCESS *)
       I: INTEGER;     (* X INDEX *)

FUNCTION RANDOM: REAL; EXTERNAL;

BEGIN (* STDEV *)
   FOR I := 1 TO MAXN DO   (* GENERATE NUMS ONCE AND FOR ALL *)
      R[I] := RANDOM;
   WRITELN('TYPE BASE, NUMBER OF RANDOM NUMBERS');
   READ(ADDER, N);
   WHILE (N <> 0) DO (* COMPUTE STD DEV BY 2 METHODS *)
      BEGIN
         A := 0; B := 0;
         FOR I := 1 TO N DO
            BEGIN
               X[I]  := ADDER + R[I];
```

```
              A := A + X[I];
              B := B + SQR(X[I])
            END;
        MEAN := A/N; V := 0;
        FOR I := 1 TO N DO
            V := V + SQR(X[I] - MEAN);
        STD1 := SQRT(V/(N-1));
        STD2 := SQRT((N*B - A * A)/(N*(N-1)));
        WRITELN(STD1, STD2);
        READ(ADDER, N)
      END
  END.  (* STDEV *)
```

The program was run on a CDC Cyber 174 (which has floating point with about 14 significant decimal digits) with the following results (note that standard deviation is a measure of the difference between data and its mean, so the size of ADDER should not change the actual standard deviation; digits in which the two methods differ are underlined).

```
TYPE BASE, NUMBER OF RANDOM NUMBERS
?       0    100
   2.7419954467600E-001        2.7419954467599E-001
?     100    100
   2.7419954467600E-001        2.7419954386522E-001
?    1000    100
   2.7419954467602E-001        2.7419954913496E-001
?       0   1000
   2.7937840294157E-001        2.7937840294159E-001
?     100   1000
   2.7937840294156E-001        2.7937840404923E-001
?    1000   1000
   2.7937840294152E-001        2.7937860327245E-001
?       0     0
```

It is thus easy to see that the first method is quite accurate, while the second (the "computational" method) is quite inaccurate

It is difficult to reason out beforehand which of these methods should be better since both involve subtracting numbers which might be of about the same size, so the following after-the-fact explanation may be somewhat suspect. Computing A - B tends to introduce much more inaccuracy than computing the individual (X[I] - MEAN)**2's, because the variations in the data tend to cancel out when everything is added up (if they did not, there would be an enormous difference between A and B and the standard deviation would also be enormous).

286

Exercises 10.2

1. Why should the size of ADDER make a difference in the results of Example 10.2.2?

2. Write a loop to do "Process X" for X = 0, INC, 2∗INC, . . ., 1, where it is not known beforehand what INC is, but only that it divides 1 evenly (in the real world, so perhaps only approximately as floating-point numbers). Do two versions, one with a FOR loop and one with a WHILE loop (that stops when X > 1 + something).

3. It is a mathematical fact that as x gets larger and larger, the quantity $(1 + 1/x) ** x$ gets closer and closer to $e = 2.7182818284 \ldots$. Explain the results of the following program:

```
PROGRAM E(OUTPUT);

    VAR N: INTEGER; (*INDEX *)
        X: REAL; (* = 10 ** N *)

    BEGIN (* E *)
        X := 1E5;
        FOR N := 6 TO 18 DO
            BEGIN
                X := 10 * X;
                WRITELN(N, EXP(X * LN(1 + 1/X)))
            END
    END.  (* E *)
```

which were (on a Cyber 174):

6	2.7182804624564E+000
7	2.7182817243111E+000
8	2.7182820397793E+000
9	2.7182723947509E+000
10	2.7183303400528E+000
11	2.7175578540066E+000
12	2.7233568554571E+000
13	2.7040748258079E+000
14	2.0350954780611E+000
15	1.0000000000000E+000
16	1.0000000000000E+000
17	1.0000000000000E+000
18	1.0000000000000E+000

4. The following is a (rather inefficient) program to compute cube roots, which disobeys rule 1 in the line marked (* ??? *). How should it be fixed?

```
PROGRAM CUBEROOT(INPUT, OUTPUT);

    VAR X, INC, R: REAL;
```

```
BEGIN (* CUBEROOT *)
    READ(X);
    WHILE (X > 0) DO
        BEGIN
            INC := -10; (* TO GIVE FIRST INC OF 1 *)
            R := 0;
            REPEAT
                INC := -INC/10;
                WHILE (R < X) DO R := R + INC
            UNTIL (R*R*R = X); (* ??? *)
            WRITELN(R);
            READ(X)
        END
END.  (* CUBEROOT *)
```

Programming Problems

10.1 Determine the approximate number of significant decimal digits on your computer by determining the largest n for which $(1En - 1) - (1En - 2)$ = 1; that is, determine the maximum number of digits for which $9 \ldots 99 - 9 \ldots 98 = 1$. (And here we want exact equality!)

10.2 Write a computer program to compute $1 - 1/2 + 1/3 - \cdots + 1/9999 - 1/10{,}000$ in four ways:

(a) Left to right as given.

(b) By computing $A = 1 + 1/3 + \cdots + 1/9999$ and $B = 1/2 + 1/4 + \cdots + 1/10{,}000$ and subtracting B from A.

(c) Using the fact that $1/N - 1/(N + 1) = 1/(N(N + 1))$, sum

$$1/(1 * 2) + 1/(2 * 3) + \cdots + 1/(9999 * 10{,}000)$$

9999 * 10,000 may be too large to be an integer on your machine so compute the terms as $(1/N) * (1/(N + 1))$.

(d) By computing the same sum as in method (c), but backward.

The correct sum to 20 decimal places (computed by method (d) using double precision arithmetic in FORTRAN on a CDC Cyber 174) is

$$0.69309718305994529692.$$

Try to explain the varying degrees of accuracy of your results.

appendix A

the STATES file

The following is a list of the STATES file which is used in several programming problems in the text. The fields are, in order, state name, population (1960 census), area, date of admission, order of admission, and capital. The numbers at the top of the file are column numbers and are a guide only. The actual first line of the file is MAINE.

0		1	2	2	3	3	3	3	4	
1		8	3	6	0	2	5	8	0	
MAINE		969265		33215		1820		23		AUGUSTA
NEW HAMPSHIRE		606921		9304		1788		9		CONCORD
VERMONT		389881		9609		1791		14		MONTPELIER
MASSACHUSETTS		5148578		8257		1788		6		BOSTON
RHODE ISLAND		859488		1214		1790		13		PROVIDENCE
CONNECTICUT		2535234		5009		1788		5		HARTFORD
NEW YORK		16782304		49576		1788		11		ALBANY
PENNSYLVANIA		11319366		45333		1787		2		HARRISBURG
DELAWARE		446292		2057		1787		1		DOVER

MARYLAND	3100689	10577	1788	7	ANNAPOLIS
VIRGINIA	3966949	40815	1788	10	RICHMOND
NORTH CAROLINA	4556155	52712	1789	12	RALEIGH
SOUTH CAROLINA	2382594	31055	1788	8	COLUMBIA
GEORGIA	3943116	58876	1788	4	ATLANTA
FLORIDA	4951560	58560	1845	27	TALLAHASSEE
MICHIGAN	7823194	58216	1837	26	LANSING
OHIO	9706397	41222	1803	17	COLUMBUS
INDIANA	4662498	36291	1816	19	INDIANAPOLIS
ILLINOIS	10081158	56400	1818	21	SPRINGFIELD
WISCONSIN	3951777	56154	1848	30	MADISON
KENTUCKY	3038156	40395	1792	15	FRANKFORT
TENNESSEE	3567089	42244	1796	16	NASHVILLE
ALABAMA	3266740	51609	1819	22	MONTGOMERY
MISSISSIPPI	2178141	47716	1817	20	JACKSON
LOUISIANA	3257022	48523	1812	18	BATON ROUGE
ARKANSAS	1786272	53104	1836	25	LITTLE ROCK
MISSOURI	4319813	69686	1821	24	JEFFERSON CITY
IOWA	2757537	56290	1846	29	DES MOINES
MINNESOTA	3413864	84068	1858	32	SAINT PAUL
MONTANA	674767	147138	1889	41	HELENA
NORTH DAKOTA	632446	70665	1889	40	BISMARCK
SOUTH DAKOTA	680514	77047	1889	39	PIERRE
WYOMING	330066	97914	1890	44	CHEYENNE
COLORADO	1753947	104247	1876	38	DENVER
NEBRASKA	1411330	77227	1867	37	LINCOLN
KANSAS	2178611	82264	1861	34	TOPEKA
OKLAHOMA	2328284	69919	1907	46	OKLAHOMA CITY
TEXAS	9579677	267339	1845	28	AUSTIN
NEW MEXICO	951023	121666	1912	47	SANTA FE
ARIZONA	1302161	113909	1912	48	PHOENIX
UTAH	890627	84916	1896	45	SALT LAKE CITY
NEVADA	285278	110540	1864	36	CARSON CITY
IDAHO	667191	83557	1890	43	BOISE
WEST VIRGINIA	1860421	24181	1863	35	CHARLESTON
WASHINGTON	2853214	68192	1889	42	OLYMPIA
OREGON	1768687	96981	1859	33	SALEM
CALIFORNIA	15717204	158693	1850	31	SACRAMENTO
ALASKA	226167	586400	1959	49	JUNEAU
NEW JERSEY	6066782	7836	1787	3	TRENTON
HAWAII	632772	6424	1959	50	HONOLULU

appendix

selected nonstandard Pascal features

In this appendix we consider four features as implemented by various Pascals. Of necessity this represents a very small sample of Pascals (there are at least 16 for the DEC PDP-11 alone) and features. The choices I have made are not to imply any endorsement or lack thereof of implementations. Features considered are the following.

1. Binding of external permanent files to internal file variables (in particular, whether this can be done dynamically during program execution; see Section 3.6).
2. Interactive I/O method (see Section 1.13.5).
3. Character array READ (see Section 1.13.4).
4. Abnormal program termination (see Section 1.14).

In each of the following sections we list first the general class of machines on which the Pascal runs, the vendor, and the particular version considered.

B.1   CDC 6000 AND CYBER 70 AND 170 COMPUTERS

(University Computer Center, University of Minnesota, Minneapolis, Minnesota 55455). Pascal 6000 Version 3 running under the NOS operating system.

    1. File name binding is via the PROGRAM statement, the standard way. Dynamic binding, of one FILE type only per program, is available through an external procedure declared by

```
PROCEDURE OPEN(VAR F: filetype; NAME: ALFA;
                        OPENFORWRITE: BOOLEAN); EXTERN;
```

Execution of this procedure would normally be followed by RESET(F) or REWRITE(F):

    2. Interactive I/O uses method A of Section 1.13.5. An interactive file variable must be followed by a / in the PROGRAM statement.

    3. This Pascal doesn't have a built-in string reading facility but one can be simulated using its dynamic array facility, as follows:

```
PROCEDURE READS(VAR S: DYNAMIC ALFA);
    VAR I: INTEGER;
    BEGIN (* READS *)
      I := 1;
      WHILE (I <= HIGH(S)) AND NOT EOLN DO
        BEGIN
          READ(S[I]);
          I := I + 1
        END;
        FOR I := I TO HIGH(S) DO S[I] := '
    END; (* READS *)
```

READS can be called with any PACKED ARRAY OF CHAR as argument.

    4. Programs can be terminated with post-mortem dump by executing

```
HALT(message)
```

which prints "message" before the dump.

B.2   DEC PDP–11 COMPUTERS

Oregon Software Inc., 2340 SW Canyon Road, Portland, Oregon 97201. OMSI Pascal Version 1.2 running under RSTS/E and other operating systems.

1. The PROGRAM statement is optional and is ignored. ALL files must be associated with permanent external files via RESET(F, 'externalname') or REWRITE(F, 'externalname').

2. Interactive I/O is the lazy input of Section 1.13.4, modified in such a way that an empty line will seem to consist of one blank. Thus if we run Example 1.13.2 in this system, the result is

```
TYPE IN LINES OF INPUT
ABCDEFGH<CR>
<CR>
IJK<CR>
$<CR>

ABCDEFGH       IJK   $ (Note extra blank between H and I!)
```

3. Reading a character array works as postulated in Section 1.13.4.
4. There is no abnormal termination instruction in OMSI Pascal.

B.3   MOST MICROCOMPUTERS

Softech Microsystems, 9494 Black Mountain Road, San Diego, California 92126. UCSD Pascal Version II.0 running under its own operating system on a DEC LSI–11.

1. The PROGRAM statement is ignored. External files are associated with a file variable F via RESET(F, 'filename') or REWRITE(F 'filename'). In addition the standard forms of RESET and REWRITE are available for scratch files (which last only the length of the program run).

2. Interactive I/O is handled using a special file type called INTERACTIVE which is the same as TEXT except that what might be called *very* lazy input is used. There is not even any look-ahead when testing EOLN and EOF. Thus EOLN occurs after the end-of-line phony blank is read. This is partially compensated for by a READLN which reads until EOLN is true and then merely turns the indicator off, instead of reading another character. Thus READLN is not equivalent to any other piece of code! If Example 1.13.2 is executed with the input

```
ABCDEFGH<CR>
<CR>
```

```
IJK<CR>
$          (NO <CR>!!!)
```

the output is

```
                 ' '      '
  ABCDEFGH   IJK  $
```

(EOLNs are shifted one to the right.) Note that there is immediate input on reading of characters, so the user must take care of character erase and the like. However, on input of numbers or strings, this erasure is handled by the system.

3. UCSD Pascal has a special type STRING[N] similar to PACKED ARRAY [0 . . N] of CHAR which stores the STRING's variable length in character 0 and the characters in 1 . . N. READ(STRING variable) works much as we postulated READ(character array), except that now blank fill is not required because of a STRING's variable length.

4. Abnormal termination is handled by including a 'PROGRAM name' statement and executing EXIT(name).

B.4   DEC VAX–11

Digital Equipment Corporation, Maynard, Massachusetts 01754. VAX Pascal V2.1 running under VMS.

1. External files can be bound to file variables statically using the standard PROGRAM statement or dynamically by executing OPEN(filevariable, filename) just before RESET or REWRITE.

2. Interactive I/O uses lazy input.

3. Reading of character arrays works as postulated in Section 1.13.4.

4. Abnormal program termination can be handled with the HALT (no parameters) built-in procedure.

B.5   SPERRY UNIVAC 1100 COMPUTERS

Academic Computer Center, University of Wisconsin, 1210 W. Dayton St., Madison, Wisconsin 53706.

1. Binding of external file names to file variables is through the PROGRAM statement only. There is no dynamic binding.

2. Interactive I/O is done by lazy input.

3. There are no built-in facilities for reading a character array.

4. The STOP statement can be used for abnormal program termination.

B.6   IBM SYSTEM 360/370 COMPUTERS

Australian Atomic Energy Commission, Private Mail Bag, Sutherland, NSW 2232, Australia. Pascal 8000 Version 1.2 running on IBM System/360 under OS.

1. File binding through PROGRAM statement only.

2. There seems to be no facility for interactive I/O.

3. Character array read is implemented as in Section 1.13.4.

4. Executing the HALT procedure (no parameters) causes an immediate halt with post-mortem dump.

Finally, and rather depressingly, we have:

B.7.   PROPOSED ISO PASCAL STANDARD

(See the Bibliography for a reference).

1. File binding is through the PROGRAM statement only.

2. No special treatment of (or recognition of) interactive I/O.

3. Reading of character arrays is not included in the standard. It is possible to simulate this as in section B.1 with a slightly different syntax:

```
PROCEDURE READS(VAR S: PACKED ARRAY [LO .. HI: INTEGER] OF CHAR);
    VAR I: INTEGER;
    BEGIN (* READS *)
      I := LO;
      WHILE (I <= HI) AND NOT EOLN DO
        BEGIN
          READ(S[I]);
          I := I + 1
        END;
        FOR I := I TO HI DO S[I] := ' '
    END; (* READS *)
```

4. Abnormal termination is not included in the standard.

appendix C

a pseudo-random number generator

A good pseudo-random number generator will be different for different machines because of variations in arithmetic, precision, etc. Details for writing and testing such functions are found in D. Knuth's *The Art of Computer Programming*, vol. 2. See particularly the summary on pp. 170-73.

A compromise function which should work reasonably well (if slowly) on all computers for up to 10,000 or so numbers is as follows:

```
CONST SEED = 0.1; (* 0 <= SEED < 1 *)

VAR LASTR: REAL; (* LAST RANDOM NUMBER *)
```

```
FUNCTION RANDOM: REAL;
    CONST MPYER = 309.0; ADDER = 0.203125;
    BEGIN (* RANDOM *)
        LASTR := MPYER * LASTR + ADDER;
        LASTR := LASTR – TRUNC(LASTR);
        RANDOM := LASTR
    END; (* RANDOM *)
    .
    .
    .

BEGIN (* MAIN PROGRAM *)
    LASTR := SEED; (* INITIALIZE RANDOM' ONCE! *)
    .
    .
    .
```

RANDOM is uniformly distributed with $0 \leqslant$ RANDOM < 1. Notice that LASTR must be a global variable so that its value is preserved between calls to RANDOM.

appendix D

the WITH statement

The WITH statement can be a great convenience when manipulating RECORDS (introduced in Chapter 3). It is not used in this book, but as it is useful and its explanation a good application of contour diagrams (see Section 6.4), it will be introduced and discussed here.

The general form of the WITH statement is

```
WITH record name DO
     statement
```

("statement" is usually compound). Roughly, this has the effect of adding "record name ." ahead of each field name in "statement" where it is needed. Thus, if we have declared

```
TYPE REC = RECORD B, C, D: . . .

VAR A: REC;
```

then the statement

```
WITH A DO
    BEGIN
        B := . . .
        C := . . .
        D := . . .
    END
```

is equivalent to

```
A.B := . . .
A.C := . . .
A.D := . . .
```

The record name can be an evaluated expression; for example, it we have REC as before and declare

```
VAR  M: ARRAY [1 . . 10] OF REC;
     P:  ^REC;
     F:  FILE OF REC;
```

then WITH M[I+3] DO. . ., WITH P^ DO. . ., and WITH F^ DO. . . are all legal.

Pascal Pointer 27

Each time the "record name" part of a WITH statement changes, the WITH statement must be reevaluated.

Thus

```
I := 1;
WITH M[I] DO (* WRONG! *)
    WHILE (I <= 10) DO
        BEGIN
            B := . . .
            I := I + 1
        END
```

will process M[1] 10 times! The (probably) correct form is

```
I := 1;
WHILE (I <= 10) DO
    BEGIN
        WITH M[I] DO
            BEGIN
                B := . . .
            END;
        I := I + 1
    END
```

Similarly,

```
WITH F^ DO (* WRONG! *)
    WHILE NOT EOF(F) DO
        BEGIN
            process F^;
            GET(F) (* see Chapter 9 about F^, GET *)
        END
```

may process the first record of the file several times and miss subsequent records.

To explain exactly how the WITH statement works, we look at the contour model. First we extend it to allow RECORD variables. VAR A: REC; would be represented as in Figure D.1. Execution of a WITH statement, like entry of a procedure or function, causes a new contour

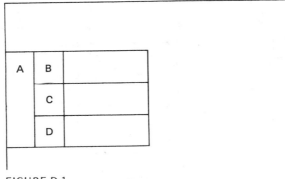

FIGURE D.1

to be created, in effect encompassing the "statement" in the WITH statement. All field names in the "record name" become the variable names in the new contour, with arrows referring back to the corresponding fields of "record name" instead of storage space of their own. Thus

```
WITH A DO statement
```

causes the contours of Figure D.2. These "variables" in the new contour act much like VAR parameters to procedures and functions. The contour model helps to explain apparent ambiguities here too. For instance, if we have declared

```
VAR B: . . .;
    A: REC;
```

then within "WITH A DO statement" we have Figure D.3, and here B alone would refer to A.B, since as usual we start in the innermost

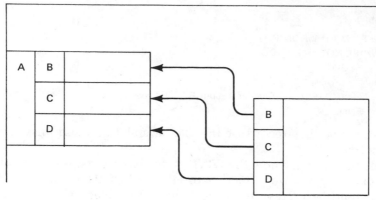

FIGURE D.2

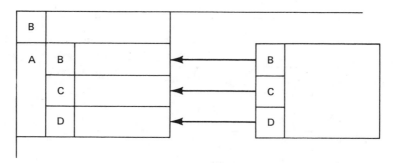

FIGURE D.3

contour looking for B and work out. The B in the outer contour would be invisible within the WITH statement. Similarly, outside the WITH statement, B alone refers to the B not in a RECORD.

A similar apparent ambiguity results from

```
VAR   A: RECORD B, C, D: ...
      X: RECORD M, B, Q: ...

      WITH A DO
          WITH X DO
              ... B ... C ...
```

Once again, contours tell the story (see Figure D.4). B is found in the innermost contour and therefore refers to X.B, while for C we must go out one contour, and so C refers to A.C. Thus

```
      WITH A DO WITH X DO ...
```

is not the same as

```
      WITH X DO WITH A DO ...
```

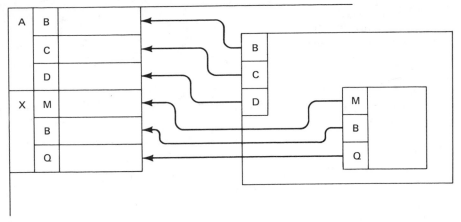

FIGURE D.4

Nested WITH statements may be abbreviated: WITH A, X DO is equivalent to

```
WITH A DO
    WITH X DO
```

(and is *not* equivalent to WITH X, A DO).

Exercises D

1. Suppose we have declared

```
VAR A: RECORD B : REAL;
                C. RECORD D, B, F: REAL END;
                G: REAL
        END;
```

Draw a contour diagram showing the situation when "statement" as follows is being executed:

```
WITH A DO
    WITH C DO
        statement
```

2. Suppose we have declared

```
VAR A, B: RECORD X, Y: REAL END; X: REAL;
```

What is printed by the segment

```
A.X := 2; B.X := 8; X := –5;
WRITELN(X);
WITH A DO WRITELN(X);
WITH A DO
    WITH B DO
```

```
        WRITELN(X);
WITH A, B DO WRITELN(X);
WITH B, A DO WRITELN(X)
```

Pascal pointers, principles, and model programs

E.1 PASCAL POINTERS

1. Literals with decimal point must have digits both *before* and *after* the decimal point.
2. 8/5 = 1.6, *not* 1.
3. Pascal *never* converts reals to integers automatically.
4. "integer variable := real expression" is not allowed.
5. If your Pascal does not have an automatic prompt, it may appear to be in an infinite loop when in fact it is waiting for input.

6. Use = for permanent assignments, in declarations; use := for (possibly) temporary assignments, in executable code.

7. Every statement must be followed by a semicolon, END, ELSE, or UNTIL.

8. There is *never* a semicolon before ELSE!

9. *Always* enclose relations in parentheses.

10. NEVER put ; after DO.

11. ALFA is spelled with an F, *not* PH!

12. NEVER use TYPE names in the executable part of your program, that is, between BEGIN and END.

13. SETs of CHARs probably will not work.

14. Always READLN just before testing EOF!

15. Sentinels are safer than EOF!

16. (Incorrect) Pascal programs often require more input than they appear to.

17. GOTO is one word!

18. FUNCTION values must be of type REAL, INTEGER, BOOLEAN, CHAR, enumerated, subrange, or pointer.

19. When assigning a value to FUNCTION name using "name := expression," the parameters to the function do not follow "name."

20. Parameters whose outside values are to be changed by a sub-program must be VAR parameters.

21. Types of parameters and function values must be simple type names.

22. If P = NIL, evaluation of P^ is a fatal error.

23. The type ^SOMETYPE should always be given a name like PTRTOSOMETYPE *before* its first use and that name only be used in declaration.

24. In FORWARD declarations, parameter and function type declarations appear ONLY in the FIRST mention of the subprogram.

25. FILE parameters to subprograms must always be VAR parameters.

26. A RECORD with variant CASE has only one END, which ends both CASE and RECORD.

27. Each time the "record name" part of a WITH statement changes, the WITH statement must be reevaluated.

E.2 PRINCIPLES

The HOUDINI Principle: Don't use magic numbers!

The SHIRLEY TEMPLE Principle: Don't get too cute!

The INSIDE-OUT Principle: Things which are done only once should be done OUTSIDE loops as much as possible.

The COWBOY Principle: Look for fundamental loops.

The PLAID Principle: Always check input for validity.

The HALVING Principle: If $n > 1$, we must replace n by n DIV 2 a total of $\text{TRUNC}(\log_2(n))$ times to get 1.

The TRIANGLE Principle: The number of points in an n by n triangle is $n(n + 1)/2$.

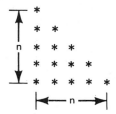

The MIKADO Principle: Make the data structure fit the application.

The MASON-DIXON Principle: Always test boundary cases.

The RECURSION Principle: Always start a recursive procedure by testing for trivial cases, and handle these nonrecursively.

E.3 MODEL PROGRAMS

Model Program 1: Read and process numbers, terminating on a sentinel.

```
CONST SENTINEL = . . .
     .
     .
     .
   READ(X);
   WHILE (X <> SENTINEL) DO
      BEGIN
         process X;
         READ(X)
      END
```

Model Program 2: Perform some process on each of A[1 .. N].

305

```
FOR I := 1 TO N DO
   BEGIN
      process A[I]
   END
```

Model Program 3:   Read items ended by a sentinel and store them in an array A[1 .. TOP], TOP a constant. Set N equal to the number of items in the array (less the sentinel).

```
N := 0; READ(TEMP);
WHILE (TEMP <> SENTINEL) AND
      (N < TOP) DO
   BEGIN
      N := N + 1; A[N] := TEMP;
      READ(TEMP)
   END
```

Model Program 4:   Read a line of characters with blank fill.

```
CONST N = ...

VAR A: ARRAY [1 .. N] OF CHAR;
    I: INTEGER;
         .
         .
    I := 0;
    WHILE (I < N) AND NOT EOLN DO
       BEGIN
          I := I + 1; READ (A[I])
       END;
       FOR I := I+1 TO N DO A[I] := ' '
```

Model Program 5:   Linear search for X in A[1 .. N]; I = 0 or A[I] = X when done.

```
A[0] := X; I := N;
WHILE (A[I] <> X) DO I := I - 1
```

Model Program 6:   Binary search A[1 .. N], in increasing order, getting A[HI] $\leqslant$ X $<$ A[HI+1] (X $<$ A[1] if HI = 0, A[N] $\leqslant$ X if HI = N).

```
LO := 1; HI := N;
WHILE (LO <= HI) DO
   BEGIN
      MID := (LO + HI) DIV 2;
      IF (X < A[MID] THEN HI := MID - 1
      ELSE LO := MID + 1
   END
```

Model Program 7: Sequentially process a linked list pointed to by FIRST.

```
P := FIRST;
WHILE (P <> NIL) DO
    BEGIN
        Process P^;
        P := P^.LINK (* P TO NEXT NODE *)
    END
```

Model Program 8: Set P pointing to the first node in the list starting at FIRST such that "P^ satisfies condition."

```
P := FIRST; FOUND := FALSE;
WHILE (P <> NIL) AND NOT FOUND DO
    IF P^ satisfies condition THEN
        FOUND := TRUE
    ELSE P := P^.LINK
```

Model Program 7s: Sequentially process a list pointed to by FIRST and ended by SENTINEL.

```
P := FIRST;
WHILE (P <> SENTINEL) DO
    BEGIN
        Process P^;
        P := P^.LINK
    END
```

Model Program 8s: Set P pointing to the first node in the list starting at FIRST and ended by SENTINEL such that "P^ satisfies condition." If no such P is found, P will be left equal to SENTINEL.

```
P := FIRST;
Make SENTINEL^ satisfy condition;
WHILE (P^ doesn't satisfy condition) DO
    P := P^.LINK;
IF (P = SENTINEL) THEN not found
```

bibliography

The following is an annotated bibliography of books and articles that may be of interest to the reader of this book. (As a rule of thumb, I would suggest that anything by Dijkstra, Knuth, Weinberg, or Wirth is worth looking into.)

Brooks, Frederick P., *The Mythical Man-Month*. Reading, Mass.: Addison-Wesley, 1975.

Useful information about large programming projects.

Cherry, George W., *Pascal Programming Structures*. Reston, Va.: Reston, 1980.

A good elementary Pascal text.

Conway, Richard, David Gries, and E. C. Zimmerman, *A Primer on Pascal* (2nd ed.). Cambridge, Mass.: Winthrop, 1981.

Another good elementary Pascal text. This is one of my favorites because of its due lack of reverence for the Pascal language.

Cook, Curtis R., and Do Jin Kim, "Best Sorting Algorithms for Nearly Sorted Lists," *Communications of the ACM*, 23, no. 11 (November 1980).

Demillo, R. A., R. J. Lipton, and A. J. Perlis, "Social Processes and Proofs of Theorems and Programs," *Communications of the ACM*, 22, no. 5 (May 1979).

A persuasive case against mathematical proofs of program correctness (see also the Gries anthology).

Dijkstra, Edsger W., "Goto Statement Considered Harmful," *Communications of the ACM*, 11, no. 3 (March 1968).

The famous letter that started structured programming.

Gries, David, ed., *Programmming Methodology*. New York: Springer-Verlag, 1978.

A collection of the most important papers on proofs of program correctness. A balanced view may lie somewhere between the view espoused here and that of Demillo and others cited previously.

Grogono, Peter, *Programming in Pascal* (rev. ed.). Reading, Mass.: Addison-Wesley, 1980.

An excellent introductory text, but not for the novice.

Hofstadter, Douglas R., *Gödel, Escher, Bach: an Eternal Golden Braid*. New York: Basic Books, 1979.

A popular, often whimsical, treatment of some of the theoretical underpinnings of computer science.

Jackson, M. A., *Principles of Program Design*, New York: Academic Press, 1975.

An excellent book on program design, particularly oriented toward business data-processing problems. Uses COBOL.

Jensen, Kathleen, and Niklaus Wirth, *Pascal User Manual and Report* (2nd ed). New York: Springer-Verlag, 1975.

The classic description of the Pascal language.

Johnston, John B., "The Contour Model of Block Structured Processes," *ACM SIGPLAN Notices*, 6, no. 2 (1971).

The original description of the contour model (see Chapter 6).

Kernighan, Brian W., and P. J. Plauger, *The Elements of Programming Style* (2nd ed.), New York: McGraw-Hill, 1978.

Excellent approach to programming; most examples use the FORTRAN language.

Kernighan, Brian W., and P. J. Plauger, *Software Tools*. Reading, Mass.: Addison-Wesley, 1976.

Develops many useful programs, including a sophisticated text editor. Uses a C-like FORTRAN preprocessor language introduced in the book.

Knuth, Donald E., *The Art of Computer Programming:* vol. 1, *Fundamental Algorithms* (2nd ed.), 1973; vol. 2, *Seminumerical Algorithms* (2nd ed.) 1981; vol. 3, *Sorting and Searching*, 1973, Reading, Mass.: Addison-Wesley.

The first three volumes of a projected seven-volume set. A bit dated but nonetheless should be owned by every computer scientist.

Ledgard, Henry F., John F. Hueras, and Paul Nagin, *Pascal with Style*. Rochelle Park, N.J.: Hayden, 1979.

Has some good things to say about programming in Pascal, but don't take it all too seriously.

Proposed ISO Pascal Standard, *Pascal News*, no. 20 (December 1980), pp. 1–83.*

Saxe, J. B., and A. Hisgen, "Lazy Evaluation of a File Buffer for Interactive I/O," *Pascal News*, no. 13 (December 1978), pp. 93–94.

Description of the method of interactive I/O assumed here (Section 1.13.5).*

Tenenbaum, Aaron M., and Moshe J. Augenstein, *Data Structures Using Pascal*, Englewood Cliffs, N.J.: Prentice-Hall, Inc., 1981.

A more advanced treatment of many of the topics of this book.

Weinberg, Gerald M., *The Psychology of Computer Programming*. New York: Van Nostrand Reinhold, 1971.

Describes what you are doing or ought to be doing when programming. Another classic.

Welsh, Jim, W. J. Sneeringer, and C. A. R. Hoare, "Ambiguities and Insecurities in Pascal," *Software Practice and Experience*, 7 (1977), pp. 685–96.

One of the best of many treatments of Pascal's failings.

Wetherell, Charles, *Etudes for Programmers*. Englewood Cliffs, N.J.: Prentice-Hall, Inc., 1978.

A wide-ranging collection of programming problems.

Wirth, Niklaus, *Algorithms + Data Structures = Programs*. Englewood Cliffs, N.J.: Prentice-Hall, Inc., 1976.

Might be considered a more advanced and more selective version of this book. Ends by developing a compiler for a simple language. Uses Pascal extensively.

*Back issues of *Pascal News* and membership in the Pascal User's Group can currently be obtained from
    Pascal User's Group
    c/o Rick Shaw
    P.O. Box 888524
    Atlanta, Georgia 30338

program index

A

Available storage list manipulation, 151-52

B

Binary search, 82-83
Binary tree, 165-66
Blackjack simulation, 207-9

C

Character string reading, non built-in:

Character string reading (*Cont.*)
with any compiler, 41
CDC, 291
standard Pascal, 294
Commas in input numbers, 27-28

D

Dice rolling simulation, 205-6

E

Equality test for trees, 169

E unsuccessfully approximated,
     286
Exponential distribution histo-
     gram, 214-15

F

Factorial function, 192

G

Group totals, 251-52

H

Hashing:
     with linear collision resolu-
          tion, 225-26
     with linked collision resolu-
          tion, 222-23
     with quadratic collision
          resolution, 227-29
Hexadecimal output conversion,
     63-64

I

Infix to RPN conversion:
     via recursion, 189-91
     via stacks, 117-18
Input deque simulation, 123-25
Insertion of text, 111-13
Insertion sort, 89-90
Interactive input tests, 41-42,
     44, 292-93

L

Largest grade determination,
     105-6

Linear search, 80-81
List insertion:
     at beginning, 140
     with deletions, 143-44
     at end, 141-42
List insertion sort, 148-49

M

Median calculation, 60-61
Merge, 257-58
Merge sort, 264-66
Merge update, 270-71

N

Node count, in a tree, 168-69
Numbers in words to value,
     237-40

P

Palindrome tester, 34-35
Print a text file in a specified
     format, 97-98

Q

Quicksort test simulation, 197-
     99

S

Simple program, 9-10
Single server queue simulation,
     217-18
Social Security calculation, 14
Standard deviation methods
     compared, 284-85

Sum:
  actual values of sums expected
    to be 1, 280
  all combinations summing to a
    given number, 107–8
  of input numbers terminated
    by a sentinel, 19
  two methods compared, 282–
    83
  with unexpected result, 273–
    74

T

Tab replacement by blanks, 66–
  67
Text insertion, 111–13
Triangle of asterisks, 21-22

general index

A

ABS built-in function, 29
Address table sort, 149–51
ALFA data type, 29
AND operation, 15–17
Array data type, 22–25, 32–33
ASCII character set, 28, 29, 33–34, 70, 264
Available storage list, 151

B

BCD character set, 28, 29
Binary operator, 116, 120

Binary search, 81–86, 88–89, 241
Binary search tree, 159–64, 241
Binary tree, 156
Blackjack simulation, 207
Boundary cases, 144
Bubble sort, 61, 67, 201
Buffer, 122, 246
Built-in functions. See Functions, built-in

C

Card sorter sort, 154
Carriage control, 7–8

CASE statement, 36-37, 49
Child, in a tree, 158
CHR built-in function, 27, 29, 35
Circular queue or buffer, 121-22
CLOCK built-in function, 197, 218
Cluster, in a hash table, 229
Collision resolution, 221, 224, 229-31
Comment, 9, 14
CONST declaration, 13-14, 30, 205
Contour diagram, 171, 299
Conversion between data types, 4-6, 32, 35

D

De Morgan's rules, 17, 20-21
Deque, 103, 123-26
Dereferencing, of pointers, 132, 165
Distribution of random numbers, 202
DIV operation, 3
Doubly linked list, 152

E

EBCDIC character set, 28, 29, 63
Empty statement, 10, 46
Enumerated data types, 31-33
Environment, 171
EOF built-in function, 39-40, 42, 44-45, 95, 246, 248, 251
EOLN built-in function, 33, 39, 41-45, 95, 236
Error exit, 46
Event, in probability, 209

EXP built-in function, 4
Expected value, 211
Exponential distribution, 212-14

F

Factorial, 192
Fibonacci numbers, 192
Field, 77
File, 77
FILE data type, 79, 94-95, 244-48, 262-63
Finite state machine, 232
Floating point numbers, 274
Floor function, 17
FOR statement, 21-22, 24, 33, 48
FORWARD declaration, 188-89, 191
Functions, built-in:
  ABS, 29
  CHR, 27, 29, 35
  CLOCK, 197, 218
  EOF, 39-40, 42, 44-45, 95, 246, 248, 251
  EOLN, 33, 39, 41-45, 95, 236
  EXP, 4
  LN, 4
  ODD, 61, 263
  ORD, 26-29, 32, 35, 263
  ROUND, 4, 35
  SQR, 4
  SQRT, 4
  TRUNC, 4, 16-17, 35
Function subprogram:
  declaration of, 71
  value type, 30, 71
Fundamental loop, 57-58

G

GET built-in procedure, 237, 245-48

Global items, 69-71
GOTO statement, 46-47, 51-54,
    57

H

HALT procedure, 46-47
Hanoi, towers of, 193
Hashing search, 220-21, 241
Histogram, 205-6, 215
Horner's method, 25

I

Identifier, 2
Independent events, 211
Inorder tree traversal, 167-68,
    176-80
Insertion sort, 89-94, 200-201,
    219
Integer data type, 2
Interactive input, 10-11, 38-45,
    290-94
Invariant of a loop, 84-85, 90,
    184-86

K

Key, 79
Keyword, 9
KWIC index, 272

L

Labels, 46-47
Law of large numbers, 211
Lazy input, 44
Leaf, of a tree, 158-59
Linear collision resolution, 224
Linear search, 52-54, 79-81,
    138-39, 142-43, 154, 241

Link, 129-31
List, 101-2
    head, 147, 153
    insertion sort, 147-51
Literal, 2
LN (natural logarithm) built-in
    function, 4
Load factor, 227
Local items, 69-71, 173
Logarithms, 4, 20, 71, 88-89,
    197
Logical order, 128, 131
Lower case characters, 29, 36
Lukasiewicz, 113-14

M

Magic numbers, 13, 128, 205,
    207
Master file, 266
MAXINT built-in constant, 2
Median, 58, 193-94
Merging and merge sort, 253,
    259
MOD operation, 3, 5
Mutually exclusive events, 210

N

NEW built-in procedure, 133-34
Nil pointer, 129, 132
Node, 129, 156
Normalization of floating point
    numbers, 275, 277
NOT operation, 15, 17

O

ODD built-in function, 61, 263
Open addressing, 224
OR operation, 15-17
ORD built-in function, 26-27,
    29, 32, 35, 263

Order:
    of character strings, 29
    of operations, 3
Order of magnitude, 87–88, 144,
    162, 185–87, 197, 241, 259
Overflow:
    in arithmetic, 276, 287
    in queues, 122, 126
    in stacks, 104

P

Packed array, 28–29
Parameters to procedures and
    functions, 69–73
    formal vs. actual, 73
    value parameter, 72, 173–75
    VAR parameter, 72, 173–75,
    263
Physical order, 128
Pointer, 128–31
    data type, 132–35
Polish notation, 113, 188
Postorder tree traversal, 167
Power operation, 3–4
Preorder tree traversal, 167
Prime number, 50
Probability function, 210
Procedure declaration, 67–69
Pseudo-random, 195
PUT built-in procedure, 245–48

Q

Quadratic collision resolution,
    230
Queue, 103, 120–23, 152–53
Quicksort, 181–87, 197–200

R

Random number generators,
    195, 197, 201–2, 295–96

Random variable, 211
Real data type, 2
Record:
    data type, 78
    in a file, 77
    variant, 267–68
Recursion, 155, 191–92
Recursive descent, 188
Relative error, 281
REPEAT statement, 15, 18–21
Reserved word, 9, 235
RESET built-in procedure, 94–
    96, 245–48, 262
Reverse Polish notation (RPN),
    113–20, 159, 188
REWRITE built-in procedure,
    94–96, 245–48, 262
Root of a tree, 156
ROUND built-in function, 4, 35
Run, in sorting, 259
Running pointer, 136

S

Sampling, 196, 207
Scalar data types, 30
Scratch files, 258
Searching:
    binary search, 81–86, 88–89,
    241
    binary search tree, 159–64,
    241
    hashing, 220–21, 241
    linear search, 52–54, 79–81,
    138–39, 142–43, 154, 241
    summary, 241
Selection sort, 93–94, 200–201,
    219
Selector, 23, 78–79
Self-reorganizing list, 154
Semicolon, 10, 12, 15, 22, 46
Sentinel:
    to end a file, 254, 270
    on input, 19–20, 24

Sentinel (*Cont.*)
    to stop a search, 54, 108,
       138-39, 160-61
Separators, on input, 38-39, 99
SET data type, 35
Shuffling, 207-8
Significant digits, 2, 275, 279,
     287
Simulation, 196, 207, 216
Single server queue, 216
Sorting:
    address table sort, 149-51
    bubble sort, 61, 67, 201
    card sorter sort, 154
    insertion sort, 89-94, 200-
      201, 219
    list insertion sort, 147-51
    merge sort, 253, 259
    quicksort, 181-87, 197-200
    selection sort, 93-94, 200-
      201, 219
SQR built-in function, 4
SQRT built-in function, 4
Stable sorting method, 92, 148
Stack, 102-4, 151-52
Subrange data type, 32
Subscript, 23, 30, 32-33
Subtree, 156

T

TEXT files, 94-95, 244-45

Top-down design, 55-58
Trailing pointer, 142, 161
Tree, 156
    traversal of, 167-68
TRUNC built-in procedure, 4,
    16-17, 35
Two-way merge, 260
Type conversion, 4-6, 32, 35
TYPE declaration, 30-31

U

Unary operator, 116, 120
Underflow, 104, 122, 126
Uniform distribution, 202
Update of a sequential file, 266-
    67

V

VAR declaration, 9, 30-31
Variants in records, 267-68

W

WHILE statement, 18-21
WITH statement, 297-302